MOTHERHOOD AND MOTHERING
IN ANGLO-SAXON ENGLAND

THE NEW MIDDLE AGES

BONNIE WHEELER
Series Editor

The New Middle Ages presents transdisciplinary studies of medieval cultures. It includes both scholarly monographs and essay collections.

PUBLISHED BY ST. MARTIN'S PRESS:

MOTHERHOOD AND MOTHERING IN ANGLO-SAXON ENGLAND

Mary Dockray-Miller

St. Martin's Press
New York

ISBN 0-312-22721-3

Library of Congress Cataloging-in-Publication Data
Dockray-Miller, Mary, 1965–
   Motherhood and mothering in Anglo-Saxon England / Mary Dockray
-Miller.
      p.   cm. (The New Middle Ages)
   Includes bibliographical references and index.
   ISBN 0-312-22721-3
   1. Mothers—England—History—To 1500.   2. Motherhood—England-
-History—To 1500.   3. Great Britain—History—Anglo-Saxon period,
449–1066.   4. Mothers in literature.   5. Motherhood in literature.
6. English literature—Old English, ca. 450–1100—History and
criticism.   I. Title.
HQ759.D63   1999
306.874'3'09420902—dc21   99–39680
                                                                      CIP

Design by Letra Libre, Inc.

First edition: March 2000
10 9 8 7 6 5 4 3 2 1

For the Hawk,
Edith Weatherby Dockray

CONTENTS

SERIES EDITOR'S FOREWORD

The New Middle Ages contributes to medieval cultural studies through its scholarly monographs and essay collections. This series speaks in a contemporary idiom about specific but diverse practices, expressions, and ideologies in the Middle Ages; it aims especially to recuperate the histories of medieval women. *Motherhood and Mothering in Anglo-Saxon England* by Mary Dockray-Miller is the thirteenth book in the series. This, the first monograph on maternity in Anglo-Saxon England, uses a large range of diverse evidence culled from saints' lives, chronicles, and charters to demonstrate modes of medieval maternal nurturance. Not surprisingly, given its grandeur and interpretive importance, Dockray-Miller uses *Beowulf* as her central text. Grendel's mother, then and now, models ways in which maternity can be both powerful and thwarted.

Bonnie Wheeler
Southern Methodist University

ACKNOWLEDGMENTS

I am indebted to many members of the community of Anglo-Saxon scholarship for assistance with *Motherhood and Mothering in Anglo-Saxon England*. I wish to thank specifically Stephanie Hollis, Paul Szarmach, and John Hill, for their detailed and enormously helpful readings of individual chapters; Karma Lochrie and Gillian Overing, for serving on my dissertation committee and challenging me to formulate my theoretical rubric; Nina Rulon-Miller and Michael Drout, for support and email; and the staffs of Lambeth Palace Library and of the interlibrary loan office at O'Neill Library of Boston College. I would like to acknowledge the editors of *Women and Language,* which published a modified version of the first section of chapter 4 in the fall of 1998 as "*Beowulf's* Masculine Queen." I would also like to thank the trustees of the British Museum, and especially Leslie Webster of the department of Medieval and Later Antiquities there, for permission to reproduce a photograph of the Franks casket on the jacket cover. My greatest professional debt is to Allen Frantzen, who first suggested I turn my maternal thinking into a book about Anglo-Saxon mothers, and who guided me along the way.

PREFACE

LOOKING FOR ANGLO-SAXON MOTHERS

"The personal is political" runs the much-maligned *cri de coeur* of the 1970s feminist movement. Yet the personal lives and circumstances of scholars, critics, and historians influence and guide their scholarship, criticism, and history, as postmodern theory has shown us.[1] I first became interested in mothers in Anglo-Saxon England when I became a mother and began to wonder how mothers of a thousand years ago raised their children, where their circumstances and problems overlapped with mine, and how they differed. I began looking for Anglo-Saxon mothers, who, it turned out, were not so easy to find.

Bede's *Ecclesiastical History of the English People* remains the logical place to begin an inquiry into Anglo-Saxon history, despite feminist historians' recent observations about Bede's neglect and distortion of the roles and activities of women.[2] In AD 731, "the Father of English History" completed his text, which presents a seamless and inevitable conversion and consolidation of the diverse pagan tribal kingdoms into a unified Christian England.

While Gillian Overing and Clare Lees have admirably demonstrated Bede's manipulation of the "maternity" of Hild of Whitby,[3] it is to another saint and another double monastery in Bede's text that I turn to elucidate the problems inherent in a search for Anglo-Saxon mothers. In Anglo-Saxon culture at large, both during and after Bede, patrilineage was the focus of most extant genealogy; such a patrilineal focus was also coupled with a usual exclusion of women's roles and names at all, erasing and eliding the biologically crucial maternal body from both the family tree and the historical focus.

In book four, Bede's *History* celebrates the monastery of Ely, founded and ruled by the virgin St. Æðelþryð. Ely demonstrates a matrilineal rather than a patrilineal succession, but Bede does not inform his readers of this unusual genealogy. Rather, he focuses on Æðelþryð's virginity and piety before revealing almost inadvertently that her sister Seaxburh was her successor as abbess. His main focus is not "sororal succession" at all but instead Seaxburh's orchestration of Æðelþryð's translation.[4] Readers of Bede's canonical, primary text are not informed that Seaxburh was succeeded by her daughter Eormenhild, who was succeeded by her daughter Werburh, a genealogy that demonstrates a transmission of power and property from sister to sister and mother to daughter through four abbesses and three generations.[5]

While I will be discussing the maternal genealogy of Ely in much greater detail in chapter 2, I want to emphasize here that Bede and/or his sources did not think this maternal genealogy worthy of inclusion in the national history. Bede's exclusion of the maternal genealogy of Ely is indicative of the place of mothers in Anglo-Saxon texts—typically, they have no place. The little-known successive abbacies of Seaxburh, Eormenhild, and Werburh show us that Anglo-Saxon mothers are traditionally excluded and hidden but that they can be found. And they can tell us, ultimately, about motherhood and mothers in our own culture as well as in theirs.

CHAPTER 1

MATERNAL PERFORMERS

M otherhood is becoming respectable, finally, in feminist circles. For years it was something to be ignored, embarrassed about, or evaded as feminists defined themselves as daughters rather than as mothers.[1] This focus shifted slightly in 1976 with the publication of Adrienne Rich's landmark study *Of Woman Born,* which differentiates between "Motherhood as Experience and Institution" (her subtitle), meaning between the patriarchal institution of motherhood, and women's actual experience of motherhood, which Rich reads to be empowering and illuminating. Motherhood as a subject of analysis has since gained legitimacy in U.S. academic feminism as the last of the baby boomers have their children and "parenting" and "families" are the buzzwords on every politician's lips.

In medieval studies, feminist theory and postmodernism have made uneasy headway into the dominant methodologies of source study and historical criticism, although physical motherhood is most often missing as a category of female experience available for scholarly inquiry. Whether one agrees with Allen J. Frantzen that "it is impossible to dismiss the revaluation of medieval evidence that feminist scholarship and gender theory have already produced"[2] or with Judith Bennett that "the medieval studies community is often indifferent and sometimes hostile to this feminist scholarship,"[3] it is safe to say that critical examination of motherhood in medieval texts has been circumscribed by patriarchal, religious conceptions of motherhood when it has appeared at all.[4] In *The Oldest Vocation: Christian Motherhood in the Middle Ages,* Clarissa Atkinson notes that "monastic authors presented 'real' or significant motherhood as a spiritual rather than biological relationship" and remarks that the very monks who exhibited the most Marian devotion also despised actual, physical mothers.[5] Atkinson argues that it was not until the late Middle Ages and the early modern period that there was some positively valued relationship between physical motherhood and concepts of holiness.[6] Such spiritual motherhood is also the focus of Caroline Walker Bynum's *Jesus as Mother,* which discusses motherhood as a trope of religious understanding, not as actual practice.[7] There is more textual evidence available about spiritual motherhood than about actual motherhood, an imbalance that likely accounts for the usual critical focus on spiritual motherhood.

In Anglo-Saxon studies specifically, "motherhood" has not been pursued as a working topic of analysis, although woman-centered feminist criticism has certainly made an impact in the field. Christine Fell's 1984 *Women in Anglo-Saxon England* provided a much-needed women's history of the period; in it, Fell argues that the overall status of women declined throughout the period.[8] Jane Chance's *Woman as Hero in Old English Literature* provided a specifically literary analysis of the various sorts of power wielded by women in Anglo-Saxon texts,[9] while in 1990 Helen Damico and Alexandra Hennessey Olsen collected a number of important critical essays about women in Anglo-Saxon culture in *New Readings on Women in Old English Literature*.[10] More theoretical gender-based readings by Gillian Overing, Clare Lees, James Hala, Karma Lochrie, and others have brought semiotics, psychoanalysis, queer theory, and deconstruction to feminist Anglo-Saxon studies.[11]

An introduction of motherhood into this critical conversation can only expand the scope of our knowledge about and analysis of the functions, places, and desires of women in Anglo-Saxon culture. Lees and Overing have examined the spiritual motherhood of Abbess Hild of Whitby, and the ways in which Bede manipulates that "maternity" in his *History*,[12] but actual motherhood in Anglo-Saxon England has received surprisingly little critical attention. Even recent work on Anglo-Saxon medical texts and obstetrical practice is focused on pregnancy, labor, and delivery, rather than on the work of mothering that continues long after an individual child is born.[13]

I argue here that three postmodern theorists, Judith Butler, Sara Ruddick, and Luce Irigaray, can provide a rubric for an examination of the maternal as a category in Anglo-Saxon texts. Butler's concept of gender performance allows a realization of the maternal as a category separate from those of masculine and feminine. Ruddick's definition of maternal work as protection, nurturance, and training of children provides specific criteria in the search for maternal performers in Anglo-Saxon texts. Finally, Irigaray's descriptions of maternal genealogy can point to successful maternal performers in Anglo-Saxon texts who leave subjectivity, agency, and power to their daughters.

Protection, nurturance, and training of children constitutes maternal work in Anglo-Saxon England, maternal work that is stymied at every turn by patriarchal Anglo-Saxon culture. In literary and historical sources, maternal performers find ways to co-opt the patriarchy that both needs and effaces maternal reproduction. Analysis of actual, rather than spiritual, mothers in Anglo-Saxon history and literature reveals strong maternal strategies used throughout the culture to protect, nurture, and teach children—sons as well as daughters. The performances of the variously related queens, saints, and abbesses of the eighth-century Kentish royal family; of Æðelflæd, Lady of the Mercians; and of the various mothers in *Beowulf* all point to a system of maternal practice preserved almost inadvertently in the textual sources of Anglo-Saxon England, a system that maternal performers manipulated to enable them to raise their children.

Butler's *Gender Trouble* and *Bodies That Matter* clarify the notion of gendered performances that are repeated to the point where they seem natural or inevitable (although they are neither). Butler says that performance, not biology, determines gender: "There is no gender identity behind the expressions of gender; that identity is performatively constituted by the very 'expressions' that are said to be its results."[14] In *Bodies That Matter,* Butler expands upon this notion of performativity, which, she emphasizes, is not a subjective, conscious "choice" by an already essentialist, humanist "self." In *Bodies,* Butler corrects misperceptions by readers of *Trouble,* stating that by "performativity" she did not mean that " . . . one woke in the morning, perused the closet or some more open space for the gender of choice, donned that gender for the day, and then restored the garment to its place at night."[15] Rather than the subject deciding its gender, "gender is part of what decides the subject." One cannot precede the other in some sort of linear progression. Genders are not constructed onto preexisting sexed bodies; gender construction is not an act that can be deemed "finished" at a certain point. The performativity of gender depends on an understanding of gender construction as an ongoing process (or performance) that is never ultimately complete.

That ongoing process depends on repetition and reinscription of "norms" of gender. Butler's arguments about the materiality of the body insist upon "the understanding of performativity not as the act by which a subject brings into being what she/he names, but, rather, as that reiterative power of discourse to produce the phenomena that it regulates and constrains." As such, what humanity has traditionally perceived as "the sexes" are, for Butler, actually "normative positions." Such a position takes its place in a "citation" of previous performances, so that performances layer one upon another to posit an illusion of determined sex. For Butler, "Performativity is not a singular 'act,' for it is always a reiteration of a norm or set of norms, and to the extent that it acquires an act-like status in the present, it conceals or dissimulates the conventions of which it is a repetition."[16]

Butler's main goal, if that term is not too teleological for such a philosopher, is examination of examples of "disidentification with those regulatory norms by which sexual difference is materialized"; for her, it is those sites of disidentification that serve to undermine what she calls "the heterosexual imperative," "the regime of heterosexuality," or "compulsory heterosexuality" that reigns in contemporary Western culture.[17] As such, norms of gender construction may seem inflexible when they are defined as "the repeated stylization of the body"; yet disidentification, or slippage from those norms, is what reveals their very unnatural constructedness and provides ways to challenge those norms. Such an "enabling disruption" overlooks or resists citations of the norm, and refuses to cite such a norm, insisting on a performance without precedent.[18]

While Sara Ruddick's *Maternal Thinking* does not state it explicitly, Ruddick ascribes to a theory of gender performance much like Butler's, especially in her argument that "maternal work" can (and should) be performed by men as well as by women.[19] That work is "to take upon oneself the responsibility of child care, making its work a regular and substantial part of one's working life."[20] Ruddick rejects such organic notions as instinctive mother-love or mother-knowledge that (some people assume) appear "naturally" upon the birth of the child; indeed, she consciously separates birthgiving from mothering as two separate kinds of work.[21] Ruddick's schema of maternal work is threefold: she argues for "the goals of preservation, growth, and social acceptability as constitutive of maternal practice." Or, as she states elsewhere, "mothers are people who see children as 'demanding' protection, nurturance, and training."[22]

Protection or preservation of a child may seem too basic to be called part of a thoughtful practice, but Ruddick points out that "In any culture, maternal commitment is far more voluntary than people like to believe."[23] While a late-twentieth-century mother may worry about traffic and kidnappers, in contrast to a medieval mother who may have worried about disease and Viking raids, mothers must actively take steps to protect their children from injury or death. The most immediate action is to feed the child; until relatively recently, the only food source for an infant was the body of a lactating woman. Ruddick argues that such action is "the central constitutive, invariant aim of maternal practice."[24]

Nurturance, the second criterion, involves shielding and guiding the child's emotional and intellectual growth. While such practice would have had different ends and different means a thousand years ago (most mothers would probably not have taught their children to read, stories about King Alfred's childhood aside), the criterion is still relevant—a mother must equip her child to live as fully as possible in the society into which he or she has been born.

Training, for Ruddick, means "to shape . . . children's growth in 'acceptable' ways" so that the child is an accepted, ideally a welcomed, member of the social group to which the mother and child belong.[25] Acceptance in a rural eighth-century village or a thriving tenth-century town or the late-twentieth-century United States all imply vastly different standards, but the maternal performer must raise her child to meet those standards. While Ruddick uses the term "train," I will be using "teach" to indicate the third term that distinguishes maternal performance. Ruddick acknowledges that "train" is "somewhat harsh," although she prefers it because of its neutrality.[26] I prefer "teach" since it more fully conveys the intellectual feat of raising a child; it connotes a reciprocity in the relationship; and it implies the wide-ranging nature of maternal practice. Ruddick sees a relationship among these three forms of practice; in keeping her child alive (protection), a mother then provides the opportunity to nurture and teach him or her in the customs of their culture.

Ruddick acknowledges that her philosophy is grounded in late-twentieth-century, white, middle-class America. Yet her ideals, she argues, permeate social and cultural boundaries in that her "primary concern is with moral claims about the responses children deserve."[27] As I have indicated above, these criteria also permeate historical boundaries; children in any age, in any culture, need protection, nurturance, and teaching to grow into socially acceptable adults, although the specifics of that practice were necessarily vastly different in the Middle Ages from what they are today. In the individual chapters that follow, I hope to show that Anglo-Saxon mothers engaged in practices like those Ruddick describes.

When these maternal performers were successful, when they protected, nurtured, and taught their children, they could create what Irigaray terms a maternal genealogy. In *Sexes and Genealogies,* Irigaray uses and then breaks down the terms and models of psychoanalysis that describe the Mother. She forces an acknowledgement that the sexuality and gender of the Mother is subversive and enigmatic, and reveals that the traditional psychoanalytic focus on the child elides that subversiveness in order to render it inoperative.

Throughout *Sexes and Genealogies,* Irigaray advocates woman's reclamation of maternal, female genealogy and a rejection of a cultural genealogy that separates the mother and daughter to make the daughter into only a mother in her husband's house.[28] She invokes a number of mythic archetypes to show how the mother-daughter bond is routinely severed in Western culture; for her, the primary myth in our culture is not Oedipus's patricide but Orestes's murder of Clytemnestra, the "original matricide" that was condoned by the gods as revenge for the murder of the father, Agamemnon.

Clytemnestra kills Agamemnon for a number of reasons, all of which identify her as a woman noncompliant with patriarchy: she has taken a lover who is ruling the kingdom with her; Agamemnon has returned with his latest mistress, Cassandra; Agmemnon had killed their daughter, Iphigenia, to get the right wind to sail to Troy (a mission devoted to reclaiming his brother's sexual rights over Helen). For Irigaray, the murder of Iphigenia, the "motive often forgotten by the authors of tragedy," is the most salient of these motives; Agamemnon, like patriarchal structure, needs violence to sever the bond between mother and daughter.[29]

This reclamation of a female genealogy, Irigaray hopes, will lead to a society in which gender difference is accepted rather than subsumed in a hopeless attempt at neutrality that is actually a veiled masculinity. The following quotation shows the immediacy of myth in Irigaray's schema of female genealogy that can lead to acknowledged sexual difference:

> But very few students of myth have laid bare the origins, the qualities and functions, the events that led up to the disappearance of the great mother-daughter couples of mythology: Demeter-Kore, Clytemnestra-Iphigenia, Jocasta-Antigone, to mention only a few famous Greek figures that have managed to leave some traces in patriarchal times.
>
> I suggest that those of you who care about social justice should put up posters in public places showing beautiful images of that natural and spiritual couple, the mother-daughter, the couple that testifies to a very special relationship to nature and culture.[30]

This mother-daughter bond can become a paradigm for women's relationships with each other as well; rather than a feared phallic mother from whom the daughter needs to separate, the mother should instead be viewed as a source of strength.

Irigaray argues that in western culture, the cult of maternity is actually "the cult of the *son's mother*" (emphasis hers), a celebration of maternity that serves to reinscribe male domination of women and male use of female reproductive capacity.[31] Most feminist dis-ease with maternity stems from such a construct; some feminists (see note 1) view maternity as a bodily submission to patriarchy rather than an opportunity for a particularly female and feminist type of practice.

Butler, Ruddick, and Irigaray, then, provide a vocabulary and criterion set for investigation of maternal performance through history. While such rubrics are helpful—indeed, they have guided my research—they also by their nature caution us against any universalization of an idealized maternal category. The vocabulary of maternal genealogy reveals new textual possibilities; it does not call for mothers to be reinterpreted as "better" than other women and all men nor for all mothers to be somehow the same throughout history and culture. I advocate here not simply a valorization of newly defined maternal practice, but an acknowledgement that such practice can exist, a practice with aims quite different from those usually ascribed to historical and literary figures.

In the chapters that follow, I analyze both mothers of sons and mothers of daughters, arguing finally that some mothers of daughters in Anglo-Saxon texts do manage to create maternal genealogies that do not merely reinscribe patriarchal desires about motherhood and property. Such desires engage in what Allyson Newton has called "the occlusion of maternity" in her analysis of Chaucer's *Clerk's Tale*. Newton argues that in the tale "the maternal . . . is appropriated by processes of patriarchal continuance and paternal succession . . . that occlude the maternality upon which lineage and succession are dependent."[32] I will be using Newton's term both to illuminate Anglo-Saxon instances of the occlusion of maternity and to seek examples of maternal genealogy that has not been occluded, even by largely patriarchal textual transmission.

Chapter 2 analyzes the familial relationships among Anglo-Saxon religious women of the late seventh and early eighth centuries. The royal abbesses of this period were almost all related to each other, by blood or by marriage, and the analysis reveals that the founding and maintenance of monasteries followed a pattern during this time: on land that she controlled, a royal widow founded a monastery with links to Frankish Gaul, then passed her abbacy to a close blood relative, who could have been either widow or virgin. This chapter provides detailed analyses of the relationships among the abbesses of Ely, Whitby, and Minster-in-Thanet, with briefer examinations of Minster-in-Sheppey, Wimborne, Barking, Lyminge, and Much Wenlock. The manuscript fragment of London, Lambeth Palace MS 427, folio 210 hints at the maternal practice of a ritual of greeting a female blood relative into such a community.

Chapter 3 reexamines the family tree of Æðelflæd, Lady of the Mercians, with an emphasis on its neglected, female side. As is usually noted, Æðelflæd was the daughter and sister of two kings of Wessex (Alfred the Great and Edward the Elder, respectively), but she also had a maternal genealogy of women who provided role models for her maternal performance of governance. This genealogy includes her grandmother Osburh, her mother Ealhswið, her paternal aunt Æðelswið, and her daughter Ælfwynn. Æðelflæd's reign in Mercia, a subkingdom of Wessex, was characterized by compromise, defense, and reduction of violence whenever possible. In addition, at St. Mary's, Nunnaminster, the female side of the West Saxon royal house may have created a monastic matrilineal genealogy like those of the great double monasteries of the seventh and eighth centuries.

Chapter 4 examines the mothers in that most canonical of Old English poems, *Beowulf,* examining their performances and speeches to provide a critical framework that reveals the active discouragement of maternal practice in the cultural world of *Beowulf*. Because of the poem's focus on men, this chapter of necessity deals with mothers of sons rather than mothers of daughters. Individual readings of each of the five mothers of in the poem—Modþryðo, Grendel's Mother, Hildeburh, Hygd, and Wealhþeow—lead to the realization that maternal performers in *Beowulf* explicitly do not want their sons to succeed to the throne. The violence of the heroic ethos is a constant threat to children, grown or not, and in the course of the poem only Wealhþeow's maternal performance is fully successful.

The content of these chapters was guided partly by availability of sources (there is a relative wealth of charters about Minster-in-Thanet, for example). More importantly, each chapter's focus is on mothers whose interactions with their children are not blurred by their relations with other textual traditions. For example, the relationship of the Virgin Mary with Christ in *Advent* (also called *Christ I*), like that of Elene with her son Constantine in *Elene,* is deeply colored by church history and patristic tradition in a way that the relative textual isolation of Wealhþeow's with her young sons is not. Similarly, each of the chapters takes an oft-studied, canonical text—Bede's *History, The Anglo-Saxon Chronicle,* and *Beowulf*—and reads against it for indications of maternal practice, often supplementing its information with other, less-read texts (the *Þa Halgan,* or the charters, or the *Chronicle of Æðelweard*).

The division between literary and historical texts is always blurry in medieval studies, especially in Anglo-Saxon texts, where "history" and "literature" frequently reside next to each other—witness the poetic sections of *The Anglo-Saxon Chronicle* or Bede's *History* as obvious examples. While this book begins with "history" and ends with "literature," I approach all of the texts with an eye to their literary structures, manuscript contexts, and critical histories. The nature of the extant textual record necessitates a focus on royal and aristocratic women, whose existences and names have been, to some extent, preserved. Throughout this study of upper-class maternal performers, there resonate, however faintly, hints of lower- and working-class maternal performers, the invisible poor mothers who endeavored as well to protect, nurture, and teach their children.

CHAPTER 2

MATRILINEAL GENEALOGY AND
MILDRIÐ'S MATERNAL LEGACY

A focus on the maternal genealogy of the seventh- and eighth-century royal Kentish saints reveals a system of maternal practice that established powerful and secure maternal strongholds throughout England. It is no accident that the abbesses of the double monasteries of seventh- and eighth-century Kent and East Anglia were all related to each other, by blood or by marriage. Roberta Gilchrist has noted that, "Medieval nunneries were liminal places—located at the physical and psychological margins of society."[1] Such liminality may have contributed a sense of separateness to the English nunneries and double monasteries of the seventh and eighth centuries that enabled their abbesses and nuns to construct maternal genealogies prominent and powerful enough to survive in the textual record, although not in highly canonical and widely read texts such as Bede's *History*.

Rather than trying to fit these double monasteries and nunneries into patriarchal schemas, as scholars have previously done, we need to see them as coexisting and working with the patriarchies of kingship and the institutional church while at the same time developing their own maternal traditions to protect, nurture, and teach the daughters of the house, who were often biological as well as spiritual daughters. A variety of textual evidences—charters, saints' *Lives,* letters, Bede's *History,* and manuscript fragments—indicates the cultural and political power these abbesses wielded outside their communities. In addition, these texts can be read to reveal maternal communities and communication within and between the monasteries. Indeed, there is textual evidence of a uniquely female ritual of consecration as a mother consecrates a royal daughter into a maternal community. This text, London, Lambeth Palace, MS 427, f.210, indicates that Minster-in-Thanet, the church of St. Mildrið, may have been the locus for a Greek-inspired maternal practice that coexisted amicably with the patriarchal church and culture.

The seventh and eighth centuries have frequently been called a golden age of English monasticism. Monika Otter stated most recently that "It has long been recognized that, particularly in England, the seventh and eighth centuries were a golden age of female monasticism, and (comparatively speaking) of women's participation in public life in general."[2] Similar comments could be culled from a variety of scholarly texts ranging throughout the past one hundred years.[3] The relative peace of the period—abruptly shattered at the end of the eighth century when the Vikings sacked Lindisfarne in 793—provided opportunity for the spread of Christian conversion, the founding of monasteries, and the development of educational and cultural endeavors. Most famous of these cultural establishments is the Venerable Bede, from whose *Ecclesiastical History* much of the information about the golden age has been taken.[4]

Among the most prominent monastic foundations in seventh- and eighth-century England were double monasteries—houses for monks and nuns—governed by an abbess, usually of royal or noble family. Historians have long noted the unusual structure that allowed a woman to govern an institution of both women and men. Many of these royal abbesses trained at the double monasteries of Chelles or Brie (also called Farmoutier) in Frankish Gaul and then returned to England to rule similarly structured foundations, sometimes built on land granted by the reigning king (a male relative of the abbess in question), more often built on land that the abbess controlled on her own through dowry rights after she became a widow. Patricia Coulstock views the double monasteries as extensions of the current royal family's political power; she argues that they were "power-bases for the royal families which sustained them" in that they provided administrative centers and served to keep lands under family control through blood links with the abbess.[5] Joan Nicholson remarks on this family connection somewhat more crudely when she says that the double monastery "provided the female element of the ruling caste with something to rule,"[6] while Jane Schulenberg argues that "the family monastery in this early period was in many ways regarded simply as an extension of the noble household."[7]

While Bede's *Ecclesiastical History* is our primary source of information about many of these double monasteries—he includes references to or narratives about Coldingham, Whitby, Ely, Lyminge, Brie, and Barking—feminist historians have recently questioned his presentation of much of the information. Nicholson remarks that "the information which modern readers seek from his text is hardly that which he set to give."[8] More recently, Stephanie Hollis, Clare Lees, and Gillian Overing have interrogated the gender-based assumptions in the *Ecclesiastical History* to show that Bede was most interested in and most admiring of virgin women who submitted unquestioningly to male ecclesiastical authority. Hollis shows that

Æðelþryð, the virgin abbess of Ely, "commands his enthusiasm" (he even writes a poem in her praise) while the achievements of abbesses like Hild are elided as "Bede . . . tells us next to nothing of the contribution to the growth of the church and the participatory role of abbesses like Hild."[9] Lees and Overing even argue that "Hild deserves to be rescued from Bede and afforded her own place in history."[10] These scholars read Bede's omissions as well as his inclusions to piece together a history of the seventh-century double monastery that not only glorifies pious virgins but also reveals the intense public involvement of the double monasteries' abbesses in political and ecclesiastical synods and councils, pastoral work, education, and care for the sick.

It is with such a skeptical eye on Bede that I begin my investigation into the double monasteries associated with the royal house of Kent, an investigation that spirals out to encompass East Anglia, Mercia, Wessex, and Northumberland. The abbesses of these houses were all related to each other by blood or by marriage, and Mildrið, the saintly abbess of Minster-in-Thanet, was distantly related to the more-famous Hild of Whitby. These female links from one house to another, I argue, allowed for the construction of a maternal genealogy that culminated in the maternal ritual preserved in the Lambeth Palace manuscript fragment.

The Christian history of the Kentish royal house begins with a woman, interestingly enough, although Overing and Lees have noted Bede's omission of that fact.[11] Æðelberht of Kent married the Frankish Christian princess Bertha and subsequently converted after Augustine's mission arrived in Kent; Bede notes Æðelberht's conversion but does not credit Bertha's influence.[12] Æðelberht's two children displayed a combination of piety and political power similar to their father's. His daughter Æðelburh founded Lyminge monastery after a marriage to King Edwin of Northumbria;[13] their daughter Eanflæd became abbess of Whitby after a marriage to Oswiu, a king of Northumbria from a bloodline different from her father's.

Æðelberht's son Eadbald ruled Kent after his father's death; Eadbald's daughter Eanswið founded and was abbess of Folkestone;[14] his son Eorcenberht married Seaxburh, who was founder and abbess of Minster-in-Sheppey as well as abbess of Ely; his second son Eormenred produced two martyred and canonized sons (Æðelberht and Æðelred), as well as three daughters associated with Minster-in-Thanet (Æbbe, the foundress, Eormenburh, and Eormengyð). (See the first of the family trees in the appendix.)

The first three generations of the Christian history of Kent, then, indicate that a veritable flurry of monastery founding was occurring in southeast England in the early seventh century, mostly involving royal princesses and widows. It is a pattern that will be repeated throughout England, as I hope to show in the following pages, and a pattern that allowed for the development of maternal genealogy in a liminal space, to return to Gilchrist's term.

Æðelþryð's Ely is arguably the most famous Anglo-Saxon foundation, and it was certainly liminal, set so deeply in swampland that it was referred to as an island. Ely demonstrates its own maternal genealogy with both a form of "sororal succession" between daughters of the same mother and of matrilineality from mothers to daughters as well. Its foundation history, although not its maternal genealogy, was preserved in Bede's *Ecclesiastical History;* the saint's cult continued well after the Norman Conquest, when Ely had been refounded as a house for men.[15] Bede tells us that Æðelþryð was the daughter of Anna, king of East Anglia (d.654); she was married twice, first to Tondberht, an ealdorman of South Gyrwe, and then to Ecgfrið, king of Northumbria. Her first marriage seems to have been short; her second one lasted for 12 years, according to Bede, but she managed to remain a virgin through both of her marriages.[16] Lina Eckenstein seems sympathetic to the age difference between Æðelþryð and her second husband, who was probably 15 years younger than she was; Barbara Mitchell realistically suggests that Æðelþryð may have been barren, and her husband had dynastic reasons for allowing her to enter a nunnery so he could take a new wife (presumably one closer to his own age).[17]

After she founded Ely, probably on land given to her by Tondberht, Æðelþryð led a life of great sanctity, died, and was discovered to have a uncorrupted body at her translation 16 years after her death. Many posthumous miracles have occurred at her shrine, Bede informs us, and he composes a poem about her virgin sanctity. David Rollason has suggested that the nuns of Ely may have known some sort of mummification techniques; he points out that "the nuns expected the saint's body to be undecayed, perhaps because they had taken steps to ensure that this would be so."[18]

Not just Bede but also the scribe of the twelfth-century *Liber Eliensis,* as well as more recent historians, has promoted Æðelþryð's cult. In the late eighteenth century, James Bentham, the prebendary of Ely cathedral, included his own version of Æðelþryð's *Life* in his history of the cathedral, illustrating it with his own copperplate engravings, one of which shows Æðelþryð robed and crowned, holding a crozier as she reads from a book, presumably the scriptures.[19] The textual focus remains firmly on the foundress rather than her successors.

Æðelþryð was succeeded by her sister Seaxburh; Bede does not bother to inform his readers that Seaxburh had founded and governed the double monastery of Minster-in-Sheppey before coming to Ely. He does note that she had been married to Eorcenberht of Kent, and it is through Seaxburh that Ely traces its connection to the royal house of Kent and its saintly maternal genealogy. Before turning to Sheppey and Kent, however, it is worth noting that Seaxburh acted as regent for her son Egberht after the death of his father;[20] she had political experience as an East Anglian princess, a Kentish queen consort, and a Kentish queen regent, and was thus well equipped to handle the administrative duties of the double house of Ely, and to effect not just her sister's translation but the ongoing maintenance of the house.

Æðelþryð's other sisters and Ely's sororal succession indicate the deep involvement of the female family members with the church. Æðelþryð and Seaxburh's other sister, Wihtburh, was translated to Ely in 974; she had founded a community in East Dereham.[21] Their two stepsisters Saeþryð and Æðelburh, Anna's daughters by another wife, were abbesses in turn at the double monastery of Brie in Gaul, revealing Ely's Gaulish connection in the web of female monastic relations.

Ely's maternal genealogy continues into the next two generations (see the second family tree in the appendix). Seaxburh was succeeded at Ely by her daughter Eormenhild, who fits the pattern of a widowed princess retiring to the monastic life at her mother's monastery. Eormenhild had married Wulfhere, king of Mercia (d.674), and borne a daughter, Werburh, before retiring first to Sheppey, to take over when her mother left for Ely, and then to Ely, to take over upon her mother's death. Her daughter Werburh followed her as abbess of Ely, although Werburh was also abbess of Sheppey, Hanbury, and Trentham, indicating either that she moved around a lot or (more likely) that she simultaneously administered a number of monasteries. While conventional historians may choose not to emphasize this pattern of maternal and sororal succession, its frequency indicates that the seventh- and eighth-century double monastery provided a system of religious matrilineage that depended on biological as well as spiritual maternity.

Sheppey seems to have been something of a training ground for the abbesses of Ely as both Seaxburh and Eormenhild ruled there, in Kent, before going to Ely in East Anglia. One folio of Lambeth Palace MS 427, the whole of which I will be discussing in much more detail later, describes Seaxburh's foundation of the minster:

And sancta Seaxburh and Sancta Eormenhild onfengon halig rifte on ðam mynstre þe is geeweden Middletune on kentlande. And þæt igland on Scæpyge hyrð into Middletune; and hit is ðreora mila brad and scofan mila lang. ða gelicode ðære halgan cwene Seaxburge þæt heo ðær binnan for myrðe and for mærðe, hyre ðær mynster getimbrode and gestaðelode, swa geo men cwædon þæt ðrittegum gearum ne gestilde næfre stefen cearciendes wænes ne ceoriendes wales. . . .[22]

[And St. Seaxburh and St. Eormenhild took the holy veil at the minster which is called Milton in Kent. And the island in Sheppey belongs to Milton; and it is three miles wide and seven miles long. Then it pleased the holy queen Seaxburh that she there might within [the isle] for pleasure and for honor for herself there build and settle a minster, so that formerly men said that for 30 years never stilled the sound of creaking wagons nor complaining slaves. . . .]

This account of Seaxburh's building project raises a number of interesting points, not the least of which is the semi-poetic nature of its alliterative rhythmic prose. It establishes Seaxburh, rather than one of her male relatives, as the founder of Sheppey (despite remarks like historian K. P. Witney's that Sheppey was "founded for" rather than by Seaxburh[23]). It also assumes the presence of slave labor: Swanton translates *wales* as "harrows," Cockayne as "wheel," but *wales* is more simply translated as "slaves," despite the discomfort twentieth-century readers may feel at the coexistence of slavery and renowned piety. Margaret Faull and David Pelteret both agree that *wales* here means "slaves," and both include this instance of *wales* in their respective discussions of slavery.[24] Seaxburh and her daughter take the veil together, indicating the joint nature of this intergenerational religious venture.

While Bede does not mention Eormenhild at all, much less her mother-daughter relationship with Seaxburh, he does reference Seaxburh's relationship with Eorcengota, her other daughter, before he discusses Eorcengota's saintliness. In true Bedan fashion, he is most interested in Eorcengota's virginity and her death, but before chronicling these he notes that "Cuius regis filia maior Sexburg, uxor Earconbercti regis Cantuariorum, habuit filiam Earcongotam, de qua sumus dicturi," (the eldest daughter of the king [Anna of East Anglia] was Seaxburh, wife of King Eorcenberht of Kent, whose daughter Eorcengota deserves special mention.)[25] *The Anglo-Saxon Chronicle* also mentions Seaxburh prominently as Eorcengota's mother in the entry under AD 640 (Bede's *History* was an important source for the *Chronicle*—thus the obvious similarity between these two texts). The E Text reads:

Her Eadbald Cantwara cining forðferde. se wæs cining XXIIII wintra. ða feng his sunu Ercenbriht to þam rice. Se towearp ealla þa deofelgyld on his rice. ond ærost Engliscra cininga he gesette Eastor feasten. þæs dohtor wæs gehaten Ercongota. hali femne ond wundorlic man. þære modor wæs Sexburh. Annan dohtor. Eastengla ciningas.

[In this year Eadbald, king of the people of Kent, died. He had been king for 24 years. Then his son Eorcenberht succeeded to the kingdom. He demolished all the idols in his kingdom. And, first of the English kings, he established the Easter fast. His daughter was called Ercongota, a holy virgin and a remarkable person, whose mother was Seaxburh, daughter of Anna, king of the East Angles.][26]

While this entry could be read as a glorification of Eorcenberht for his pious kingship and his relationship by marriage to Anna, it also defines Seaxburh not as the wife of a king but specifically as a mother of a daughter. In this, her only mention in the *Anglo-Saxon Chronicle,* Seaxburh is a *modor.* Her daughter Eorcengota was a nun and eventually the abbess at Brie (Farmoutier), revealing a Gaulish connection for Sheppey; Eorcengota's aunt Æðelburh, her mother's sister or half sister, was abbess there, and the maternal genealogy of Brie expands from mother-daughter to mother's sister–sister's daughter.[27]

This pattern of maternal genealogy plays out at Whitby as well. Whitby, founded by Hild and home to Cædmon, the (in)famous "Father of English poetry" boasts its own maternal genealogy elided by Bede and most historians. While Lees and Overing are concerned to "rescue" Hild from Bede—and a noble endeavor it is too—I wish to argue that Hild engaged in maternal practice quite different from those Lees and Overing (and Bede) ascribe to her.

Lees and Overing take Bede to task, quite rightly, for not giving Hild enough credit for her work at Whitby. Like Stephanie Hollis, they argue that Bede was uncomfortable with a woman in charge, especially in charge of cultural production, and Bede effectively wrote Hild out of much of her own history. Lees and Overing point out that Bede begins his narrative of Whitby with Hild's death, effectively killing her off before he discusses the Synod of Whitby (which she hosted and attended) and Cædmon's gift of poetry (which she recognized and encouraged). Feminist historians who have written recently on Hild tend to assume she was a widow when she entered the monastic life at the age of 33 (Christine Fell notes that Bede "rarely misses the opportunity to use the title 'virgin' but Bede never calls her one" while Hollis notes the inapplicability of "Bede's predilection for the persecuted virgin model of female sanctity" to Hild's life).[28] They celebrate Hild's administrative skills, her encouragement of learning, and even our "warm awareness of a human personality" in Hild.[29]

Hild has, then, to some extent, been rescued from Bede. Her maternal genealogy has not, however, and it is here that I now turn. If Hild were a widow—and she probably was—then Whitby begins to fit the pattern of a monastery founded by a widow, and Fell and others have suggested that Hild used land from her dowry or widow's inheritance to found Whitby. The connection to Frankish Gaul is provided by Hild's sister Hereswið, who went to Chelles as a widow, where Hild herself was bound when called back to Northumbria by Aidan (as Bede tells us).[30]

Whitby's dynasty of biologically related abbesses is somewhat murky; Bede is a bit vague about Hild's parentage, stating that she was of noble birth (nobilis natu erat) and that she was the daughter of Hereric, who was a nephew of King Edwin of Northumbria (d.632). Bede names Hild's mother when discussing the hagiographically commonplace vision by the saint's mother of the saint's future greatness, but Breguswið's connections to the East Anglian and Northumbrian royal families, although there must have been some, are not included in Bede's narrative. There is some confusion about Hild's sister Hereswið, whom Bede terms the mother of Ealdwuld, king of the East Angles. She was most likely married to Anna's brother Æðelric, although Anna himself had a wife named Hereswið (mother of Æðelþryð, Seaxburh, and Wihtburh). Hild, then, had royal connections to the thrones of East Anglia and Northumbria. It is through these connections that she builds her maternal genealogy.

Hild's kinswoman Ælfflæd succeeded her as abbess of Whitby, thus illustrating again the maternal pattern of biological succession. It seems that Ælfflæd and her mother Eanflæd may have held some sort of joint abbacy for a few years between Hild's death (AD 680) and Eanflæd's. Hild's exact relationship to Ælfflæd is hard to determine—while many scholars simply refer to her as Hild's niece (which would fit the patterns of maternal genealogy quite nicely),[31] we cannot place exactly Hereric's or Breguswið's relationships to Edwin or Æðelburh of Northumbria (Eanflæd's parents). Eckenstein states that Hild was baptized with Eanflæd at Easter 627,[32] and while Bede is vague about exactly how Hereric is Edwin's nephew (by marriage? through a sister? a brother?), Eanflæd and Hild were, at least by marriage, first cousins once removed, thus making Ælfflæd Hild's first cousin twice removed. It is possible and even likely that the tangled web of royal relationships and marriages also provided a closer connection, and Ælfflæd may indeed have been Hild's niece.

Hollis argues that Ælfflæd of Whitby may have been even more politically prominent than Hild, and Hollis uses the Life of Gregory written at Whitby during Ælfflæd's rule as well as the Life of Cuthbert and the Life of Wilfrid to show her "active involvement in both royal and ecclesiastical politics."[33] While Ælfflæd may indeed have advised bishops and saints in her role as her aunt(?) Hild did before her, Ælfflæd's succession to Hild's place, especially her sharing of that place with her mother for a brief time, indicates that maternal genealogy was thriving at Whitby just as it was at Ely and Sheppey.

One interesting aspect of Eanflæd's and Ælfflæd's monastic life is their choice of Whitby rather than Lyminge, the monastery founded after Edwin's death by Æðelburh, Edwin's queen and Eanflæd's mother. It would seem that for maternal genealogy to hold true, so to speak, Eanflæd should have gone to Lyminge. But Æðelburh of Lyminge, also called Tata (d.647), was not succeeded by her daughter in a monastic maternal genealogy; her daughter went to Whitby instead. Eanflæd also could have settled at her cousin Eanswið's monastery at Folkestone in Kent (Eanswið was the sister of Eorcenberht and thus Seaxburh's sister-in-law). The reason for her Northumbrian choice, it seems, is male intervention—Ælfflæd went to Whitby as a child at her father's direction, and Eanflæd chose to reunite with her daughter at Whitby rather than to honor the memory of her mother at Lyminge or to settle with her cousin at Folkestone. Eanflæd's range of monastic options with female blood links, however, provides further illustration of the spread of these matrilineally linked double monasteries.

Eanflæd did not have an easy childhood. Bede narrates the horror of her father Edwin's death and Æðelburh's flight back to Kent (she was the daughter of Æðelberht, king of Kent) with Eanflæd and Paulinus, her bishop. Eanflæd returned to Northumbria to marry Oswiu after he converted to Christianity. Bede details how Oswiu dedicated their daughter Ælfflæd to Christ to fulfill a vow made before a battle, and Bede twice refers to Ælfflæd's virginity as he tells of her life as nun under Hild, although he does not mention the biological relationship between Hild and her new student.

There is archaeological as well as textual evidence for Ælfflæd's childhood at Whitby; excavation there unearthed a stone slab that may have marked either Ælfflæd's grave or the site of her translation; Charles Peers and C. A. Ralegh Radford reconstruct the inscription to read AELFLEADA/ QUAE AB INFANTIA/ CONSILIATRIXQUE VAS, Ælfflæd who from infancy (was) a Conciliator and Vessel (of God), and suggest that another slab below it contained the word *electa,* chosen.[34] These various rereadings and findings, then, show that Hild, Eanflæd, and Ælfflæd make up a maternal genealogy of Whitby, much like those of Ely and Sheppey.

These discussions of the royal monasteries of Ely, Sheppey, and Whitby, then, reveal a pattern of maternal genealogy, a pattern of biological relation unique to double monasteries headed by women. While there were houses founded for men only in the seventh and eighth centuries, any monastery open to women was a double monastery headed by an abbess.[35] The single-sex houses seem to demonstrate no such pattern of biological succession in the abbacy. I take as my examples the most famous early Anglo-Saxon houses for men only—Benedict Biscop's Monk Wearmouth and Jarrow, and Sts. Peter and Paul at Canterbury (later St. Augustine's). Bede's *Ecclesiastical History* informs us that Benedict Biscop, founder and first abbot of Monk Wearmouth, was succeeded by Ceolfrið, Bede's current abbot. Ceolfrið is called Benedict's "companion and fellow worker" in book four—*cooperatore ac socio eiusdem operis;*[36] evidently the relationship between the men did not include a biological link. Benedict Biscop also served as abbot for two years at Sts. Peter and Paul in Canterbury before he founded Wearmouth in 674.[37] Following Benedict was Theodore's companion Hadrian, definitely not biologically related to Benedict; Hadrian was succeeded as abbot by his pupil Albinus. While a metaphorical paternal relationship may have existed between Hadrian and Albinus, a biological one certainly did not.

Perhaps the influence of Irish asceticism and the stringency of the Benedictine Rule combined to encourage the selection of chaste men as abbots for men-only houses, perhaps chaste men like Bede who had been confirmed in the monastic life from a young age. While Bede does reveal the existence of "family monasteries," which certainly would have involved biological relations among the officers of the house and their successors, he includes them to disparage them as tax shelters rather than as places of devotion and learning. The great double houses of Ely, Whitby, and Sheppey are obviously comparable in such regard to Jarrow, Wearmouth, or Canterbury, but their matrilineality differentiates them from the men-only great houses. For the men's houses, no complementary pattern of "paternal genealogy" seems to exist. The double monastery consistently presents itself as a house with links to Frankish Gaul, founded by a royal princess or widow as its first abbess, then passed to her biological sister, daughter, or niece, who is as likely to be a widow as a virgin. Minster-in-Thanet, the preeminent house of the female royal Kentish saints, fits this pattern as well.

Matrilineality at Minster-in-Thanet

David Rollason has termed the group of texts describing Minster-in-Thanet the "Mildrith Legend," although the scope of these narrative genealogies goes far beyond Mildrið, the virgin-saint-princess who was Thanet's second abbess. Examination of the legend's texts as well as of charters and the *Anglo-Saxon Chronicle* indicates that Minster-in-Thanet was a peaceful and powerful institution, governed matrilineally so that mothers invested daughters with power, whether temporal or spiritual, within or without the walls.

The textual sources for the history of Minster-in-Thanet are varied and problematic. Rollason does an admirable job of sorting, sourcing, and comparing them in his important study *The Mildrith Legend: A Study in Early Medieval Hagiography in England.* None is contemporary with the founding of the monastery itself, although some of the texts' sources may be, and the texts cannot agree on something as seemingly basic as Mildrið's mother's name. Hollis argues that the most originary of the extant texts is the mid-eleventh-century Old English fragment, London, British Library, MS Cotton Caligula A.14, which breaks off before Mildrið comes to Thanet.[38] Other texts include a *Life* of Mildrið by the twelfth-century Goscelin of Canterbury, a section of the *Historia Regum,* a *Life* of Æðelberht and Æðelred (Mildrið's cousins), and the interesting text called *þa Halgan* because of its heading—*Her cyð ymbe þa halgan þe on Angelcynne restað.* The *þa Halgan* text is part of the *Liber Vitae* of New Minster and Hyde Abbey, British Library, MS Stowe 944. The text combines a genealogy of the royal house of Kent with a list of resting-places of its saints. A typical section reads, "ðonne wæs Ymme, Eadbaldes cwen, Franca cynges dohtor; and hig begeaton sancte Eanswiðe, þe æt Folcanstane restað" [then Ymme, daughter of the king of France, was Eadbald's queen, and they begot Saint Eanswið, who rests at Folkestone].[39] Rollason shows that this text has a Kentish origin (unsurprisingly) that cannot be dated more precisely than 725–974 (the *Liber Vitae* dates to circa 1031).[40] Because of the Kentish origin, relative completeness, and possible early date for the text, I will be using it as the primary text in this study, although I will judiciously refer to other texts of the legend as well. A brief outline of the Minster-in-Thanet foundation story runs along these lines:

Eorcenberht and Eormenred were the two sons of Eadbald, king of Kent (d.640). Eorcenberht, who succeeded his father on the throne, married Seaxburh and had Egberht (among others). Eormenred had two sons (Æðelberht and Æðelred) and at least two daughters (the texts are unclear here), Eormenburh and Eormengyð. Eafe/Æbbe may be another daughter of Eormenred, although some texts equate her with Eormenburh.

Egberht succeeded to his father's throne in 664, and sometime between 664 and Egberht's death in 673, his cousins Æðelberht and Æðelred were murdered, either at his direction or by the machinations of one of his advisors.

Their sister Æbbe/Eafe/Eormenburh had been married to Merewalh, a son of Penda and subking of the Maegosaeton. After they had four children, they separated amicably because of the love of God, and Æbbe went to Kent at Egberht's summons to collect *wergild* (literally, man-price) for her dead brothers. She chose land on Thanet, built a minster dedicated to St. Mary there, and sent her daughter Mildrið to Chelles for training. Her other daughters also entered the monastic life—Mildburh as abbess of Much Wenlock in Shropshire, Mildgyð in an unspecified monastery in Northumbria. Her son died in childhood.

At Chelles, Mildrið resisted a marriage arranged for her by the abbess to one of the abbess's kinsmen, and after a series of legendary events, including controlling tides and leaving footprints on a rock of her homeland, Mildrið returned to Thanet to be consecrated by Archbishop Theodore and take her mother's place as abbess (thus dating her consecration to before

690, the year of Theodore's death). She was celebrated for her piety and wisdom as well as her miracles. She died between 732 and 748, when her successor Eadburh translated her remains from St. Mary's to the new church of SS. Peter and Paul.

A number of the aspects of maternal genealogy are immediately apparent. The minster is founded on land obtained through her male kin by a previously married woman, whom I will call Æbbe throughout this chapter (Eafe/Æbbe/Eormenburh is called Æbbe in the reliable charters relating to the lands of Minster-in-Thanet). The connection to Frankish Gaul comes through Mildrið's education there. Mildrið's mother passes control of her monastery to her daughter. Other female kin are at Minster-in-Thanet as well, I shall argue—and Thanet's connection with Theodore shows its possible connections with Greek rather than Roman practices, as discussed in the canons of Theodore's *Penitential.*

Thanet, like Whitby and Ely and Sheppey, provided a forum for maternal practice at the same time that it participated in the institutional patriarchies of church and state. Minster-in-Thanet is absent from Bede's *History,* although he does describe Augustine's landing on the island of Thanet and Æðelberht's initial meeting with the missionaries there. Thus, Thanet already had holy and historical significance when its founding abbess established her monastery there. Thanet must predate Ely, for Ely was founded in 673 (the year Egberht died); Thanet was probably somewhat contemporary with Sheppey, as Egberht's mother Seaxburh founded her monastery after finishing her regency for her son (probably in the late 660s).

The later, male-authored texts of the *Legend,* as Rollason terms them, do not indicate the varied power of the monastery and its abbesses in the political turmoil of late-seventh-century England, although Hollis argues that the legend originated at Thanet and in its original form celebrated the female genealogy and accomplishments of the house at the same time that it reasserted the monastery's title to its lands.[41] Charter evidence indicates that the minster prospered even in a time of constant turnover on the throne. While Viking invasion was still far in the future, the kings of Kent, Wessex, and Mercia fought almost continuously to establish dominance of the land south of the Humber river. The *Anglo-Saxon Chronicle* is more likely to note that a king "was slain" than that he died, and the dominance of Æðelberht of Kent (d.616) was not continued by his descendents, who were variously dependent on and invaded by the other kings throughout the century.

Kent was the site of numerous invasions and conflicts at the end of the seventh century.[42] In 676, when Minster-in-Thanet was probably less than

ten years old, the *Chronicle* records that "Æþelred Myrcena cining oferher-
gode Centland" [Ethelred, King of the Mercians, ravaged Kent]. Similarly,
in 686, the year after Hloðere's death, "Ceadwala ond Mul his broðor
forhergodan Cent" [Ceadwalla and Mul his brother ravaged Kent]. The
following year matter-of-factly reports one of the most horrifying of the
Chronicle's entries: "Her Mul wærð on Cent bærned. ond oðre XII men
mid him. ond þy geara Ceadwala eft forhergode Cent" [In this year Mul
was burned in Kent and 12 other men with him, and in this year Cead-
walla again ravaged Kent]. The *cantwara* then paid 30,000 pence in wergild
in 694 to Ine for Mul's death so that Wihtred, Egberht's son, could solidify his kingship.

Throughout this turmoil, Æbbe and her daughter continued to solidify
their claims to their holdings and secure privileges for their monastery that
would protect them from rapid change in secular leadership. While we
have no extensive narrative like Bede's to guide us, or even from which to
rescue Æbbe and Mildrið, charter evidence indicates their involvement
with the secular world and the influence they wielded there, outside their
walls.[43]

Six charters show grants of land from four different kings of Kent to
Æbbe for land in and around Thanet island, indicating her ability to nego-
tiate with the variety of male power figures in the region. Birch charter
#44, issued by Lotharius, king of Kent (Seaxburh's son Hloðere, Æbbe's
cousin), grants the land of Sudanie in the island of Thanet to Æbbe in 678;
this may well confirm the original grant by Egberht recorded in the *Legend* texts, including *þa Halgan*. S. E. Kelly suggests as much in her discussion of the Thanet charters, arguing that we should view the early,
repetitive charters in the series as a set "regarded . . . as the title-deed for
the core of Minster's early endowment." It seems reasonable to argue that
Æbbe wished to confirm her holdings with the new king, who was also
her cousin. Kelly points out that "Land first provided by an invader needed
all possible guarantees."[44]

Later charters indicate Æbbe's similar maneuverings to maintain clear
title to the monastery's land. While the *Anglo-Saxon Chronicle* indicates that
there were two kings in Kent, Wihtred and Swaefheard, in its entry for 692,
these charters show that there were more than two men calling themselves
king of Kent in the early 690s. Barbara Yorke has shown the intricate structure of dual kingship in Kent in the early Anglo-Saxon period, with a king
of west Kent subordinate to a king of east Kent; Yorke's analysis substantially clarifies the murky historical record.[45] Birch charters #35 and #40
are issued by King Osuuine to Æbba wherein he grants her and her
monastery rights to land in Sturrey (#35) and on Thanet island (#40). The
land on Thanet is termed "quam aliquando Yrminredus possidebat" [that

which Eormenred (Æbbe's father) had possessed]. Both #35 and #40—dated by Sawyer to circa 690—are witnessed by Suebard, presumably one of the "kings" mentioned in the *Chronicle,* who also issues charters #41 and #42 to Æbbe as king of Kent. While all of these charters have been somehow corrupted in their textual transmission, they are all ultimately indicative of "genuine seventh-century documentation," according to Kelly, the most recent scholar to discuss them in detail.[46] Archbishop Theodore, who is also invoked in #44, witnesses #35, lending the imprimatur of the church to the transaction; it is interesting to note that Æbbe witnesses none of the charters granting and confirming land to her, perhaps indicating a reluctance on the part of the king(s) and the archbishop to allow a woman to ratify anyone's business, even her own.

Suebard as king issues his own charters, #41 and #42, to Æbbe, which confirm and enlarge the grants by Egberht, Lotharius, and Osuuine, using the same language, and invoking Theodore's counsel (even though he was probably dead by the time Suebard could call himself king of Kent). Suebard's charters to Æbbe grant her land in Sturry (previously granted by Osuuini), Sudanie (previously granted by Hloðere), and Botdesham. Osuuini is listed as a witness to charter #42, indicating that the balance of power between him and Suebard had been reversed, although Kelly suggests they may have been joint kings.[47] Æbbe, then, can be seen to wield enough influence to have her land grants chartered and confirmed by whichever man was styling himself king at the time; Sawyer and Kelly date charters #41 and #42, as well as #35 and #40, to circa 690, indicating that all four of them were issued within a short time.

Æbbe also seems to have had a good working relationship with Wihtred, who was king of Kent from 694 (when the Kentish people paid Mul's wergild to Ine) to his death in 725. Since Wihtred was the son of Egberht, Æbbe's cousin, he was Æbbe's first cousin once removed. He and his queen jointly granted land called Humeratun on Thanet island to Æbbe in July of 694 (Birch #86); Kelly has thoroughly dispelled any doubts about the authenticity of this charter.[48] Kinigitha the queen also witnesses the charter, an anomaly that indicates Wihtred's acceptance of the participation of women in public affairs. Kinigitha seems to be the first female witness to an authentic charter;[49] despite many charters granting land to women, women do not witness the documents until Wihtred's reign, perhaps lending ammunition to historians who view Wihtred as "unduly dominated by women."[50] It is interesting to note that Æbbe, not Mildrið, is the abbess of Thanet (*Æbbe abbatisse de menstre*) in Wihtred's charter #86 of 694, indicating a flaw in the *Legend*'s texts about Mildrið's assumption of her mother's role upon her consecration. While most of the *Legend* texts state that Mildrið was consecrated by Theodore and took over as abbess directly after her consecration, charter #86 indicates that Æbbe was still very much the abbess of Minster-in-Thanet four years after Theodore's death.

There is a possibility that Æbbe and Mildrið engaged in the maternal practice of a joint mother-daughter abbacy at Thanet like that of Eanflæd and Ælfflæd at Whitby. Æbbe is called abbess in a charter of 694; Mildrið is called abbess in the documents of the Bapchild Synod, dated to 694–696 (both discussed later in this chapter). We may want to reason that Æbbe died in the interval between the creation of these two documents. However, Wihtred charters land at Haeg in Kent to *Eabbe abbatissae* in 697 (Birch #96). While Kelly addresses some problems with this charter, she concludes that "a genuine charter underlies the extant text" and accepts identification of Eabbe with Æbbe, thus allowing the intriguing possibility of joint mother-daughter abbacy in Kent as well as in Northumbria.

The record of the Bapchild Synod, a much neglected piece of Anglo-Saxon history, shows that Mildrið continued to develop the minster's good working relationship with the current king. Like her mother, she bulwarked the privileges of her monastery against the possibilities of political turmoil—she was the beneficiary of grants from Æðelbehrt (Birch #141), Eadberht (Birch #846) and Æðelbald (Birch #149). Rollason has discussed the possibility that the royal monasteries of Kent served as centers for a *regio,* or specific administrative region of the kingdom, and that thus the abbesses were in some ways the deputized officers of the kings, to whom they were related by blood.[51]

The record of the Bapchild Synod, however, indicates that Wihtred formally relinquished much of the administrative power of the monasteries, perhaps in a power-brokering move that helped to ensure his kingship in the chaos of late-seventh-century Kent.[52] The document appears in a number of places, including an abbreviated Old English form in the F Text of the *Anglo-Saxon Chronicle.*[53] Mildrið and her minster(s) figure prominently in the Latin version of this document, which confirms previous grants and privileges to the kingdom's monasteries by previous kings, guarantees the right of the archbishop to appoint abbots and abbesses to those monasteries, and exempts the church from most of the customary taxes due to the king.[54]

While church historians may be most interested in the confirmation of the archbishop's right to appoint abbots and abbesses, the maternal genealogist is most interested in the flow of power between Mildrið and her second cousin the king. The listed monasteries are "Upmynster, Raculf, Suðmynster, Dofras, Folcanstan, Limming, Scepeis, et Hoe"; Mildrið was abbess of "Suðmynster" and possibly of Lyminge as well (as I will discuss later). This document confirms, then, all previous land grants and privileges to Minster-in-Thanet for the duration of Wihtred's reign, thus protecting the monastery from any erroneous claims to its holdings.

In addition, Mildrið is a witness to the Latin form of the document (Birch #91) along with four other abbesses, demonstrating yet again Wihtred's propensity for including women in his administration. Mildrið's name is first among the abbesses, indicating the prominence of her position; about the others—Æðeldriðae, Ætte, Wilnoðae, and Hereswyðae—we know nothing, unless this "Ætte" is identical with the "Eabbe" of charter #96 and thus possibly Mildrið's mother. Also in the witness list are Wihtred; his queen Werburga (Kinigitha, Wihtred's queen of 694 and charter #86, seems to have been replaced); Archbishop Berhtwald; "Æðelberht and his brother Eadberht" (presumably the sons of Wihtred—Wihtred was succeeded by Æðelberht); Bishop Tobias; and nine *presbiteri* (whose names come after those of the abbesses). This witness list shows Mildrið in exalted company, maintaining the economic security of her minster.

While the Bapchild Synod documents show Mildrið's involvement at the highest levels of both church and state, the possibility of her involvement in other monasteries is also indicated by charter evidence. Rollason discusses the possible joint nature of the monasteries of Thanet and Lyminge, and while his evidence dates from the ninth century,[55] charter evidence shows that Mildrið held land at Lyminge in 724, thus indicating that Thanet had some, if not full, control of Lyminge in the first quarter of the eighth century.

Such control would accentuate the pattern of maternal genealogy in the royal monasteries of Kent. Lyminge was founded by Mildrið's great-great aunt Æðelburh, whose daughter Eanflæd became abbess of Whitby. Witney suggests that Mildrið's aunt Eormenburg was abbess at Lyminge after she became a widow; Mildrið may have taken over after her aunt's death, if Witney is correct.[56] In 724, Wihtred's son Æðelberht granted land around the river in Lyminge to "Mildrithae religiousae abbatissae" (Birch #141). It is significant that the charter does not say to which minster Mildrið belongs; in the other charters that name her in the text, she is "Mildrede abbatise in Thaneto" (Birch #88) or "Mildrithae religiosae abbatisse . . . in insula Thanet" (Birch #149) or "Mildrithae abbatissae de Menstre" (Birch #150). This land grant in Lyminge from the son of the reigning king to his first cousin once-removed hints that Mildrið, like her cousin Werburh who governed a number of monasteries, may have been abbess of Lyminge and Thanet simultaneously. Such a position would indicate the extent of her political influence to be even greater than earlier supposed; it also indicates the explicitly matrilineal nature of the abbess's position in this monastery. In this analysis, the formulaic phrase of the land grant in the charters—"do Mildrithae religiosae abbatissae et venerabili familiae ejus" [I give to Mildrið the religious abbess and her venerable family]—takes on new meaning, as the biological and spiritual meanings of *familiae* blend and collapse into one another.

The charters as well lead us to the continuation of the maternal genealogy at Thanet. The texts I shall group together as the "ship charters" introduce the figure of Eadburh, Mildrið's enigmatic successor who, I will argue, forms the third in the matrilineage of Thanet.

Like the land grant charters, the ship charters show the ability of the abbess of Thanet to confirm her rights with the current king. The charters, a series of five similar documents that relieve the abbess of Minster-in-Thanet of the duty to pay tax on a ship, are issues of Æðelbald of Mercia, Offa of Mercia, and Eadberht of Kent.[57] The first, Birch #149, relieves Mildrið, termed "Mildrithae religiosae abbatissae . . . in insula Thanet," of the tax on a ship in the port of London. Kelly dates this charter to 716/717, in the early part of Æðelbald's reign.[58] This charter is tantalizing in its hints of a commercial aspect of Mildrið's monastery management: Why did an abbess need to have a ship that docked at the port of London? Was she selling goods or crops produced on monastery lands in the city? Did she own the ships? Did they travel on the open ocean or just in the riverways from Thanet to London? While we cannot answer the questions that this charter raises, the charter itself shows us that Mildrið was a shrewd businesswoman who used her connections with the political establishment to the financial benefit of her minster.

The second charter, Birch #150, indicates similar management strategies. Kelly argues that #150 actually predates #149, if only slightly, and suggests that the toll exemptions were drawn up in Kent and carried to Mercia for ratification by the king-overlord.[59] Like #149, #150 is issued by Æðelbald to "Mildrithae abbatissae de Menstre" and exempts the ship from tolls in all of Æðelbald's territory "ut ubique in regno nostro libera de omni regali fiscu et tributo maneat" [so that (the ship) might remain in our reign free of all kingly tax and tribute]. These two charters from Æðelbald to Mildrið show that she exerted power in the traditionally patriarchal realms of trade and taxes—this abbess's work included not only spiritual but also commercial and political ventures.

The third of the Thanet ship charters remits half of the tax for one ship—"dimidium vectigal unius navis"—from Æðelbald to Eadburh, Mildrið's successor. The charter, Birch #177, is dated reliably to 748, for it mentions Mildrið's translation in that year to the new church on Thanet. It shows that Eadburh was expanding Thanet's fleet, as it refers to a ship recently acquired by Minster from someone named Leubucus. Since the other grants (#149 and #150) were supposed to be valid for all of Æðelbald's reign, this charter shows that the community at Minster was deeply engaged in ship trading, with two or possibly three ships (although Hollis reads the charter #177 as a replacement of the ones granted to Mildrið— and thus a tax increase on the monastery[60]). Eadburh receives a tax ex- emption for half of the usual dues rather than Mildrið's whole (totam exactionem navis), indicating that perhaps Æðelbald was ready to make some concessions to the abbess of Thanet but also felt that, with more than one ship engaged in commerce, she could well afford to pay some, if not all, of the usual fees.

The last two ship charters are actually confirmations of the earlier grants, and again they illustrate the ability of the abbess to work to the minster's advantage with the current king. Æðelbald of Mercia obviously had enough power in Kent to charter ship-tax exemptions in the 730s and 740s; similarly, Offa of Mercia confirms in charter #188 the same privi- leges to Abbess Sigeburga of Thanet in 759. He invokes Æðelbald's char- ter to Mildrið—"illam donationem quam gloriosis Ethilbaldus Deo omnipotenti gratiarum persolvens actiones, Mildrithae abbatissae de navis onustae transvectiones censu"—and then confirms the same rights upon "Sigeburgae ejusdem monasterii abbatisse" [Sigeburga the abbess of that same minster].

Similarly, Eadberht of Kent two years later remits taxes to Sigeburga for two ships (duarum navium) at Sarre in Kent in Birch #189. The exemption also refers to a third ship being built at Minster, which Eadberht exempts from tolls at Sarre and at Fordwich. He invokes both Æðelbald (sicut a reg- ibus Merciorum Æðilbaldo) and Offa (rege Offan), indicating the ongoing na- ture of these transactions. The ship charters show that the abbesses of Thanet managed trade routes and commercial ventures for the benefit of the minster at the same time that they engaged in pastoral work, provided education, and furthered their own spiritual studies.

Eadburh, Mildrið's successor, did much more for Thanet than expand its fleet; under her direction, Thanet was a school for the highest sort of cul- ture, Latin religious poetry, as well as a center for book production. Eadburh of Thanet is traditionally identified with the Eadburh of the Boniface cor- respondence, an abbess of a rich and varied house; most scholars accept that identification.[61] Witney, for example, refers to Eadburh as "a highly articu- late person, the close friend and correspondent of St. Boniface."[62] In con- trast, Patricia Coulstock argues that the "Edburga" of the Boniface correspondence, at least the one noted in Lioba's letter of 732 to Boniface (discussed in detail later), should be identified with Tetta, whom Rudolf of Fulda identifies as Lioba's mentor at Wimborne. Coulstock's evidence for this, however, is Rudolf's insistence on the exclusivity of Lioba and Tetta's bond—and Hollis has shown that Rudolf had a political and religious agenda of his own.[63] Lioba need not have had only one teacher to have had a special bond with Tetta, and we know definitively that Eadburh was abbess at the proper time at a wealthy, royal monastery on the coast (for relatively easy access to the continent). Hence, I will accept the usual identification of Boniface's Eadburh with Thanet's Eadburh. Rollason states: "Minster-in-Thanet may also have been well equipped from a cultural and scholarly viewpoint. Boniface, the 'apostle of Germany,' corresponded with an abbess called Eadburg who was active in the first half of the eighth century and may have been Mildrith's successor as abbess of Minster-in-Thanet. Boniface's correspondent was clearly the head of a very learned and literary house. . . ."[64] These letters make it abundantly clear that Eadburh was doing more at Thanet than building ships. Five letters in the Boniface correspondence are relevant to Eadburh's rule there. They have mostly been read to reveal the level of cultural attainment at the monastery, as indeed they do. They also reveal the links among the monasteries of southern England, and show that maternal and matrilineal connection flourished between the minsters as well as within them.

Letters from Boniface to Eadburh requesting and thanking her for books are those most frequently cited to show the level of cultural production at Thanet. In 735 or 736, Boniface thanks Eadburh for the gift of books she had sent him and asks for her prayers.[65] A second letter, dated 735, thanks Eadburh not just for books but also for clothes—indicating that Thanet produced cloth as well?—before Boniface asks her to make a copy of the Epistles of Peter in gold letters. He sends the materials for this project along with the letter.[66] The Thanet scriptorium, then, had the ability to produce work of the highest level. Eadburh was more than simply a book-provider for Boniface, however; another letter from him to her asks simply for her prayers, and reveals some of the danger of Boniface's position; he speaks of "struggle and grief, fighting without and fear within" as he asks her to pray to keep him safe.[67] Such correspondence is enlightening about both Boniface's mission and Thanet's production abilities, but sheds no light on Eadburh's matrilineal connections to Thanet and other monasteries.

Two other letters in the Boniface correspondence, however, do hint at maternal connections and performances. These are a long letter from Boniface to Eadburh about a mystical vision experienced by a monk at Much Wenlock and a shorter letter from Lioba asking for prayers and instruction. These letters tie Eadburh, through the Boniface correspondence, to three other double monasteries in England. While I remarked earlier on the connections of Thanet with Whitby, Ely, and Sheppey, through these letters of Boniface to Eadburh and Lioba to Boniface, three more houses—those of Much Wenlock, Barking, and Wimborne—become tangentially related to Thanet as well.

Much Wenlock, the residence of the visionary monk, was the house founded by Mildburh, Mildrið's sister. Boniface calls it *monasterio Milburge abbatissae,* the monastery of Abbess Milburga, indicating that she was still Much Wenlock's abbess in 716, the date of the letter.[68] The monastery's originary charters have been gathered together in a first-person narrative (called "St. Mildburg's testament") that purports to be the dictation of Mildburh herself.[69] Mildburh was not the first abbess of Wenlock, despite her family's involvement in its founding; she seems to have been expressly trained for the position of abbess by the first abbess, Liobsynde, whose name indicates her Frankish nationality (the *Oxford Dictionary of Saints* simply states that Liobsynde came from Chelles[70]).

At Much Wenlock parts of the maternal genealogical pattern reassert themselves: Much Wenlock, like Thanet, Whitby, Ely, and Sheppey, was a large and prosperous house with a connection to Frankish Gaul, governed by a royal abbess on land given to her by a male relative. Other than the "testament," early records of Much Wenlock are practically nonexistent, so we have no way of knowing if Mildburh was able to establish a maternal genealogy there as her mother and sister did in Thanet.

Boniface's letter describing the vision to Eadburh also draws the monastery of Barking into the web of related foundations. He states that he heard about the vision at Much Wenlock from Hildelith of Barking, indicating some correspondence between Much Wenlock and Barking as well. Barking is famous in Anglo-Saxon studies as the home of the original readers of Aldhelm's notoriously abstruse *De Virginitate,* which is dedicated to the nuns of Barking. That text is frequently cited as evidence that nuns in the "golden age" had educations as stringent as their brothers'.[71]

Barking was founded by St. Earcenwald for his sister Æðelburh (adding another Æðelburh, of Barking, to the previously discussed Æðelburh of Brie and Æðelburh of Lyminge) in the second half of the seventh century; the *Oxford Dictionary of Saints* says of Æðelburh of Barking: "Of a wealthy (possibly royal) family and sister of Erkenwald, Ethelburga was quite likely the owner, as well as the ruler, of Barking. A late tradition says that Erkenwald invited Hildelith from Chelles to be prioress and future abbess of Barking; her difficult task was to teach Ethelburga monastic traditions while retaining a subordinate role."[72] Since Æðelburh is not called virgin, we can suppose that, like Hild and Seaxburh and Æðelburh of Lyminge and Æbbe, Æðelburh had been married before entering the monastic life. Whitelock states that, "It is probable that Eorcenwald was a member of the Kentish royal house, for it is only in this that the Frankish name-element *Eorcen* is met with."[73] Barking, indicated by the Boniface correspondence to be communicating with Mildburh's Much Wenlock, was ruled by a (possibly Kentish) princess who had been married before; its connection to Frankish Gaul came from the famous Hildelith.

The last of the Bonifatian letters I will discuss—the one that illuminates ties between Thanet and Wimborne—is one of the few texts from Anglo-Saxon England that we know definitively to have been written by a woman. Lioba, also called Leofgyð, was an Anglo-Saxon nun who traveled to Germany at Boniface's request and became abbess at Bischofsheim (d.782). Her *Life* was written only 50 years after her death by Rudolf of Fulda, and thus we have a relatively large quantity of probably accurate information about her life, although Hollis has exposed much of Rudolf's gender-based desires about nuns in general and Lioba in particular, as I noted earlier. Lioba's letter to Boniface dates to circa 732, while she is still in England. In the letter, Lioba names her parents—Dynne and Æbbe—and reminds Boniface that her mother is his blood relation. She asks Boniface for his prayers, and also asks him to comment on the style of her letter and some poetry she sends him.

Lioba's letter also describes Eadburh as a teacher, something of interest to the maternal genealogist looking for information. Her last sentence before she closes the letter and copies out her poem reads, "Istam artem ab eadburga magisterio didici, quae indesinenter legem divinam rimare non cessat" [I have learned this art from Eadburh, who still does not cease to examine divine law].[74] The most important information here is that Eadburh was a teacher at Thanet as well as its abbess and ship manager. Since the date of Lioba's letter is circa 732 (when Mildrið was still alive), we can extrapolate that Eadburh's succession was based on her teaching as well as on her administrative ability and blood ties to the royal house. Eadburh was not only a teacher but also a scholar, conducting her own investigation into divine law.

While Rudolf narrates Lioba's training at the double monastery of Wimborne, Lioba's reference to Eadburh places her at Thanet as well. It would seem she went from Thanet to Wimborne before going to the continent; she provides the link from Thanet to the most famous double house of Wessex, founded in 718 by Cuthburh, sister of Ine of Wessex (Wimborne's Cuthburh is traditionally associated with the Cuthburh of Barking named in Aldhelm's preface to *De Virginitate*).[75] Wimborne itself engaged in maternal practice: Cuthburh had been married to Aldfrið of Northumbria before founding Wimborne; Cuthburh's sister Cwenburh followed her as abbess; the sisters were followed by "Tetta," the abbess-teacher whom Rudolf identifies as Lioba's mentor at Wimborne. While Coulstock wants to identify Tetta (a nickname) with an Edburga of Wessex, she also notes that it could have been a nickname for either of the first two sister-abbesses; Rudolf identifies Tetta as *soror regis,* thus connecting her to the West Saxon royal house and relating her by blood to Cuthburh and Cwenburh, if she is not identical to one of them.

The Bonifatian correspondence, then, produces genealogical links from Thanet to three more double monasteries; it provides information about Eadburh's instructional and study habits; it hints at the high level of cultural production in Eadburh's monastery. It cannot, however, place Eadburh *biologically* in a maternal genealogy of Thanet. She was certainly related in some way to the Kentish royal house, for both parts of her name are found in the alliterative traditions of the Kentish royal family—Eadbald and Æðelburh, brother and sister, are just two examples. To place her in the genealogy, if only tentatively, we must first examine a previous inquiry into Eadburh's relationship to the Kentish royal house and then enter into a disagreement among eleventh- and twelfth-century monks about the relics of Mildrið and Eadburh.

K. P. Witney has used Eddius's *Life of Wilfrid,* supposed scribal error in *þa Halgan,* a letter from the Boniface correspondence, and a poem of Alcuin to argue that Æbbe's sister Eormengyð was really named Eangyð. This Eangyð, Witney argues, was married to Centwine, king of Wessex, and one of their children was Eadburh, who succeeded Mildrið as abbess of Thanet.[76] Witney's logic is tenuous in parts, especially in his rejection of the *þa Halgan* text that clearly states that "Ermengyð hyre moddrie mid hyre wunode oþ hyre lifes ende" [Eormengyð her (Mildrið's) maternal aunt lived with her until her life's end]. Michael Swanton, like Witney, presents Eadburh as the daughter of Centwine of Wessex,[77] although Swanton does not explain his presentation of this genealogical construction. If Witney and Swanton are correct, however, Eadburh would be Mildrið's cousin, Æbbe's niece, and thus a biologically appropriate link in Thanet's maternal genealogy.

Another possibility for Eadburh's relationship to Mildrið and Æbbe can be teased out from the dispute over Eadburh's and Mildrið's relics. Rollason has used the disagreement between the monks of St. Augustine's Canterbury and St. Gregory's Priory to show the source relationships among the various texts of the Mildrið Legend.[78] The version originating at St. Gregory's Priory (which claimed the relics of both women in the late eleventh century) had several "mistakes" in it, which Goscelin seized upon in his defense of the Canterbury claim to Mildrið's relics (St. Augustine's seemed rather less interested in Eadburh).

These mistakes include the claim that Eadburh was Mildrið's great-great aunt, a daughter of Æðelberht I, the Kentish king who received Augustine's mission in 597. In his treatise *Libellus contra inanes sanctae virginis Mildrethae usurpatores,* Goscelin points out the chronological impossibility of Mildrið's great-great aunt's translating Mildrið's relics. I would like to note here that which has been previously unremarked—that Mildrið may have had a great-great aunt Eadburh who was a daughter of Æðelberht. The þa Halgan text notes that Æðelburh founded Lyminge, "and þar nu resteð, and sancta Eadburh mid hyre" [and there now rests, and St. Eadburh with her]. While this Eadburh may be Mildrið's successor, the þa Halgan's approach is usually much more chronological than such an inclusion would allow. A reference to Eadburh of Thanet in the same sentence with Æðelburh of Lyminge (d.647) would be completely incongruous to the nature of this text. It is much more likely, although ultimately unprovable, that this first Eadburh mentioned in þa Halgan is a previously unremarked daughter of Æðelberht, perhaps by another wife or concubine, whose memory was still alive enough that the writers of the St. Gregory's Priory text mistook Æðelberht's daughter for Mildrið's successor.

While such speculation may partially elucidate an eleventh-century scribe's mistake, it brings us no closer to the relationship between Mildrið and her successor Eadburh. I would like to suggest here that Eadburh may indeed have been Æðelberht's daughter, as the monks of St. Gregory's Priory claimed—simply the daughter of a different Æðelberht.

The "other" Æðelberht in the Kentish royal legend is one of the murdered princes, Æðelberht and Æðelred, the brothers of Æbbe for whose wergild she took Thanet. Gordon Ward's work on King Osuuini points out that when one thinks about Ecgberht or one of his thanes murdering the brothers, "One can't help being reminded of the Princes in the Tower at a much later date and this may lead to a subconscious supposition that Ethelbert and Ethelred were children. This was not the case. They were certainly at least twenty-four years old. . . ."[79] Ward continues to note that their sister Æbbe had had four children by the time her brothers died. Æðelberht, son of Eormenred, then, could very well be Eadburh of Thanet's father, and the claim of the monks of St. Gregory's Priory that Eadburh was Mildrið's proavia[80] could result from confusion among Æðelberhts (the powerful king and the murdered prince) and their daughters, both Eadburhs (the semi-forgotten daughter of a ?concubine and the abbess of Thanet).

While both Witney's and my own conjectures about Eadburh's parentage are ultimately unprovable, both show Eadburh of Thanet to finalize her monastery's maternal genealogy. As Æðelberht's or as Eormengyð/Eangyð's daughter, she is Mildrið's cousin, living in the monastery founded by her aunt, inhabited by another aunt or possibly her mother (Eormengyð), and working with her cousin to maintain their institution.

Maternal Performance in the
Lambeth Palace Manuscript Fragment

These monastic, maternal genealogies, however, invite questions about replication of patriarchy. If the queens and princesses merely replicated their fathers', brothers', husbands', and sons' dynastic aspirations, they were performing patriarchally, not maternally. If their goals were acquisition of money, political power, and cultural prestige, they were merely female versions of the dynastic ebb and flow of power outside the monastery. Were these biologically related women, who were also "sisters in Christ," engaging in maternal performance? I have shown the establishment of a pattern—that a widow founds a house with a connection to Gaul on land from her dowry or from a male relative that passes to a biological daughter, sister, or niece. Does that performance within that pattern qualify as a maternal one? As Sara Ruddick would put the question, do these women protect, nurture, and teach?

My answer is an unqualified yes. First, the monastery afforded these women protection in the civil violence of the seventh and eighth centuries. That uncloistered women were not exempt as targets in dynastic feuds is indicated by the 697 entry in the *Anglo-Saxon Chronicle:* "Her Suð-anhumbre ofslogon Ostryðe. Æðelredes cwen. Ecgfrides swustor" (in this year the Southumbrians slew Osþryð, Æðelred's queen, Ecgfrið's sister). Osþryð was also the sister-in-law of Æðelþryð of Ely. The protection provided by the monastery came from both God and the power of the male kin of the reigning abbess. It was by the Vikings, not the various lords of the English kingdoms, that the double monasteries were destroyed and the nuns killed.[81]

That nurturance and teaching flourished in these monasteries is indicated by far more than Goscelin terming Eadburh an *alma virgo*.[82] Thanet had the wealth necessary for the leisure to teach and nurture; the abbess who gathered titles to land and exemptions from ship taxes was also creating opportunity for security and learning. We see Eadburh teaching and studying, presenting herself as a role model to younger nuns like Lioba. We know that the nuns who went to Gaul came back expressly to teach what they had learned to others—the *þa Halgan* text notes that Mildrið was sent to Chelles "þæt heo þone wisdom þar geleornode, þe man on þam mynstre healdan scolde" [so that she there might learn the wisdom that a person in a monastery should know]. Even the record of the Bapchild Synod shows Mildrið securing the privileges of the monastery to protect it in a time of uncertain kingship.

Such maternal performance is indicated in the manuscript fragment that is now London, Lambeth Palace, MS 427, folio 210. In this fragment, we see a mother protect, nurture, and teach her daughter in a ritual that, I argue here, consecrates the daughter into the maternal genealogy of the house. The ritual seems specifically maternal in that it excludes the presence of the bishop, a presence usually required.

Before turning specifically to folio 210, it will be necessary to place it in its manuscript and textual context. Its manuscript context is a paleographical puzzle—Lambeth 427 is a late tenth- or early eleventh-century interlinearly glossed psalter. Helmut Gneuss includes it in his list of psalters that could have been used either for the divine office or for teaching purposes.[83] The first 182 leaves are a Latin psalter with Anglo-Saxon glosses in smaller letters above the Latin. On folio 183b are the first 15 lines of an Anglo-Saxon hymn or prayer.[84] The Canticles fill folios 184 to 202a; 202b to 205b contain a fourteenth-century litany of saints. Folios 206 to 209 are blank (except for some scribbling and some antiphons on folio 209b) but quite evidently originally attached to the first 205 folios because of their size, color, and texture.

Folios 210 and 211 are markedly different from the others. Although they are the same size, they are a much darker yellow-brown than the previous folios. Ker goes so far as to list them in his *Catalogue* as a manuscript separate from folios 1 to 209.[85] The handwriting and lineation are different from those of any of the previous folios. The puzzle stems from the connection between the two parts of MS 427: when were folios 210 and 211 joined to the rest? A bit of the first sentence on folio 210 was copied onto folio 209b sometime in the fifteenth century, showing that these leaves were added onto the psalter at some time before that.[86] Beyond that, we have no way of knowing who put the pieces together, when or where it happened, and whether the distinct sections were made to be put together, an intriguing possibility. My own examination of the manuscript reveals at least two folios missing between 211 and the endleaf. Scrawled diagonally across the back of the endleaf, in small and clear letters, are two Greek words (παντα αδηλα), which translate roughly to "everything undeclared," something quite true about the history of this manuscript.

While the actions described on folio 210 involve a mother and daughter, the narrative of that leaf is unclear and seemingly unconnected to that of folio 211, which contains the narrative of Seaxburh's building of Sheppey, quoted earlier, as a part of a Kentish royal genealogy that seems to follow the same patterns as *þa Halgan*—Hollis even argues that folio 211 is "a fragment of a variant version of the text which is known as *þa Halgan.*"[87] Ker groups folios 210 and 211 together as "Two non-adjacent leaves of a history of St. Mildred and other Kentish royal saints."[88] Similarly, Cockayne presents them as two leaves of the same narrative text, implying that the connecting information between the leaves is simply missing.[89]

Swanton argues as well for a close connection between the Lambeth leaves and London, British Library, Cotton Caligula A.xiv, ff.93–130, another Kentish royal genealogical narrative that begins with the heading "13 July, the birth of St. Mildred, virgin." While Cockayne includes and discusses this text as well, Cockayne does not assert, as Swanton does, that the Cotton Caligula text and the Lambeth leaves represent parts of the same narrative.[90] Hollis relates Lambeth folio 211 to Cotton Caligula A.14 because, in her terms, they both contain "a genealogy of the founder-abbess and the daughter who succeeded her, followed by an account of how the founder gained by her own efforts an independent legal title to the monastery's land."[91] The Cotton Caligula text reads like an expanded version of þa halgan, and the majority of the surviving section focuses on the murder of the brothers and the summons to "Eafe" to collect their wergild. If this text were devotional reading for Mildrið's feast day, it would be a very long reading indeed; more than six folio sides are already full of narrative, which breaks off imperfectly before Eafe has even received full title to Thanet. Mildrið is mentioned as her daughter, but the sections about Mildrið's education at Chelles, her triumphant return home to her consecration, and her miracles—if they were ever included—are now missing. To judge from the length of the extant text, the complete narrative may have been three to four times the length it is now.

While Swanton writes his own narrative links to connect the three fragments, he also notes that the language of the Lambeth leaves is "a regular form of literary late West Saxon" while that of the Cotton Caligula text is "much less regular." In addition, the handwriting of the Lambeth leaves is "somewhat later," according to Swanton, than that of the Cotton Caligula text. These disparities seriously call into question, in my view, his argument that the three separate texts represent a single "genuine Canterbury tradition in a relatively pristine state."[92] Since the three sections were probably never linked in one narrative manuscript, we cannot assume that they originally formed parts of one long genealogical narrative centered on Mildrið. The two Lambeth folios have some sort of a textual relationship with the Cotton Caligula text, but not necessarily a close one. Rollason views the Cotton Caligula and Lambeth folios as separate; he advises that "it is more justifiable to regard them as fragments of different texts" even as they represent the "single literary tradition" of the Mildrið Legend.[93] Hollis, most convincingly, places the fragments as varied parts of a women-inspired and -created Thanet tradition.[94]

If the Cotton Caligula text does not directly relate to Lambeth 427, folio 210, the question remains of how Lambeth 427, folio 210, relates to its folio 211. Rollason discards folio 210 entirely from his groupings of the *Legend* texts, including only folio 211. He argues: "Cockayne was also wrong to regard f.210 of Caligula A.xiv [*sic*—this is a mistake for Lambeth 427] as part of the same version of the Mildrith Legend. The Old English fragment on this leaf contains an account of an unnamed girl's consecration as a nun by her mother and her humility and piety; but it bears no relationship to any other version of the Mildrith Legend and the sense does not run on between it and either the Lambeth fragment [f.211] or *S. Mildrið* [the Cotton Caligula text]."[95]

Despite Rollason's reservations, Folio 211 has much in common with the *þa Halgan* text, as scholars have long noted. It begins with Eadburh's succession to Mildrið; this is followed by a section on the daughters of Anna—Æðelþryð, Seaxburh, and Wihtburh—that contains basically the same information in the same order as the complementary section of *þa Halgan*. The narrative of the building of Sheppey, discussed earlier, follows the "Daughters of Anna" section and represents part of a tradition different from that of *þa Halgan*. The narrative could be construed as quasi-complete as it does not break off in mid-sentence. How folio 211 relates to folio 210 is another matter.

Ker, Swanton, and Cockayne all assume that folios 210 and 211, while originally unadjacent, are from the same text. Rollason's argument about the lack of relationship to other legend texts ignores the physical nature of the folios, which do indeed seem to be from the same original manuscript. Ker presents the two folios as one entry in his catalogue; they have the same handwriting; they have the same ruling. Despite Rollason's argument, it seems that folios 210 and 211 are two parts of the same work, a text somehow part of the Mildrið *Legend*. Rollason tentatively ascribes a Minster-in-Sheppey origin to folio 211 (because of its expanded narrative relating to Sheppey),[96] and it is quite likely that the two now-adjacent Lambeth folios represent a Minster-in-Sheppey version of the legend.

Hollis's recent work on the fragments concludes that two leaves were from different texts—folio 211 a version of *þa halgan,* as I have noted, and folio 210 a fragment from a lost life of Mildrið.[97] Hollis uses the later texts of Mildrið's *vita* to show that a welcoming ritual of Mildrið by Æbbe most likely formed part of the original legend written at Thanet for Mildrið's translation in 748. Hollis's argument, while more source-focused than mine, serves to stengthen my own reading of folio 210, and I will be working with it throughout the following analysis.

Folio 210 presents what I call a maternal ritual of consecration—a ritual that underscores the maternal performance of founding and maintaining a minster that will provide protection, nurturance, and teaching for daughters and other female relatives. Ambiguities in the text of folio 210 stem mostly from the feminine pronouns in the first half of the text, which runs thus:

> Benedicta et beata sis semper in aeternum et in thronum Dei connumerata et computa sis cum choris virginum. ða hyre modor hi mid þyssere bletsunge hyre ðus onfangen hæfde, heo hy aþenedum limum ætforan þam halgan wefode astrehte, and hy mid teara agotennysse to Drihtne gebæd. ða heo hyre gebed geendod hæfde, heo up astod and to hyre modor cneowum onbeah. And heo hy ða mid sibbe cosse gegrette, and ealle ða geferrædene samod. And hy hire wæter to handa bæron, æfter regollicre wisan.

> [May you always be blessed and holy in eternity and may you be numbered in the throne of God and counted with the chorus of virgins. When she, her mother, with this blessing thus had received her, she stretched her out before the holy altar with prostrated limbs, and prayed to the Lord with shed tears. When she had ended her prayer, she stood up and bowed to her mother with her knees. And she then with a peace-kiss greeted her, and all the fellowship together. And they bore her water for her hands, according to canonical custom.][98]

The pronouns make this introductory section confusing: Who stretches out before the altar? Who kisses whom? Whose hands are washed? And for that matter, what are these women doing? Why are there no men around (except perhaps vaguely in the *geferrædene*—Cockayne suggests as much[99])? While both Cockayne and Swanton have some interesting suggestions, both are much too definitive and much too anxious to solve the puzzle of this text. Its ambiguity, I will argue, is its most intriguing and most important aspect.

Cockayne and Swanton have vastly different "answers" to the puzzle of folio 210. Cockayne assumes that the folio depicts Mildrið's consecration as nun by her mother, and remarks of the benediction that begins the folio, "it is surprising that we find it spoken by Domne Eafe, the abbess" since of course the benediction is usually spoken by the priest in charge and other *Legend* texts tell us that Mildrið was consecrated as a nun by Theodore. Cockayne briefly examines a number of other consecration rituals only to conclude, "With none of these do I see much resemblance in our text."[100] These limitations do not stop him from translating the first *heo* of folio 210 as "Mildrith."[101]

Swanton, on the other hand, thinks that Seaxburh prostrates herself before the altar in a ritual of guest-greeting. He states:

> This sequence does not represent, as the subsequent ambiguity of pronouns might suggest, the admission of Mildrid as a nun. It is the abbess Seaxburh who prostrates herself before the altar; this, like the bringing of water, the

> kiss of peace, and the recital of the first of the psalms cited, is simply part of
> the formal reception of a guest required by the Benedictine rule. . . .
> Mildrid was later admitted as a nun by the archbishop. . . . [102]

Swanton seems to think that Seaxburh is greeting her mother (or her daughter?) to Sheppey. While Hollis thinks that Swanton has mistaken "Seaxburh" for "Eafe" here,[103] Swanton's desires for the folios to contain one smooth narrative make it likely that he did mean Seaxburh, since Seaxburh is named on folio 211. Part of Swanton's reading is accurate— the Benedictine Rule does direct abbots to greet guests with a prayer, prostration, a kiss of peace, and water for hand-washing. Even the prescribed psalm, *Suscepimus, Deus, misericordiam tuam in medio temple tui,* is one of the three sung by the abbess-mother in Lambeth 210. While David Knowles argues that Augustine probably did not have the Rule with him when he came to Kent in 597,[104] the similarities in segments of the ritual between the Benedictine Rule and the Lambeth 210 fragment show that the Kentish nuns had access to some version of the Rule that included chapter 53, "De Hospitibus Suscipiendis."[105]

The amalgamation of the consecratory blessing and the guest-reception ritual suggests, perhaps, that the abbess was greeting her daughter into the community both as a nun and as an outsider coming in. Hollis argues as much when she reads this folio as a narrative about Mildrið's reception to the community by her mother, pointing out that "The logic of the comparison to Christ's dedication in the temple requires that we accept fol. 210, at the very least, as an account of an abbess formally receiving a postulant as a member of her community."[106] Hollis's identification of the figures as Mildrið and Eafe (Hollis's referent for Mildrið's mother) is likely but not certain, however. The mix of sources and references in the text, complicated by the vague pronouns, makes sure identification of the purpose of the ritual and its performers impossible. Neither Cockayne nor Swanton, nor even Hollis, has any actual evidence to prove that these women are Seaxburh and Hereswið, Seaxburh and Eormenhild, or Æbbe and Mildrið.

If we accept that Lambeth 210 and 211 are parts of a larger and more complicated version of a Kentish royal genealogy than those now extant—a version that focused on the women of the house, and that detailed their lives, relationships, and accomplishments—then the beauty of folio 210 is that *heo* and *hyre modor* could refer to any of a number of mother-daughter "couples," to return to Irigaray's language with which this study began. *Heo* and *hyre modor* could be Seaxburh and Hereswið, Seaxburh and Eormenhild, Eormenhild and Werburh, Æðelburh of Lyminge and Eanflæd, Æbbe and Mildrið, or even Eadburh and Eormengyð, if we follow Witney's arguments.

The ambiguities of the text also leave open the possibility that these pronouns refer to women lost to history, or the possibility that the pronoun references are deliberately vague because this sort of ceremony was one performed numerous times in the Kentish minsters.

It is this last possibility that I wish to suggest, not in the definitive way of Swanton and Cockayne, but as a speculation about textual ambiguity. In this text, a mother consecrates and greets a daughter with some of the same words that a bishop would use in a nun's consecration and with parts of the Benedictine reception of a guest. There is no reason that such a reception and consecration should or could supersede that of the (arch)bishop; there is no reason Mildrið could not have participated in both and been consecrated by Archbishop Theodore (into the conventional church) and by her mother (into their maternal community). Such a ritual may have satisfied a need determined at least partially by lack of male authority figures to provide vestiture of religious vocations; Hollis points out that Mildrið probably returned from Chelles when the archbishopric was vacant (between the death of Deusdedit in 664 and Theodore's arrival in 669–70), a time when "abbesses must necessarily have assumed responsibility for the formal admission of members to their communities."[107]

Hollis ties the occlusion and disappearance of this ritual in the later Latin sources to the general decline in women's monastic power and sanctity from the seventh and eighth centuries to the Conquest and beyond; her conclusions certainly do point to the mid-eighth century as a probable date for the source of folios 210 and 211. Folio 210 may indeed refer only to Mildrið and Æbbe, but its pronouns without referents hint that this maternal ritual of consecration (to use my term) or admission (to use Hollis's) was not a ritual uniquely constructed for Mildrið. It may have been used before and after her consecration by a number of mothers with their biological and spiritual daughters.

While Mildrið was likely admitted to Thanet before Theodore's arrival in Kent, as Hollis remarks, the enduring nature of the ritual—its recording in hagiographic narrative—may owe something to Theodore and his connections to Mildrið and Thanet. Archbishop Theodore came to England in 669 at the request of Pope Vitalian. Theodore was from Taursus, and Stenton remarks on the "remarkable nomination" of an "aged scholar from Asia Minor" to the post of Archbishop of Canterbury. Theodore was accompanied by Hadrian, to whom Vitalian had first offered the archbishopric, and Stenton suggests that part of Hadrian's job was to see that Theodore "should not introduce any Greek perversities into the teaching of his church." While Theodore's career in Canterbury is varied and fascinating, it must suffice here to examine only a section of his penitential and his relationship with Thanet.[108]

Part of Theodore's mission was to establish uniformity and union within the English church, and to that end he caused to be made what is called *Theodore's Penitential*—a guide for priests hearing confession that also lists guidelines about church policy and administration. The authenticity of this document—which Stenton notes has an "extremely complicated" transmission history[109]—has been generally agreed upon by scholars, who basically accept the text's internal information that the *Penitential* was compiled at Theodore's direction and under his supervision.[110] While most source studies focus on the relation of the *Penitential* to Irish ascetic traditions, Thomas Charles-Edwards has recently argued for a Mediterranean rather than a Celtic slant to the *Penitential's* theology.[111] One section of this text can be read to inform the narrative of Lambeth 210; his canons *De Ritu Mulierum vel Ministerio in Æcclesia* (Of the Rite of the Women, or Their Ministry in the Church) suggest that perhaps Hadrian was not quite as successful as he could have been in keeping Greek "perversities" (Stenton's word) out of the English church.

The brief section *De Ritu Mulierum* substantiates much feminist historical scholarship on the golden age double monasteries. Just as Hollis, Lees and Overing, and Fell all suggest that Hild and abbesses like her engaged in substantial pastoral duties, the first of Theodore's canons about the rites of women states that:

> Mulieribus, id est, Christi famulabus licitum est in suis ecclesiis lectiones legere et implere ministeria quae conveniunt ad confessionem sacrosancti altaris, nisi ea tantummodo quae specialiter sacerdotum et diaconum sunt
>
> [It is permissible for the women, that is, the handmaidens of Christ, to read the lections and to perform the minsteries that appertain to the confession of the sacred altar, except those that are the special functions of priests and deacons].[112]

This canon seems to sanction public reading and teaching, care for the sick, pastoral counseling, even preaching—all activities that feminist historians have read into Bede and other narratives. The *Penitential* here suggests that Theodore recognized the value of such work. The second canon prohibits a woman from prescribing penance—perhaps suggesting that some women were doing so?—while the third notes that women may receive communion *sub nigro velamine,* under a black veil.

It is Theodore's fourth and final canon of *De Ritu Mulierum* that may hearken to Lambeth 210, and it reads "Mulier potest oblationes facere secundum Grecos, non secundum Romanos." McNeill and Gamer translate, "According to the Greeks a woman can make offerings, but not according to the Romans." The primary meaning of *oblationes,* offerings, can encompass a wide variety of acts and gifts—bread, fruit, flowers, the Eucharist, even estates and property.[113] The acceptability of women who make offerings in the Greek tradition is indicated by the mid-sixth-century San Vitale frescoes in Ravenna, in which Justinian and his empress Theodora approach the altar through the narthex bearing gold and jewel-encrusted vessels that hold the bread and wine.[114]

In the Benedictine Rule (to which the Kentish abbesses had access, Lambeth 210 shows), the word *oblationes* is used when discussing the offering of a son to the monastery by parents; chapter 59 closes by noting that "cum oblatione offerant filium suum coram testibus" [with offerings, they offer their sons with witnesses].[115] Such intermingling of the offering of gifts and the offering of a postulant suggests that the child so offered could be construed as part of the *oblatio.* Hollis calls the ritual detailed on folio 210 at least "the formal reception of a postulant."[116] Indeed, the Modern English cognate of *oblationes,* oblate, means, "one dedicated to the religious or monastic life," and I wish to suggest here that the mother of Lambeth 210—Æbbe or Seaxburh or Eormenhild or another woman—is indeed making an offering, creating an oblate, just as the final canon of Theodore's section *De Ritu Mulierum* says she might, if she follows Greek rather than Roman custom.

It is likely that the Kentish monasteries at the end of the seventh century would do so, since Theodore was their archbishop and close friend. Legendary tales of his consecration of Mildrið aside, he or his office is invoked in the majority of the land charters to Minster-in-Thanet; he certainly was in close contact with both the political and the monastic structures of Kent. His Greek background would have predisposed him to such a ritual for a woman who wished *facere oblationes* and engage in such a ritual with her daughter; his own *Penitential* provides that information. While such a ceremony may have been distasteful to more conventional Roman preference, Theodore would have seen such a ritual to complement rather than threaten a more traditional consecration. The existence of such a mother-daughter consecration need not preclude the more conventional consecration; it merely indicates a parallel structure within the maternal community.

Patriarchy and Maternal Ritual

Such coexistence is the hallmark of maternal community in the double monasteries of seventh- and eighth-century Kent. Scholars have tended to assert the power and prestige of the double monasteries and their abbesses, thus quantifying those institutions in patriarchal terms. And indeed this is legitimate practice, for the evidence does demonstrate the considerable political and financial influence of abbesses like Mildrið or Seaxburh. But such patriarchal examination of the minsters excludes the maternal practice that protected, nurtured, and taught the biological and spiritual daughters of the house. This study of the Kentish monasteries has shown that biological maternity and relationship was a major factor in the community of a minster.

Lees and Overing suggest as much at the conclusion of their essay on Hild, although I wish to revalue the conclusions of their argument. They seem to think that the royal abbesses give much more to patriarchy than they receive from it, stating, "the saintly royal women maintain the family, even' within their cloistered environments, and their family maintains them, with an eye firmly on dynastic interests," as well as "While we may balk at the description of 'high-ranking servant,' the status and power of such aristocratic women is clearly coopted in the service of patriarchy." In addition, they state that the abbesses "remain Anglo-Saxon mothers, whether literally, spiritually, or both."[117] Lees and Overing, I think, are reacting to a cheerleading sort of feminism that celebrates feminine power in the monastery without looking at the structures in which that power participates.[118]

Without being naive, I hope I have shown here that it is possible to "maintain the family" without becoming a high-ranking servant of patriarchy. That Æbbe, Seaxburh, Eormenhild, and Mildrið served dynastic interests by providing royal reproductive and administrative services is beyond a doubt. But they also established a maternal community that Lees and Overing, it seems, disparage or overlook. The maternal genealogy of the royal Kentish minsters is not just a female reinscription of a patriarchal genealogy. The Lambeth folio demonstrates that the royal women of the minsters had established maternal structures separate from those of the institutional church and state.

Abbesses used their minsters to perform a maternal practice—they governed their houses in which lived their daughters, nieces, cousins, and sisters. To consecrate a daughter into a royal minster was to dedicate her to God but also to insure that she would not die in childbirth, that she would not be slaughtered in a feud, and that she would not go hungry or cold. Such a maternal consecration allowed the daughter the privileges of education, access to the best available medical care, and a relative self-determination and control of her life's choices. These goals, amply fulfilled by the abbess-mothers of seventh- and eighth-century Kentish monasteries, were the goals as well of the queens of Wessex and Mercia two hundred years later, and it is to maternal performers in the age of Alfred and Viking invasion that I now turn.

CHAPTER 3

THE MATERNAL GENEALOGY OF ÆÐELFLÆD, LADY OF THE MERCIANS

Despite the wealth of scholarship about the historical sources and narratives of Wessex and Mercia at the end of the ninth century and the beginning of the tenth century, these sources have never been seen to present a woman's narrative, much less a maternal one. And with good reason—the various annals' entries about the Alfredian and post-Alfredian wars with the Vikings, the charters' endless lists of men's names in various land grants, and the propagandist bent to Asser's *Life of Alfred*—all are relentlessly focused on the men who wielded power in this tumultuous period of English history. Only Æðelflæd, Lady of the Mercians, has occasioned some scholarly interest as a participant in this military and patriarchal ethos; her command of the Mercian army after her husband's death has led to extensive critical inquiry into the level of cooperation between her and her brother, Edward the Elder, who became king of Wessex when their father Alfred died.

The narratives surrounding King Alfred, who ruled Wessex from 871 to 899, an age of repeated Viking incursion, include a number of female figures who are presented and have been read as very typical "peace pledges," female bodies traded from one country or tribe to another in marriage as part of diplomatic maneuvering. The marriage of Alfred's sister Æðelswið is an obvious example of such a transaction; after a description of a joint campaign in 853 of Æðelwulf, king of Wessex, and Burgred, king of Mercia, against the Welsh, the *Anglo Saxon Chronicle* states that "ond þæs ofer Eastron geaf Æðelwulf cyning his dohtor Burgrede cyninge of Wesseaxum on Merce" [and after that Easter, King Æðulwulf gave his daughter to King Burgred from Wessex to Mercia].[1] Æðelswið is not even named in the text; her importance is as a seal of the alliance between the two kings.

The model of maternal genealogy outlined in my introduction provides a different rubric for examination of the women in and around Alfred's life, however, and the concomitant shift of focus from one of nation building to one of protection, nurturance, teaching, and female-female relationship can elucidate a maternal genealogy of the royal houses of Wessex and Mercia. In that genealogy, four generations of maternal figures work to protect, nurture, and teach their children in the face of Viking attack and more domestic masculine aggression. Æðelflæd, Lady of the Mercians, finally constructs a maternal genealogy so firm that it briefly appears, if somewhat enigmatically, in patriarchal history.

Osburh

Osburh, mother of Alfred, is probably the most famous mother in Anglo-Saxon history. The story of her award to him for learning a book of Old English poetry has been referenced by countless scholars in a variety of disciplines. The narrative appearing in chapter 23 of Asser's *Life of King Alfred* tells us that Alfred's mother showed him and his brothers a book of Saxon poems and told them that she would give the book to the brother who first could learn (*possit discere*) the book.[2] Alfred, of course, won the prize, thus beginning his illustrious career as a man of letters.

Osburh appears in no primary sources other than Asser's *Life of Alfred,* and the integrity of that text has recently been questioned, the latest development in a centuries-long scholarly saga of inquiry into Asser's reliability. As A. S. Cook stated almost one hundred years ago: "The authenticity of the Life was impugned by Thomas Wright in 1841, by Sir Henry Howorth in 1876–77, and by an unknown writer in 1898, and it became somewhat the fashion to regard it as the production of a later period. . . . The doubts of its authenticity have been satisfactorily dispelled by the two eminent scholars who have most recently discussed the difficulties, Plummer and Stevenson."[3] Dorothy Whitelock added her voice to the debate in her 1967 Stenton Lecture, "The Genuine Asser," in which she affirmed the authenticity of the text as a late-ninth-century production by the Welsh bishop Asser, who was attached to Alfred's court.[4] In his recent controversial biography of Alfred, Alfred Smyth argues that Asser's *Life* is a forgery, probably by the tenth-century Bryhtferth of Ramsey.[5] While Smyth's methodology and conclusions have been questioned and even derided by respected scholars of Anglo-Saxon culture,[6] Allen Frantzen has found a convincing middle ground to argue that that text has "a ninth century core . . . augmented by hagiographical commonplaces."[7] It strikes me that certain portions of Smyth's argument, if not his final conclusion, raise important questions about the real-life basis for Asser's text.

While I will follow Whitelock and her supporters in accepting the basic authenticity of Asser's text as a narrative written by a contemporary companion of King Alfred, Smyth's discussion of Asser's chapter 23 is thorough and thought-provoking as well as immensely relevant to any analysis of Osburh. Smyth argues that this scene is folkloric and apocryphal, noting folkloric themes that the piece demonstrates, such as "youngest brother alone succeeds on quest" or "learning or reading in a remarkably short time by magic or miracle."[8] Smyth also does some chronological figuring and reasons that the scene must have taken place before 855, when Æðelwulf returned from Rome with his new bride Judith, daughter of Charles the Bald, an event noted in the *Anglo-Saxon Chronicle*. Asser himself says that Alfred was born in 849 (Smyth prefers 847 or 848), so by Asser's reckoning Alfred was six, at most, when he learned to read Old English poetry. Smyth does not discount the possible reading ability of a child so young (despite his constant references to the six-year-old Alfred as an "infant"), but points out that by 855 Alfred's brothers, who were supposedly present for the book competition (Asser uses the plural *fratribus suis*), were all much too old to be spending time "learning together at their mother's knee."[9]

Smyth observes that Alfred's oldest brother, Æðelstan, was probably already dead, having served as sub-king of Kent from circa 839; Æðelbald was fighting alongside Æðelwulf, their father, by 851; Æðelberht was ruling a section of the kingdom by 855. These three, at least, were in 855 fully grown, not clustered around Osburh competing for a schoolboy's prize. Smyth argues that only Æðelred was close enough in age to have been there as well. As part of his larger argument that Asser's *Life of King Alfred* is a tenth-century forgery, Smyth then states that "The sole point of this apocryphal tale was to glorify Alfred at the expense of his brothers" and demands "recognizing the impossibility of this episode having really happened."

Smyth is correct to assert that chapter 23 is an exercise in the glorification of Alfred over his brothers, but this propagandist nature does not discount the authenticity of the core of the anecdote, that Osburh provided the impetus for Alfred to learn to read English. Smyth concedes that the tale provides evidence for the educational level of Anglo-Saxon aristocratic women: "Indeed, if the folk-tale of the book prize in the *Life* of Alfred has anything of value to offer historians, it is surely that it was considered appropriate for an author to portray aristocratic women in pre-Conquest England as being personally involved in the education of their sons."[10] While Smyth states that there is "nothing inherently improbable" in the idea that Osburh supervised the education of her sons, I would argue that this idea is the core of truth in the folkloric tale, that Osburh most certainly did supervise the education of her children. The tale assumes Osburh's ability to gauge the accuracy of Alfred's recitation of the Saxon poems (*saxonicum poematicae artis librum*). Therefore, she must have been literate in the vernacular if not in Latin.

Chronology also favors the notion of Osburh's literacy as attested in chapter 23. Asser dates his text to 893, almost 40 years after the events of chapter 23 supposedly took place. Those 40 years would be enough time to add the "folkloric" elements that Smyth disparages to the tale, while contemporaries at Alfred's court, including Alfred himself, would find the folktale in general agreement with their memories of Osburh as a literate woman who kept close watch on the education of her children.

I say "children" rather than "sons" as Smyth does because there is no reason to eliminate Æðelswið from Osburh's lessons. While Æðelswið was married by the time of the supposed events of chapter 23, Asser's phrase *fratribus suis* could be translated "his siblings"; *frater* can encompass both genders in the plural.[11] It is more than likely that before her marriage Æðelswið learned "at their mother's knee" with her brothers Alfred and Æðelred; like her brothers, Æðelswið demonstrates basic literacy in her witnessing and issuing of charters, discussed later.

Osburh, then, can be viewed as a maternal performer who teaches, even if not a maternal performer who offers book prizes in the year 855 to five brothers. She herself was probably literate and passed her learning on to her children, male and female, for a literate mother would see no impediment of sex in teaching her daughter how to read.

Scholarly remarks about Osburh are usually asides, marginalized references to the mother of a great king. Assumptions about her include her marriage to King Æðulwulf, the father of Æðelstan, Æðelbald, Æðelberht, Æðelred, Æðelswið, and Alfred. Scholars also tend to assume that she died sometime before 857, when Æðelwulf returned from a journey to Rome with Judith, who is not named in the *Anglo-Saxon Chronicle,* but is noted only as "karles dohter Francna cining" [daughter of King Charles of France].

However, Smyth has again engaged in chronological calculation that shows the unlikelihood that Osburh was the mother of Æðulwulf's older children. Since Alfred's oldest brother, Æðelstan, was sub-king of Kent eight or nine years before Alfred was even born, he "must have been at least twenty-four years older than the infant Alfred." Smyth suggests that "it is likely that Æðelstan, his brothers Æðelbald and Æðelberht, and perhaps their sister Æðelswið, were the children of a different mother."[12] Smyth's chronological conclusions make sense—if she were the mother of a grown man who was ruling Kent in 839, Osburh would have had to have been born in 805 at the very latest, thus bearing Alfred in her sixth successful pregnancy in her mid-forties, an unlikely scenario.

I would not include Æðelswið in the group of Alfred's half-siblings, however. While perhaps my own desires for Osburh to have a daughter cloud my judgment, it seems that Æðelswið's birth was probably circa 839, so she would be 14 at her marriage in 853; the eight- or nine-year span between her and Alfred is not too great for Osburh to have borne them both. My chronological rendering of Æðelwulf's children's births indicates that Osburh was probably the mother of his three youngest children— Æðelswið, Æðelred, and Alfred—placing them in her schoolroom and under her tutelage after his first three children were already grown.

That she bore children to Æðelwulf does not mean that she was married to him as his consecrated queen, however. Asser never calls her queen or even Æðewulf's wife; he calls her Alfred's mother (*mater eiusdem*[13]), and notes that "quae erat filia Oslac, famosi pincernae Æðeulwulfi regis" [she was the daughter of Oslac, the famous cup bearer of King Æðelwulf]. Pauline Stafford has noted the propensity of Anglo-Saxon kings to take and discard concubines and wives with alacrity in an expedience of serial monogamy.[14] While Asser is at pains to emphasize Osburh's noble lineage, she is not a king's daughter (like her successor Judith) and is not a consecrated queen, meaning that Osburh's claim to the king as husband was not strong. While most historians assume that Osburh had died by 857,[15] it actually seems quite reasonable that, in a scenario like those described by Stafford, she was more simply dismissed from his sexual service after 857 with the appearance of the Frankish princess.

Æðelswið

Osburh's daughter Æðelswið married the Mercian king Burgred to seal the Wessex-Mercia alliance in 853, as I noted earlier. She lost her queenship to the Vikings in 874 when they drove her husband out of Mercia. The *Anglo-Saxon Chronicle* says that the Viking army "þone cyning Burgræd ofer sæ adræfon ymb xxii wintra þæs þe he rice hæfde ond þæt lond all geeodon" [drove that King Burgred over the sea after 22 winters in which he held the kingdom and they went over all that land]. The *Chronicle* also tells us that Æðelswið, who is called "Æðelswið cuen sio wæs Ælfredes sweostor cyninges" [Queen Æðelswið who was King Alfred's sister] rather than Burgred's wife, died in 888 in Pavia; the F manuscript specifically says she was on her way to Rome.[16] Æðelswið and Burgred are commemorated in the northern Italian *Liber Vitae* of Brescia (Brescia, Biblioteca Querianiana G.VI.7, fol.27v), heading a list that also includes the names of five men and three women, all English. It is tempting—and logical—to suppose that these ten made up the deposed king's party enroute to Rome, stopping at Brescia along the way and making a contribution so as to be remembered in the monks' prayers.[17]

The transition from queen to refugee must have been dramatic for Æðelswið. Archaeological and charter evidence shows that Æðelswið was an active partner in her husband's kingdom, worthy of the title *cuen* accorded her by the *Anglo-Saxon Chronicle*. Like her much more famous niece, Æðelflæd, Æðelswið reigned in Mercia, participating in the government of the realm with her husband Burgred.

Æðelswið's continuing presence in the affairs of the kingdom is attested in 11 charters dated to 855–872. Two of these are of doubtful authenticity, although the use of Æðelswið's name in a forgery indicates acknowledgement of the usualness of her inclusion in an important transaction. Of the remaining nine, six are charters of her husband, which she witnesses; two are joint charters of Burgred and Æðelswið, which they witness as well as issue; the last is a charter of Æðelswið alone.[18]

In every one of these charters she is styled "Æðelswið Regina," indicating her power to transact and ratify the business of the kingdom; in only one extant charter of Burgred (which is "not of unimpeachable genuineness") does she not appear in the witness list. An appropriate contrast is with the witness lists of the charters of King Edward (Æðelswið's nephew and Alfred's son); in the one charter where his wife does appear as a witness, she is styled "Elffled conjunx regis" [Elffled the wife of the king].[19]

Æðelswið's textual appearances indicate a queen who helped to carry out the affairs of state, regulating land and financial transactions among the powerful persons and institutions of Mercia—the king and queen, the bishop of Worcester, Gloucester Abbey, and various individual thegns and monks. While the *Anglo-Saxon Chronicle* tries to depict her initially as a commodity traded between her father and husband to seal their alliance, she actively helped to shape the community that she ruled.

Another indicator of Æðelswið's power comes from the archaeological record. One of two extant rings from the mid-ninth century is inscribed with her name. The ring, now in the British Museum, is made of gold with niello. Its main section depicts an *agnus dei* in a quatrefoil, the subject indicated by the letters A and Ð on either side of the animal. The lamb has more in common with Lindisfarne bestiaries than with farm livestock, however, and two similarly fantastic animals grace the sides, or "shoulders" of the bezel. Leaf and dot patterns fill the spaces around the bezel and within the quatrefoil. The inscription on the inside of the ring fills three lines: +*EA / ÐELSVIÐ / REGNA,* with the final "N" and "A" formed less substantially than the other letters in order to make room for them.[20]

The purpose of the ring, which was plowed up in Aberford, near Sherburn in Yorkshire, remains unclear. Æðelswið's ring has been discussed most often in connection with a ring of her father, Æðelwulf, which is inscribed "ETHELVVLFR" (the "T" is upside down and a cross over the leg of the "R" indicates "rex"). David Wilson argues that these two ninth-century royal rings "must be seen not as the personal rings of the monarch whose name is inscribed on them, but rather as gifts of that monarch to a person or institution."Wilson reasons that "it would be too much of a coincidence to have the personal rings of two Anglo-Saxon monarchs . . . in a period when inscribed rings are in any case rare."[21] It seems to me that having two gift rings given away by Anglo-Saxon monarchs would be equally coincidental. R. I. Page does not directly contradict the argument of his editor in his essay included in Wilson's book, but he does state: "Owner formulae are common on jewelry, and it is therefore reasonable to take the names on these rings as those of the owners.The objection to this is a statistical one; it is surprising to find two royal owners of the three rings in this section. The possibility must therefore be considered that the Æðelwulf and Æðelswið rings record, not the owners', but the donors' names."[22] In his discussion of the catalogue's third ninth-century ring, Page assumes that the inscribed name (Bvredrvð) is the name of the owner.[23] Page, then, leaves open the possibility that the Æðelswið ring was worn by the queen rather than given by the queen.

Leslie Webster agrees with Wilson's argument and states in her commentary in an exhibition catalogue that "like the Æðelwulf ring, it [the Æðelswið ring] signifies a royal gift or symbol of office, not a royal possession."[24] None of these scholars has remarked on the unusual size of the ring, which is too small to be an arm-band or bracelet but too large to fit on a finger, even the finger of a very large man. My own examination of the ring (in its case in the British Museum) suggests that its owner, whoever she or he was, probably wore it on a chain around the neck. While we can never be completely sure of the purpose of the ring, we can know that it signified Æðelswið's power and prestige in Mercia when she was queen, whether she wore it or gave it away. The ring served as a symbol of her own power and piety, indicated by the valuable material and religious yet insular design. If indeed it was a gift from Æðelswið, the ring indicates her status as "ring-giver," and her ability to bestow treasure on her followers.

Æðelswið disappears from the historical record for 16 years after this relatively well-documented career as an administrator and power figure in Mercia. She helped to rule Mercia for 21 years, from 853 to 874. She presumably helped to decide to pay off theVikings with danegeld in 868, 872, and 873—payments noted enigmatically in the *Anglo-Saxon Chronicle* in a variation of the form (from the 868 entry) "Mierce friþ namon wiþ þone here" [the Mercians took peace with the army]. The queen's reaction to the expulsion of her husband (and herself) from Mercia is not recorded. The only other textual source for her life is the *Anglo-Saxon Chronicle*'s entry of her death in 888: "Æðelswið cuen sio wæs Ælfredes sweostor cyninges forþferde ond hire lic liþ æt Pafian" [Queen Æðelswið, who was King Alfred's sister, died, and her body lies at Pavia]. She may have been on her second Roman pilgrimage; Webster suggests that Æðelswið "probably accompanied him [Burgred] to Rome," in 874, and the inclusion of her name in the Brescia *Liber Vitae* (discussed earlier) suggests as much.[25] She certainly could have made such journeys; the *Anglo-Saxon Chronicle* documents numerous trips from Alfredian England to Rome.

In the years intervening between her first presumed trip and her death in Pavia, there is no record of her to attest to her residence in Italy or anywhere else. It is most likely, given the exigencies of travel and solitary living for women, that she would have lived with her brother before setting out on a pilgrimage in 887 or 888 to retrace the route she probably traveled with her husband before his death. The *Chronicle* text defines her, after all, as "Alfredes sweostor" rather than Burgred's wife or a pilgrim or an Italian resident, indicating a continuing association of the two figures in the mind of the annalist.

We have no evidence that Æðelswið and Burgred had any children, but her possible lack of biological motherhood does not necessarily indicate a lack of maternal performance. Æðelswið, deposed queen of the Mercians, may have been an important influence in the development of her niece Æðelflæd, who was to be the next queen of Mercia. Æðelflæd, indeed, exercised power like her aunt's from the very beginning of her marriage. Don Stansbury suggests this relationship,[26] and it allows a vision of maternal teaching and mentoring, from one royal woman to another. While her initial appearance in the *Anglo-Saxon Chronicle* indicates Æðelswið's passivity in the face of her father's and husband's diplomacy, the rest of the historical record shows a woman with power, prestige, and acumen in the face of Viking onslaught.

Ealhswið

Æðelswið's sister-in-law, Ealhswið, doubly links the Mercian and West Saxon maternal genealogies. Asser tells us that Ealhswið was the daughter of a Mercian princess,[27] so Ealhswið was related to Burgred by blood as well as to Alfred by marriage. David Sturdy's description of the Mercian–West Saxon relationship in the tenth century as having "the atmosphere of an expanded family business" accurately shows the variety of intermingling between the families.[28] Asser dates Alfred's marriage to 868, while Æðelswið had been in Mercia since 853; it is more than likely that Ealhswið, of the Mercian royal family, knew her queen and her future sister-in-law quite well at the time of her marriage. Again, there is no hard evidence to confirm the existence of this relationship in the extant texts, but a maternal genealogist will see it in the chronology and marital relationships as they are made clear in patriarchal texts.

Ealhswið came from Mercia into a country where, Asser tells us, the queen did not wield power; textual evidence confirms Ealhswið's lack of involvement in the "family business" when Alfred was king. While she does appear as a witness in one charter supposedly issued by Alfred, Sawyer's references and annotations term this charter a "clumsy twelfth century forgery."[29] She does not appear in any authentic charters from Alfred's reign, even as a witness; she is not named or even referred to in the *Anglo-Saxon Chronicle* until after her husband's death. Asser focuses on the anomaly of Judith's active queenship in Wessex when, in chapter 13 of the *Life of King Alfred,* he states, "Gens namque Occidentalium Saxonum reginam iuxta regem sedere non patitur, nec etiam reginam apellari, sed regis coniugem, permittit" [for the race of the West Saxons does not allow the queen to sit next to the king, nor even to be called 'queen,' but concede (her to be called) 'wife of the king']. Asser cites the tale of the vicious Queen Eadburh who killed her husband as the reason for the West Saxon queen's lack of power (chapters 14 and 15). Eadburh's supposed criminality aside, Ealhswið's lack of appearances in the textual record from Alfred's reign indicates that her position in Wessex, unlike that of her sister-in-law in Mercia, was not as a participating, reigning partner of the king.

After her husband's death, however, Ealhswið becomes active in the textual record, perhaps indicating that the queen dowager as king's mother had access to power denied the king's wife. Stafford suggests as much in her essay "The King's Wife in Wessex, 800–1066," although her discussion focuses on the queens of the later tenth and eleventh centuries. Stafford notes that "To marry into the West Saxon ruling family in the ninth century was to sink into obscurity. . . . Ninth-century West Saxon women are cloaked in silence" even as she argues that in succession disputes among sons of different mothers, "Success could bring the coveted position of queen mother."[30]

In that position, Ealhswið becomes an active participant in West Saxon administration. In 901, she witnesses a land grant from her son King Edward to Malmesbury Abbey; she is termed *mater regis.* Interestingly enough, this is the charter (noted earlier) also witnessed by Edward's wife Elffled, who is called *conjunx regis.*[31] It seems that by the time of this charter (901), women of the royal family had a more active part in the "family business," even if they were not styled queens as Æðelswið was.

Ealhswið also had the power of the property owner after Alfred's death. Alfred's will has been discussed by scholars primarily in relation to his attempt to nullify the claims of his brothers' sons to the throne.[32] In it, he leaves the bulk of his property to his sons, both in land and cash; his brothers' sons receive portions comparable to what he leaves to his daughters and his wife. Alfred states as the last of his land bequests: "Ond Ealhswiðe

þone ham æt Lambburnan ond æt Waneting ond æt Eðandune" [and to
Ealhswið (I give) the home at Lambourn and at Wantage and at Eding-
ton].[33] Ealhswið would have had the responsibility of managing the estates
or arranging for them to be managed; she would have received the income
from the estates as well.

In addition to the land, Ealhswið received cash from her husband; Alfred's structuring of his cash bequests makes clear the divisions among his
family members in his mind. Rather than simply listing a name and an
amount, Alfred leaves "minum twam sunum an þusend punda ægðrum fif
hund punda," [to my two sons a thousand pounds, five hundred pounds to
each]. After grouping his sons together, he makes the same odd sort of
group of his daughters and his wife: "minre yldstan dehter ond þære
medemestan ond þære gingstran ond Ealhswiðe him feowrum feower
hund punda ælcum an hund punda" [to my oldest daughter and to the
middle and to the youngest and to Ealhswið, four hundred pounds to those
four, one hundred pounds to each]. Alfred's will makes plain his differen-
tiation between male and female heirs with no regard for a possible en-
hanced status for Ealhswið as widow. The cash he leaves her, coupled with
the estates, probably ensured financial security for her after his death.

That financial security also enabled her to found and endow a nunnery,
and it is in the records of Nunnaminster, or St. Mary's Abbey, that Ealhswið's fleeting influence is most strong. Florence of Worcester and abbey
tradition both credit Ealhswið with the abbey's foundation;[34] the boundaries of a parcel of Ealhswið's land, roughly corresponding to the abbey's
land in the early tenth century, are preserved on the penultimate folio of a
prayer-book, London, British Library, MS Harley 2965. The boundary description begins, "þæs hagan ge mære þe ealhswið hæfð æt Wintan ceastre
lið up of þæm forda . . ." [the hedge-boundaries that Ealhswið has at Winchester lie up off the ford . . .] and continues to describe the landmarks of
the property.[35] This boundary description indicates Ealhswið's involvement
both with the book and with the abbey.

The book itself is probably ninth century and may have been owned by
Ealhswið at some point; its only editor, Birch, even refers to some feminine forms of words to suggest it was made by a woman.[36] The contents
indicate use for private devotion rather than public reading; the unusual,
personal nature of the book necessitates the literacy of its owner.[37] The
gospel narratives of the Passion begin the book; they are followed by
groups of prayers of invocation, prayers about the life of Christ, and prayers
on judgment. Some of these prayers are metrical, others more prosaic. Interestingly enough, some medical charms appear at the end of the manuscript;[38] the land boundaries on folio 40b are followed by three short
prayers on the interior endsheet.

The land boundaries are entered in a hand different from and later than that of the rest of the texts; Smyth indicates that the hand of the scribe who included the boundaries is markedly similar to that of Scribe One of the Parker MS of the *Anglo-Saxon Chronicle*. Smyth also notes that the main verb in the passage is in the present tense, indicating that Ealhswið "has" this land and is still alive, and thus dating the boundary entry to before 902.[39] Birch suggests that "the MS probably was acquired by that royal lady not long after its preparation."[40] The dating of the boundary entry in a book that may have been Ealhswið's personal devotional suggests that she was living at the nunnery—on what was still her own land—before her death and had already made plans to leave the land and the book to St Mary's. This founding of and residence in a nunnery by a royal widow echoes the establishments of the double monasteries in Kent in the seventh century, and Nunnaminster, like Thanet and Sheppey, becomes a haven for female members of the royal family, as I will show.

Thus, the charters, the bequests, and the nunnery foundation all point to a woman who became an active member of the community after her husband's death. The maternal genealogist sees Ealhswið not, perhaps, as "silenced" before 899, but busy with activities not of interest to the male authors of textual evidence. Ealhswið probably had five small children by the time of Alfred's retreat to Athelney in 878. Asser states that she had other children "qui in infantia morte" [who died in infancy].[41] Ealhswið's maternal concerns must have occupied her before her husband's death. She raised her surviving children even as she grieved for the babies who died in infancy. Under the constant threat of Viking attack, she must have attended to their most basic needs of food and shelter and clothing. Asser indicates that her children were all relatively well educated; in the tradition of her mother-in-law Osburh, Ealhswið, literate in Latin and the vernacular, probably introduced her young children to reading.

Ealhswið's success in her maternal performance shows in the varied pursuits of her grown children. Ealhswið never had to grieve for the violent death of a child, particularly unusual in the violent world of late-ninth-century England. Her five children all prospered. Edward, her oldest son, ruled after his father until his own death in 924. Her younger son, Æðelweard, died in 920 without encountering any of the pitfalls likely to ensnare a younger son; Æðelweard received a large inheritance (although not quite as large as his brother's) from Alfred and seems to have supported his brother's kingship with no hint of revolt.[42]

Asser tells us that Æðelweard "sub diligenti magistrorum cura traditus est" [was given under the diligent care of the teachers], and while Asser gives Alfred the credit for this excellent choice of schooling—"admirabili regis providentia" [by the admirable foresight of the king][43]—the example of Osburh in the same text indicates a mother's involvement in the education of her children. Alfred was fighting Vikings, making peace treaties, and fortifying borders; while he may have "supervised," it is most likely that Ealhswið made the more daily, and more enduring, decisions about Æðelweard and the others' educations. Chapter 75 even contains echoes of chapter 23, the book-prize folktale; Edward and Ælfþryð are said "psalmos et Saxonicos libros et maxime Saxonica carmina studiose didicere" [to have learned by study psalms and Saxon books and especially Saxon poems]. While the word for "poem" has changed—*poematicae* to *carmina*—the root of the verb used is the same: *discere* is the present infinitive, *didicere* the perfect infinitive of *disco.*[44] It stands to reason that Ealhswið would have taught her children in the same way that Osburh did; her literacy, indicated by the possible book ownership discussed earlier, was part of her legacy to her children.

Ealhswið's daughters, like her sons, prospered. The career of the oldest, Æðelflæd, Lady of the Mercians, is discussed in detail later in the chapter as part of this maternal genealogy. Her youngest daughter, Ælfþryð, married Baldwin II, the count of Flanders, sometime in the 890s. She inherited estates from her father, and thus controlled property; she wielded enough power in Flanders that she was able to dictate the place of her husband's burial. A forged eleventh-century charter purports to grant land in Kent from *elstrudis comitessa* to Ghent Abbey, indicating a cultural memory of a powerful countess whose name could be invoked to validate land transactions. Ælfþryð named her daughter after her mother, hinting at her own understanding of maternal genealogy.[45]

Ealhswið's middle daughter, Æðelgifu, entered the religious life at Shaftesbury Abbey. There is some scholarly disagreement over the exact nature of Æðelgifu's religious calling. A land charter of King Alfred to Shaftesbury alludes to some sort of infirmity; the charter has been deemed "suspicious," or "spurious," although the detail of Æðelgifu's illness may or may not be authentic.[46] The charter exists both in Latin and in Old English; the relevant text reads as follows:

> . . . and mine dochte Agelyue forð mid þare erie in to þan menstre for þanne hie was on broken i hadod . . .
>
> [and my daughter Agelyue forth with that grant into that minster because she was in a state of misery]
>
> . . . Aylevam filiam meam cum eiusdemque cogente infirmitate in eadem æcclesia facta est sanctimonialis . . .
>
> [and it is determined that my daughter Ayleva with that same [grant] with confining infirmity into that same assembly of purity]

This "charter" is dated to 871, only three years after Alfred's marriage. In 871, Æðelgifu, his third surviving child, was probably not yet born. Alfred seems to be providing for an infirm daughter, but the "spurious" nature of the charter indicates a later dispute over the land in which one side tried to use Alfred's paternal concern to document land rights.

It may well be that Æðelgifu was infirm, and the forgers were simply drawing on an oral tradition. Such a state, however, would conflict with the usual description of Æðelgifu as abbess of Shaftesbury Abbey. In his chapter 98, Asser states that Alfred founded Shaftesbury and installed Æðelgifu as abbess: "in quo propriam filiam suam Æðelgeofu, devotam deo virginem, abbatissam constituit" [in that (foundation) he placed the abbess, his own daughter Æðelgifu, a virgin devoted to God]. Smyth points out that "if Æðelgifu were indeed a weakling, she would have offered poor material for establishing a fervent community about to enforce the rigour of the Benedictine Rule."[47] In keeping with his argument against Asser's as an authentic text, Smyth seems to think that Shaftesbury Abbey was in fact founded by Edgar. Abbey tradition also, however, claims Alfred's daughter as its first abbess, although there is notorious confusion between Æðelgifu the daughter of Alfred and Ælfgifu the wife of Edmund (king from 939 to 946).[48]

Whether Æðelgifu was a semi-retarded or invalid nun or a rigorous, devout abbess, she spent her days in a religious foundation. While Æðelgifu's mother is not recognized in Asser's text, Ealhswið's maternal performance must have contributed to ensuring that this daughter—the one who did not marry—would spend her days ensconced in a community, perhaps one somewhat like those matrilineal monasteries of seventh- and eighth-century Kent.

Ealhswið, then, can be read as a maternal performer who managed to raise five successful children in the most difficult of circumstances. Ealhswið probably spent substantial amounts of time with her sister-in-law Æðelswið; she was a literate woman who probably owned books; after her husband's death, she used her property and influence to found a renowned nunnery, which ultimately housed some of her female descendents, as I shall note at the end of this chapter. Examination of Ealhswið's appearances in the textual record and deduction about her activities from descriptions of the actions of her family members leave us with a picture of Ealhswið, not as Alfred's silenced queen whom Asser does not bother to name, but as an influential and successful maternal performer.

Æðelflæd

Ealhswið's and Alfred's oldest child, Æðelflæd, has received more scholarly attention than any other historical, secular woman from Anglo-Saxon England. As I noted in the beginning of this chapter, scholarly discussion about her has focused on the level of cooperation between Æðelflæd and her brother Edward, who was king of Wessex. I hope to show here that Æðelflæd, while she did cooperate to some extent with her brother, directed her energies towards defense, compromise, and reduction of violence.

A brief overview of Æðelflæd's life is in order. Æðelflæd married her father Alfred's ally, Æðelred, the ealdorman of Mercia, sometime in the 880s. Like her aunt Æðelswið, Æðelflæd played an active role in the government of Mercia, witnessing and issuing charters and participating in the *witan,* or council, of Mercia. She also seems to have participated in the government of Wessex, as she witnessed a number of her brother Edward's charters after he became king in 900. Sometime in the early years of the tenth century, Æðelred of Mercia became incapacitated, and Æðelflæd took over most of the government, including defense against the continuing Viking attack. Her husband died in 911, and she continued ruling Mercia as a sub-state of Wessex until her own death in 918 (I will be using the dates of the *Mercian Register* as opposed to the problematic dates of the other *Chronicle* texts; F. T. Wainwright has convincingly shown the accuracy of the *Register* dates[49]).

The record of her rule is preserved in the *Mercian Register,* a set of annals included as a separate section in two of the Anglo-Saxon Chronicle manuscripts (B and C). Charles Plummer has called these entries the "Annals of Æðelflæd";[50] Paul Szarmach has provided more extensive evidence to show that the *Mercian Register* has a "unique origin" that was probably Latin.[51] These entries document the studied defense of Æðelflæd's kingdom during her husband's illness and after his death. The information of the *Mercian Register,* combined with entries from fragmentary Irish annals,[52] indicate that from 907 to 918 she fortified her borders with tenacity and ingenuity, building fortresses and securing cities at Chester, Bremesbyrig, Scergeat, Bridgnoth, Strathclyde, Tamworth, Eddisbury, Warwick, Chirbury, Weardbyrig, Runcorn, Brecenanmere, Derby, and Leicester. The people of York had also agreed to submit to her rule, but she died before she could claim the city.

While historians cannot now place some of these fortifications, a map of the known fortifications shows Æðelflæd and her brother Edward building a continuous string of fortresses across the midlands. Wainwright views their work as a consciously planned joint effort: "Together they planned and worked for the destruction of the independent Danish armies in England, and their collaboration was highly successful."[53] At her death, Æðelflæd left Mercia significantly more secure and stable than it was at her marriage.

Collaboration with the men in her family seems to have been a characteristic of Æðelflæd's method. Her first charter appearance is as a witness to a land grant from Æðelred to the see of Worcester dated 880; Stevenson notes that the indiction date of the charter would date it to 887 rather than 880. In this charter, Æðelflæd is termed *conjunx.*[54] A twelve-year-old, married Æðelflæd (her parents were married in 868) witnessing government documents does seem somewhat improbable, and Stevenson's suggestion of following the indiction date seems sound. This first textual evidence, when dated to 887, indicates Æðelflæd, married by age 19, working in cooperation with her father's and husband's plans. Æðelred is "dux . . . merciorum cum licentia et inpositione manus Ælfredi regis" [leader of the Mercians with the license and placement by the hand of King Alfred].

Tetxual evidence indicates other substantial collaboration in Æðelflæd's life—ten extant and probably authentic charters show Æðelflæd working with her husband, her father, and her brother (after their father's death) to administer the affairs of the realm. Three times she witnesses charters of her husband; once she witnesses the business of the Mercian *witan;* two charters are jointly issued with her husband; she and her husband witness two of Edward's charters and jointly issue one with him; she and her husband are the recipients and witnesses of a charter of Bishop Werferth.[55] While I will be discussing some of these charters in detail later, it suffices here to say that their existence and quantity show that Æðelflæd was deeply involved in the governance of the realm, both in Mercia and in Wessex.

Æðelflæd's cooperation with the men of her family, then, is not in dispute; it is the extent of and willingness behind that cooperation that has ignited scholarly debate about her role in the crucial years of the early tenth century. Wainwright argues that she was completely acquiescent to her brother's plans of total domination of England; in his landmark 1959 essay, "AEthelflaed, Lady of the Mercians," Wainwright concludes that Æðelflæd "acquiesced willingly in the subordinate role allotted to her and . . . supported her brother's schemes loyally and energetically."[56] Wainwright points most emphatically to the virtual erasure of Æðelflaed's career in the Wessex-based manuscripts of the *Anglo-Saxon Chronicle,* which do not include the *Mercian Register.* Wainwright sees this erasure as a "blanket of official silence" because Edward knew that "her reputation could be used with effect by nationalists who hoped to revive the independent kingdom of Mercia."[57]

Catherine Karkov argues for a similar interpretation through the coins minted in Mercia during Æðelflæd's reign. While Mercian coins were all attributed to *Edwardus Rex* on the obverse, the unusual reverse motifs (of a tower, the hand of God, or a flower/rosette) indicate a sense of independence in Mercian coin making. Karkov reads the tower motif as a reference to Æðelflæd and Æðelred's defense of Chester within the gate of the city (which I discuss later). She states that these coins "were not intended to question Edward's authority" but that he stopped their production after Æðelflæd's death because they "did have a specifically Mercian significance, one that Edward was not about to let circulate free from the control of his powerful sister."[58] Following Wainwright, Karkov assumes cooperation and collaboration—"joint leadership"—between the brother and sister that necessitated the suppression of the record of the sister's power after her death.

Such suppression is also evident in the *Chronicle* of Æðelweard, an eleventh-century annal compiled by West Saxon ealdorman Æðelweard for Matilda, the abbess of Essen who was the granddaughter of Emperor Otho I and of Edith, daughter of Edward and niece of Æðelflæd. Æðelweard writes his *Chronicle* at Matilda's request so that she will know of her illustrious English ancestors; it is notable that he did not include any details from the *Mercian Register* in his book. While he was working from a manuscript similar to the A Text of the *Anglo-Saxon Chronicle,* in addition to other sources, some of the information, especially battle details, seems to come from oral or orally transmitted sources. His knowledge is such that "from 893 to 946 Æðelweard is an independent source," and Æðelweard seems to show a proclivity for glorifying Edward much as the original *Anglo-Saxon Chronicle* glorified Alfred.[59]

For the maternal genealogist, Æðelweard's omission of Æðelflæd's role in consolidation of Mercia and Wessex against the Vikings is striking. While Joan Ferrante notes that he "emphasizes . . . the importance of women and marriages in their heritage," she also states that this *Chronicle* "sees history primarily in terms of notable events like battles and successions."[60] Battles and successions, in Æðelweard's terms, are male. I venture to state that the *Chronicle of Æðelweard* is the only historical text from Anglo-Saxon England written expressly for a woman—and that woman was a descendent of Æðelflæd. Yet Matilda learns nothing about her illustrious great-great aunt Æðelflæd; the exploits of Edward and Æðelred are detailed (especially in the 890s, when Edward is depicted as noble warrior prince), but Æðelweard does not mention that the two men are also brothers-in-law. Æðelweard's only mention of Æðelflæd is at her death, when he calls her "regia soror" (the royal sister), and notes that she was buried at Gloucester (where Æðelred was buried eight years before, but Æðelweard leaves that connection to the reader, declining to point it out himself).

I suggest another conspiracy of silence here—Æðelweard, for all his good intentions, did not present this German abbess, his kinswoman, with a portrait of an energetic and military-minded female ancestor because he was interested in glorifying the men of the family. He wanted to make Matilda's history known to her, and for Anglo-Saxon male writers, even those writing for women, that history is the history of men. It could be argued that he did not have the material of the *Mercian Register* available to him, but it is preposterous to think that a man who knew specific details about battles with Vikings in the 890s would not have known, at the very least, that Æðelred was married to Edward's sister. Each of Æðelweard's chapters in book four is arranged around the rule of a king; Æðelflæd quite literally did not fit into his schema.[61]

Wainwright's argument about the extensive collaboration between Æðelflæd and Edward has been generally accepted. In 1974, H. P. R. Finberg stated that Æðelflæd "collaborated loyally and effectively. . . . [She] acted in perfect accord with her brother."[62] More recently, David Sturdy, in a recap of the "family business" (his phrase), echoes Wainwright when he argues that the combination of the *Mercian Register* and the *Anglo-Saxon Chronicle* "makes it clear that brother and sister were following carefully laid plans and commanding closely co-ordinated armies."[63]

Wainwright has been questioned recently, most notably by Stephanie Hollis, who argues that Æðelflæd "appears rather to have established for herself an autonomous kingdom which her brother Edward regarded as threatening to his interests when he became king of Wessex."[64] Stansbury as well reads antagonism in the maps where others see cooperation; while his armchair psychology seems quaintly inadequate (Stansbury suggests that Edward sought out conflict to prove he was greater than his great father[65]), he does point out that Æðelflæd and the Mercians had to guard against Edward as well as against the Vikings. The fortresses Æðelflæd built served to strengthen the Mercians against the possibility of West Saxon incursion as well as against Viking attack. Stansbury emphasizes that they had reason to be wary—Edward summarily took Oxford and London from Æðelflæd when her husband died.[66]

The titles used to describe Æðelflæd in the extant sources, finally, point to an uneasy collaboration between the siblings. I argue that Wainwright is correct is ascertaining the suppression of Æðelflæd's achievement (apparent in the *Chronicle of Æðelweard* as well as in the *Anglo-Saxon Chronicle*) but he displays undue naivete in his assumption of her acquiescence to that suppression. Most frequently, Æðelflæd has no title at all in textual sources, indicating that the accustomed language of patriarchal texts did not know how to describe her accurately. Titles or descriptions that are provided indicate her unusual power in a world of men, and to hear her described as "queen" must have made her brother very nervous.

In the *Mercian Register*, the text most definitively pro-Mercia and pro-Æðelflæd, Æðelflæd is three times (in 912, 913, and 917) referred to as *myrcna hlæfdige*, the Lady of the Mercians (it is from this epithet that Wainwright took the title of his essay). Her husband Æðelred, a sub-king of Alfred and later of Edward, is termed *myrcna hlaford* in the 911 annal, and it seems that Æðelflæd's title is the feminine version of the title of her husband, indicating the same sorts of power and responsibility, as well as the same sorts of obligation to her brother, Edward, king of Wessex. She is not termed *cwen* in the *Chronicle*, however, and *hlæfdige*, like *hlaford*, shows her subordination to her brother, who is repeatedly styled *cyng* or *cyning* throughout the main section of the *Anglo-Saxon Chronicle*. Twice in the *Mercian Register* (at the entries for 910 and 916), Æðelflæd is referred to simply by her name, as if no further explanation is needed. Hollis refers to the "matter-of-fact style" in which the Register recounts Æðelflæd's achievements;[67] there seems to be no need to reinscribe her as *hlæfdige* at each entry in the same way that her brother's kingship is continually reinscribed with his title.

In addition to this sense of familiarity, however, is a sense that Æðelflæd escapes reinscription and definition, that she is not so easily placed in the patriarchal schema. The *Mercian Register* entries that do not even specifically name her point up this element of dislocation in Æðelflæd's performance in the text. The entries from 914 and 915 use a sentence structure that elides the subject of the verbs and allows the annalist to eliminate Æðelflæd from the long list of fortresses she fortified in the second decade of the century. The entry for 913 includes the subject *Æðelflæd Myrcna hlæfdige,* and the subject is assumed in the entries of 914 and 915:

> 914. Þa þæs oþre geare þa æt Eades byrig on fore weardne sumor. Ond þæs ilcan geres eft on ufeweardne hærfest þa æt Wæring wicum.
> 915. þa ðæs oþre geare on ufan midne winter þa æt Cyric byrig. Ond þa æt Weard byrig. Ond ðy ilcan gere foran to middan wintra þa æt Rum cofan.

> [914. Then in the next year that at Eddisbury in the beginning of summer. And in that same year again toward the harvest time that at Warwick.
> 915. Then in the next year in the middle winter that at Chircury. And that at Weard-burgh. And in that same year before the middle of winter that at Rumcorn.]

Æðelflæd's presence hovers around these entries even as they do not specifically name her. Fortification of five separate fortresses in the space of two years would be a substantial contribution to national defense by a man or a woman, but the sentence structure of the *Mercian Register* leaves the achievement strangely depersonalized, as if even the pro-Mercian annalist cannot quite believe what he is writing.

The A Text and the other manuscripts of the "main" Anglo-Saxon Chronicle bear out this discomfort, when Æðelflæd is called *Æðelflæd his swystar* in the record of her death and Edward's subsequent takeover of her lands. The A Text must finally acknowledge the extent of Æðelflæd's power in order to glorify Edward and his growing kingdom; at 922 (a mistake for 918), after recording Æðelflæd's death, the entry states that "him cierde to eall se þeod-scyppe on Myrcna lande þe Æðelflæde ær under þeoded wæs" [to him (Edward) in leadership submitted all those in Mercian land which before was under the rule of Æðelflæd]. Æðelflæd again has no epithet to define her.

Similar lack of an appropriate title is apparent in the charters. Æðelflæd sometimes shares her husband's titles (as in charter #608, where they are described as *hlafordas*) or participates in a plural verb or adjective that describes them both (as in charter #587, where they are *gubernantes,* or #606, where they *tenuerunt* the land). Birch #632 is the only charter that calls her *regine,* in the header of a land grant renewal. The text of the charter is in the first person and reads, "ego Æðelfled . . . gubernacula regens Merciorum"; in the text, she does not style herself queen but "governor." J. A. Robinson has argued convincingly that the charter is a "corrupt copy of a genuine document."[68] The anomalous use of the title *regine* among the other West Saxon and Mercian documents under consideration suggests that the header and title are part of the text's corruption.

Most often in the textual record, Æðelflæd is simply not described, and the omission is made more glaring by the seemingly endless and thorough lists of names of charter witnesses from the period (890 to 918), most of whom have titles or epithets. Edward is always *rex,* Æðelred is almost always *dux* or *ealdorman;* the lists usually contain a number of priests, whose ranks are noted by *minister* or *episcopus* or *presbyter,* and other titles include *frater regis, diacon,* and *ðegn.* Æðelflæd is simply listed as a name, and the lack of an epithet makes her stand out in the witness list. She is there, but she cannot be classified by the system in which she performs.

The only document that authentically calls her "queen" is a fragmentary Irish annal about which little is known. It forms the fifth and last section of the *Fragmentary Annals of Ireland,* an Old Irish annal for which the original manuscript is lost. While much of the annal deals with Irish history, parts of it deal with the exploits of Vikings who traveled from Ireland to western England. The entries numbered 429 and 459 (in Radner's edition) are narratives of two of Æðelflæd's victories against such Irish-based Vikings. While I will discuss her tactics in these and other military actions later, what concerns me here is the assumption of the Irish annalist that Æðelred was a king and Æðelflæd a queen. She is termed a *riogan* (with the variants *rioghain* and *bainrioghan*), and the annalist is at pains to explain that Æðelred the king was "in a disease" so the queen commanded the defense of the city. Æðelflæd is termed queen of the Saxons, not of the Mercians, indicating a perception of her power beyond that depicted in the "official" narratives of the *Chronicle* texts. The annalist describes Æðelflæd nine times as *riogan* (or one of its variants), making clear his perception of her power in the Chester area. Edward may have wanted Æðelflæd to acquiesce in her cooperation with him, to the point where he instructed his chroniclers to leave her out of *his* history, but the evidence of the Irish annals indicates her independent power, military operations, and diplomatic initiatives.

This survey of Æðelflæd's titles indicates that she was ultimately indescribable within the terms of the patriarchal texts that have preserved a hazy record of her achievements. She was not called queen by her own culture—although a "foreign" culture saw her as one (indeed, the *Fragmentary Annals* do not mention Edward at all). She is defined in terms of her relationships to men—as Alfred's daughter, Æðelred's wife, Edward's sister—as indeed she operated within those rubrics for much of her career. But the lack of specific textual reference to her, even in the *Mercian Register*, indicates how Æðelflæd and her work—as I will argue at the end of this chapter, her maternal work—could not be described. Perhaps the most accurate reference to Æðelflæd is simply *heo,* she, the pronoun that describes her at her death in 918: "ðy eahtoþan geare þæs ðe heo Myrcna anweald mid riht hlaford-dome healdende wæs" [in the eighth year in which she with legal lordship was holding dominion in Mercia].

Æðelflæd has not received the amount of critical attention that her fictional counterparts have. The feminist history movement has, by and large, passed her by. Once Wainwright defined her (quite positively) as a loyal and silenced collaborator with her brother, she became something of a sidebar rather than the main focus of any historical inquiry (Stansbury's book is the notable exception). However, Jane Chance and Stephanie Hollis have both discussed Æðelflæd in relation to their arguments about women, power, and the church in Anglo-Saxon England.

Chance draws on William of Malmesbury when she argues that Æðelflæd "became influential and respected probably because she abstained from sexual contact after the birth of her first child."[69] Chance's source is William of Malmesbury's twelfth-century *De Gestis Regum Anglorum,* which states:

> And here indeed Ethelfled, sister of the king and relict of Ethered, ought not to be forgotten, as she was a powerful accession to his [Edward's] party, the delight of his subjects, the dread of his enemies, a woman of an enlarged soul, who, from the difficulty experienced in her first labor, ever after refused the embraces of her husband; protesting that it was unbecoming the daughter of a king to give way to a delight which, after a time, produced such painful consequences.[70]

William continues with praise of her city building and of her advice to her brother. Chance reads this section of William's text as evidence that Æðelflæd was an example of "the chaste queen" (Chance's term) in her argument that women needed sexual purity to wield power without approbation in Anglo-Saxon England.

While William is notoriously unreliable as a source, even for events closer to his own time, common sense indicates that his remark about Æðelflæd's sexual choice probably has some historical validity. Not only is first labor notoriously difficult for most women, but Æðelred's mysterious illness may have sexually incapacitated him as well, leaving Æðelflæd chaste by default rather than by design, with both a sick husband and memories of a horrific labor and delivery.

Hollis, who interprets Æðelflæd as a threat to Edward, postulates Æðelflæd's positioning herself as a type of Church Militant. Hollis's focus is the position of women in the church and in secular society of Anglo-Saxon England; she argues that "Rulers like King Alfred's daughter Æðelfled [sic] . . . would certainly seem to have lent themselves more readily to the typology of the Church Militant than they did to Marian idealization as mediators of the peace that passes understanding."[71] Hollis's evidence for this connection is slim; earlier in her book, she states (incorrectly) that the *Mercian Register* dates the beginning of Æðelflæd's fortification campaign to the Eve of the Invention of the Cross, 912.[72] The campaign had actually begun in 910 at Bremesburh, thus reducing any possible religious significance of the fortification at Scergeat as a "first." Hollis's provocative and engaging view of the Anglo-Saxon world is circumscribed by her focus on Christianity and its typology; it may be that Æðelflæd consciously imitated figures like Elene and set the date for the fortification of Scergeat to coincide with the Inventio Crucis. It may also be that early May was a good time of year to begin a building plan and a handy reference point for the annalist. We cannot know, and thus should not place undue religious significance on the use of liturgical feast days as calendar markers.

In contemporary sources, Æðelflæd impresses the reader as an effective and methodical administrator and military leader. Whether she viewed herself as a type of Church Militant or Chaste Queen cannot be proven— but we can show that she managed governmental affairs with a vision for the future; that she excelled at the managerial side of military command; and that she was decisive and aggressive in her use of military force—but that she always was engaged in defense, never in conquest.

Æðelflæd's administrative abilities are shown most clearly in three charters, all of which have been judged authentic by prominent Anglo-Saxon scholars. All three indicate a productive working relationship among

Æðelred, Æðelflæd, and Werferth (the bishop of Worcester) dedicated to heightening the security of Worcester. The first charter, Birch #574, is dated to 896, when Alfred was still alive and very much in evidence, as the proceedings of the *witan* are "dyde be Ælfredes cyninges gewitnesse ond leafe" [done by the cognizance and leave of King Alfred].[73] It is an admirable example of compromise between secular and religious power, and shows the desires of the council to issue decisions "ge on londum ge on ma þara þinga þe heo on forhaldne weran" [about lands and other things in which they (the Mercian people) were in injury]. In it, Werferth states that he wants granted back to the church some land about which there was confusion of title. Florence Harmer, citing Plummer, suggests that this *witan* was convened specifically to sort out "confusion caused by the inroads of the Danes between 892 and 895."[74] The current occupant of the land, one Æðelwald (who seems to be a land-holding priest with a son, as he is designated *mæssepreostes* in the witness list), does not dispute the bishop's claim but asks that he and his son might hold the land from the church for their lifetimes. Æðelred, Æðelflæd, Werferth, Æðelwald, and his son Alhmund, as well as some other *aldormannes,* are witnesses. The charter shows an equitable and mutually agreeable solution to issues of land title in the confusion after war.

The second charter, Birch #579, similarly indicates congeniality among the three powerful figures. The charter grants privileges from Æðelred and Æðelflæd to Worcester Monastery after they "for Wærferþes bisceopes bene heora freonda" [at the request of Bishop Werferth their friend] built a borough, or fortress, at Worcester.[75] The charter seems to have been composed at a time when the fortification has just been completed and its maintenance is under discussion; the borough was probably completed sometime in the 890s. Alfred is again mentioned in the document, indicating a date before his death in 899. The monastery will have half of the rights of lordship—including half of the money collected from fines and taxes (excepting the salt tax)—to compensate the community for a variety of masses and prayers to be said for Æðelred's and Æðelflæd's souls. More immediately, the money will ensure that "þy arlicor on þære stowe beon mæge ond eac þy eaðr be summum dæle þæs heordes helpon" (it may be more pleasant in that place and thus more easy to help for a certain part of that group). The language, while not as clear as we might like, indicates that the money from the rights will be used to improve the general standard of living throughout the community—I use the word "community" not in the religious sense, but in the secular one.

After all, the charter states that the borough was built *eallum þæm folc to gebeorge,* for the protection of all the people, not just those in Worcester Monastery. The contents of the charter indicate an intermingling of the concepts of spiritual and physical protection, that Æðelflæd and Werferth and Æðelred perceived the political and the religious as overlapping realms, where mutual good will and cooperation would achieve worldly and spiritual benefits for all parties, including the working classes, about whom we know so little from this period of history.

The third charter in question, Birch #608, again shows such cooperation and overlap between the two segments of society. Æðelflæd and Æðelred are titled *hlafordum* in the grant of land to them by Werferth. The lands are quite extensive, both within and without the town walls, and include riverfront, pasture, and farm land. There is no clearly stated reason for this grant, except that the community at Worcester "wilniað him to þæt hi syn eigðer ge hlafordes freond ge þara hina ge þære cyrcan" [they (the monks) wished for them that they (Æðelred and Æðelflæd) might be the friend of the Lord and of their community and of their church].

It seems most likely that this bid for friendship is actually an acknowledgement of the need for protection, and by accepting the land, Æðelred and Æðelflæd were tacitly understood to take responsibility for protecting it, its inhabitants, and the local church. I will discuss one of the more interesting features of charter #608 later: in it, Werferth designates Ælfwynn, Æðelflæd and Æðelred's daughter, to hold the land after their deaths. Æðelflæd's seeming equality of stature in this document—she and her husband are always referred to in the plural—may stem from a number of factors, including the death of her father (which probably reduced the impact of the king of Wessex on the affairs of Mercia) and the illness of her husband.

But as Stansbury points out,[76] Æðelflæd's importance must be attributed to her own skills as well as to her unique situation as the wife of an invalid and as daughter and sister to a king; while the dynamics of the relationships among the men in her family certainly contributed to her position in Mercia, her own abilities ultimately must have served to consolidate and enlarge that position. These three charters all show Æðelflæd to work toward compromise, to ensure the safety of the general population, and to respect the abilties and rights of the religious and secular powers in her realm. The charters reveal Æðelflæd's skill as a negotiator and administrator.

Her administrative skills were useful in another arena as well: that of military management. The *Mercian Register* lists the boroughs, or fortresses, she built from 910 to 918. (Stansbury gives her joint credit, with Æðelred, for fortifying Oxford, London, Gloucester, Worcester, Hereford, and Shrewsbury as well.[77]) I have discussed the sentence structure of the *Register* that elides Æðelflæd's accomplishments in the years of the second decade of the tenth century; nevertheless, the text does preserve the names of the fortified cities. I list them, with the year completed:

910: Bremesbyrig
912: Scergeat and Bridgnorth
913: Tamworth and Stafford
914: Eddisbury and Warwick
915: Weardbyrig and Runcorn

The *Mercian Register* lists other cities and towns in connection with Æðelflæd, but these are the ones listed with singular active verbs: *Æðelflæd getimbrede* these nine fortresses. Fortification of a town was of course a task requiring numerous skills, large numbers of workers, and a lot of money. But the *Mercian Register* gives Æðelflæd all the credit.

Thus we must read the text to tell us that Æðelflæd planned, supervised, and paid for nine large construction projects in the space of six years. Perhaps the two-year interval between the first and second fortresses gave Æðelflæd a chance to learn from her experience at Bremesbyrig and develop a system that enabled her to build two fortresses per year for the next four years. The fortress project, taken as a whole, is a daunting task that required knowledge of materials, building techniques, worker management, and military necessity. It shows Æðelflæd to be a perceptive and dedicated manager.

Textual evidence gives us a vision of Æðelflæd, then, as superior administrator and manager, a leader who could balance the competing needs of religious and secular communities into a fortified and prosperous whole in the face of both foreign and domestic threat. This in itself would be worthy of celebration. In addition, however, Æðelflæd proved herself militarily, in a role usually reserved for men. She used military force when the situation warranted—but always in defense, never in conquest. That distinction, ultimately, is the key to Æðelflæd's maternal performance.

The combined sources of the *Mercian Register* and the *Fragmentary Annals of Ireland* show that Æðelflæd engaged in military action five times. While the narratives of the *Fragmentary Annals* have been termed "pseudohistorical" or "historical legend" by their most recent editor,[78] independent confirmation of the skeleton of the narratives provides some measure of reliability, at least for the Æðelflæd entries. Taken together, the texts reveal a military leader with creativity, subterfuge, and aggression. Æðelflæd's main goal throughout her active military career seems to have been to achieve victory as quickly as possible at the smallest cost to her side.

In 907, the *Mercian Register* enigmatically informs us that *Her wæs Lig cester ge edniwod,* here Chester was restored. The corresponding *Fragmentary Annal* gives the details. Wainwright has argued that, despite the dubious nature of the text, the *Annals* narrative "represents a genuine tradition of great antiquity," and he reaffirms a 907 date for the first sequence of

Æðelflæd events in the *Annals*.[79] While the entry is too long to quote in full, the following summary indicates Æðelflæd's involvement in a campaign for which the *Mercian Register* gives her no credit:[80]

Inigmund and his band of Norwegians were driven out of Ireland by the prayers of an Irish holy man. They came to Æðelflæd [here the annalist notes Æðelred's sickness to explain why they went to her rather than to him], asked for land, and were given land near Chester. Inigmund then wanted to possess the city itself, and convinced other Norwegians and some Danes to ally with him to take Chester. Æðelflæd found out about their plans, garrisoned Chester, and refused the Vikings' demands to surrender the city. On Æðelred's advice, the Saxons left the city gates open on the declared day of battle and concealed fighters just within the gates. Part of the troop lured the Vikings into the gates, which were then locked so that the Vikings could be "frightfully slaughtered."

The remaining Danes were tricked by Irish spies among the Danish hosts; the Saxons convinced the Irish to pretend that they [the Irish] could set up a meeting for the Danes with Saxon traitors from within the city. When the Danes went to this "meeting," the Saxons killed them.

The remaining Norwegians had besieged the city by undermining the walls, and the Saxons threw large rocks upon them to stop their digging work. Boiling ale and water followed, with a final sally of beehives, "which prevented them from moving their feet and hands because of the number of bees stinging them." The Norwegians then retreated.

While parts of the narrative (especially the beehives) seem like legendary additions, Wainwright has argued convincingly that the *Fragmentary Annals* narrative "represent . . . a genuine contemporary account of historical events."[81] Within this history, a number of details stand out, most prominently the use of trickery. The plan to lure the Vikings into the seemingly unprotected city and the plan to ambush the Danes at a parley are both presented without a trace of shame or dishonor; indeed, both situations are narrated as if celebrating the clever deceit of the "Saxon" king and queen. The immediate goal of Æðelflæd and Æðelred in "restoring Chester" was to regain control of the town and the surrounding countryside as quickly as possible at the smallest cost to themselves. It is important to note that Æðelflæd and Æðelred had no objection to peaceful settlement; it was only in reaction to the Vikings' plan of conquest that the *hlafordas* used force.

Æðelflæd's second military appearance, which similarly demonstrates cold-blooded slaughter of the enemy, trickery, and determination in a defensive situation, is also narrated in the *Fragmentary Annals*. A summary of the action shows its similarities to the battle at Chester (although there are no beehives):[82]

Both Danes and Norwegians attacked the Saxons [*sic*]. The "king of the pagans" died during the battle and the remaining "greatly esteemed earl," Oittir, led the remainder of the Vikings into a forest in retreat. The queen [Riogan] directed the Saxons to surround the wood, cut down all the trees, and then slaughter the Vikings who had no place to hide. After this battle, *Edeldrida* [*sic*] entered into an alliance with the Irish and the Welsh against the Vikings so that they would come to each other's aid in case of Viking attack.

This annal is not clearly dated in the Irish text. The most probable date is 911, when the D manuscript of the *Anglo-Saxon Chronicle* informs us that the Earl Ohter was killed in a battle; the *Chronicle* battle, however, was directed by Edward (although he was not actually present—*sende he his fyrd,* he sent his army to the battle), and Æðelflæd is not mentioned. Her absence from the *Chronicle* text is likely explained by the "conspiracy of silence" about her in the Wessex-based manuscripts. The coincidence of the names Ohter/Oittir does not conclusively prove that the *Fragmentary Annals'* battle in the forest is the same as the 911 *Chronicle* battle, although the idea is intriguing. However, we can safely date the battle in the forest between 907 and 918, between the restoration of Chester and Æðelflæd's death.

The battle in the forest indicates that Æðelflæd was fierce and unceasing in her defense of her kingdom. She is given sole credit for the victory: "Ra marbhaid tra amlaid sin na paganda lasin Rioghan, go ro leath a clu ar gach leith" [the pagans were slaughtered by the Queen like that, so that her fame spread in all directions].[83] She shows no qualms about slaughtering an army in retreat, and devises the ingenious if perhaps apocryphal strategy of cutting down the trees so that the "pagans" will have no place to hide. The treaty arrangements that conclude the annal indicate Æðelflæd's diplomatic skills; while the Welsh were more usually the enemy (as they were 50 years before when Æðelflæd's grandfather Æðelwulf and uncle Burgred fought against them), Æðelflæd is able to convince them to put aside their usual differences in the interest of an alliance against a common menace from beyond the Mercian/Welsh shoreline.

Æðelflæd's military leadership is indicated three times in the *Mercian Register,* although the possibility of her command in the D Text 911 annal shows that she may have been in command at other battles as well. In 916, she ordered a retaliatory action against the Welsh, her erstwhile allies, for the murder of an abbot:

916. Her wæs Ecgbriht abbud unscyldig ofslegen foran to middan sumera. on xvi. kl IVL. þy ilcan dæge wæs sce Ciricius tid þæs ðroweres. mid his geferum. ond þæs embe þreo niht sende Æðelflæd fyrde on Wealas. ond abræc Brecenan mere ond þær genam ðæs cinges wif feower ond ðritiga sume.

[916. Here was the innocent Abbot Ecgbriht slain with his companions before midsummer on June 16, on the same day was the feast of St. Cyriacus the martyr. And three nights after this Æðelflæd sent a force into Wales and destroyed Brecenanmere and there took the king's wife, one of thirty four.]

Æðelflæd here demonstrates a sense of revenge that indicates strength but also mercy and an avoidance of violence. She takes hostages in response to murders. For the lives of a high-ranking man and his companions, she takes as hostage a king's wife and 33 others, and presumably receives some sort of ransom for their return to Wales. The annal, terse as it is, conveys a sense of outrage that a religious figure was slain *unscyldig,* and the reader is left with the distinct impression that it would be best to let Æðelflæd's friends travel unmolested, as she is wont to destroy a city in retaliation for their deaths.

In 917, Æðelflæd leads an army again, this time losing four of her retainers as she "begeat" [seizes] the fortress at Derby, which had been held by the Vikings since 874. It is important to note that this a reclamation, not an expansion, of territory. Again, this action is not noted in the *Anglo-Saxon Chronicle,* but the *Mercian Register* tells us that:

917. Her Æðelflæd Myrcna hlæfdige Gode fultum gendum foran to hlæf mæssan begeat þa burh mid eallum þam ðe þær to hyrde, þe ys haten Deoraby. þær wæron eac ofslegene hyre þegna feower ðe hire be sorge wæron binnan þam gatum.

[Here Æðelflæd, Lady of the Mercians, through the help of God further before the faith mass seized the fortress that is called Derby, with all those who were subject to it. There were also slain within the gates her four thegns who(se deaths) were grievous to her.]

Derby, "one of the five great midland strongholds" of the Vikings, was probably only lightly garrisoned, since most of its force was fighting Edward further to the southeast. Æðelflæd's attack accomplished a dual purpose: she relieved some of the pressure on her brother, and she made the first deep cut into the unified front of Danish fortresses comprised of Leicester, Stamford, Lincoln, Nottingham, and Derby.[84] The individual note of the great grief she feels at the death of her four retainers imparts a sense of attachment to her fighters as well as an implication that Æðelflæd felt the results of violence deeply and personally.[85]

Another of the five in the string of Danish fortresses, Leicester, fell to Æðelflæd in 918, shortly before she died. Like Derby, the campaign for Leicester was a reestablishment rather than an expansion of Mercian territory.

The lessons of Brecanmere and Derby had been well learned by the residents of Leicester, however, and the *Mercian Register* states that:

> 918. Her heo begeat on hire geweald mid Godes fultume on fore weardne gear gesybsumlice þa burh æt Ligra ceastre. ond se mæsta dæl þæs herges þe ðær to hirde wearð under þeoded. . . .
>
> [Here she seized in her domain with God's help in the early part of the year peacefully the fortress at Leicester. And the most part of the army which had been in that retinue came under (her) dominion. . . .]

The surrender of Leicester *gesybsumlice* seems to contradict Æðelflæd's seizure of the city (the verb *begeat* is used to describe her actions in both Derby and Leicester). The 918 annal also informs us that the Viking-controlled city of York was ready to submit to her as well, but she died before she could accept their submission. The 918 *Mercian Register* entry shows that Æðelflæd's aggressive, decisive, and merciless tactics in the early years of the tenth century had paid off to the point where her opponents were ready to surrender to her without a contest.

Ælfwynn

Æðelflæd, then, was a capable administrator, a thorough and successful manager, and a victorious military leader. She was also a mother, and it is in the intersection of that maternal performance with her other roles that I am most interested. It is her maternal performance—her protection, nurturance, and teaching of her daughter Ælfwynn and ultimately of her kingdom—that reveals a set of objectives different from those of her brother Edward. Æðelflæd lengthens and develops the maternal genealogy begun by her grandmother Osburh and continued by her mother Ealhswið and her aunt Æðelswið so that it appears, albeit briefly and enigmatically, in the text of the *Mercian Register.*

Textual evidence reveals Ælfwynn, who was probably born in the late 880s or early 890s, to have been involved in the government of both Mercia and Wessex; the maternal genealogist links Ælfwynn not just to her mother but to her grandmother Ealhswið and possibly to her cousin Eadburg. Ælfwynn was Æðelflæd's only surviving child; if we are to believe William of Malmesbury, Æðelflæd abstained from sex after Ælfwynn's birth in order to avoid the pain of labor. Before examining Ælfwynn's appearances in the textual record, it is important to note and refute a basic misogynist and anti-maternal assumption that pervades the historical record and that may have indirectly colored historians' views of Ælfwynn. Lois Huneycutt and others have effectively debunked the "myth of medieval indifference to children," and Huneycutt has also shredded the "belief that a woman with responsibility in the public arena cannot be an effective parent," a belief definitively not confined only to study of the Middle Ages.[86]

As late-twentieth-century readers, and as maternal genealogists, we need to keep our vision of Æðelflæd as mother as an integral part of her other roles. We cannot and should not assume that because Æðelflæd was deeply involved in national politics she would not or could not rear and educate her child—her own grandmother and mother provided her with maternal models. We need to see Æðelflæd *as mother* to lead armies and make treaties and administer land. Her maternity is not a sidebar but an integral segment of the main narrative.

Her daughter Ælfwynn is not the only child Æðelflæd mothered. Her nephew Æðelstan, Edward's son who ruled England from 924 to 939, was fostered at the Mercian court. Wainwright suggests that Edward promoted this arrangement so that Æðelstan would have a good relationship with the Mercian lords whom he would someday rule.[87] The arrangement also suggests the interesting possibility that Æðelflæd could accrue to herself some of the power of the "mother" of the future king that Stafford discusses.[88]

Ælfwynn appears four times in the textual record, and each appearance shows her to be an integral part of her mother's political vision. She is a witness to charter #603 (Birch), wherein Edward records a deed for Æðelfrid of land from Æðulf to his daughter Æðelgyð. The charter is interesting for a number of reasons. It is a rerecording of a deed that had been lost in a fire. Edward issues the record at the request of Æðelfrid, whose relationship to Æðulf and Æðelgyð is not recorded. The story of the fire and the ratification of the deed are on one side of the folio in Latin; the boundaries of the land (in Old English) and the witness list (with Latin epithets) are on the reverse side.[89] Æðelred and Æðelflæd are the second and third witnesses, after *Eadweard rex,* although they have no identifying epithets; the other witnesses are mostly designated *episcopus* or *comes.* Three other witnesses are not designated. These include Osferð, who Sturdy suggests might be related to Edward's grandmother Osburh because of the similarity in their names;[90] Æðelweard, who is most likely Edward's brother who never ruled; and Ælfwynn, the daughter of Æðelflæd and Æðelred, niece to the king. The authenticity of charter #603 is not in doubt,[91] and Ælfwynn's witnessing of the charter indicates her involvement with land transactions at an early age—she was probably in her mid-teens in 903.

Charter #608, dated 904, is discussed earlier as an example of Æðelflæd's administrative ability and her relationship with Werferth and Worcester Monastery; it also shows Ælfwynn's involvement with the administration of Mercia. The land deeded from Werferth to Æðelflæd and

Æðelred will pass to Ælfwynn for her life before reverting to the monastery: "gif Ælfw[ynn] leng sy þonne sy hit swa unbesacen þa hwile þe heo lifige" [if Ælfwynn may be (living) longer, then it (the land) thus will be undisputed for her while she lives (Ælfwynn's name is abbreviated)]. Ælfwynn will hold the land—and the responsibility for its protection— after her parents' deaths. The assumption within the document is that Ælfwynn will be as capable a landlord or protector as her parents. As Stansbury points out, the residents of Worcester would have had ample opportunity and precedent to ask for another protector to be designated; that they agreed to or even requested Ælfwynn to succeed her mother and father as protector of the city shows their faith in her ability.[92]

Ælfwynn's final charter appearance occurs in the witness list of Birch #632. Ælfwynn witnesses the renewal of a land deed; her entry in the list has been corrupted by conflation with the title of the bishop Ælfwine. The two entries read thus:

> Ego Ælfwyn episcopus consensi ond subscripsi.

> Ego Ælfwine episcopus consensi ond subscripsi.

Most scholars assume that the later copyist erroneously doubled the epithet for the similar names; while her inclusion as the second witness in the list perhaps does not indicate that Ælfwynn is "her mother's deputy governor," as Sturdy suggests, it does show that she is a prominent part of the workings of Mercian government and a person with enough stature to be included in such a transaction.[93] In 916, Æðelred had been dead for five years; Ælfwynn's inclusion in the witness list shows her working with her mother in an administrative capacity. It implies that Æðelflæd taught her daughter statecraft.

Ælfwynn's final textual appearance, in the 919 entry of the *Mercian Register,* does not identify her as Æðelflæd's daughter, however. Just as previous maternal genealogies I have discussed have been elided or evaded in written sources, the maternal genealogy of Æðelflæd and Ælfwynn is left to the discernment of the reader, as Ælfwynn is called *Æðelredes dohtor Myrcna hlafordes,* the daughter of Æðelred, Lord of the Mercians. I consider a daughter's appearance at all to show the strength of this genealogy—indeed, she is named in a separate sentence: *seo wæs haten Ælfwyn.* Anglo-Saxon texts tend not to refer to daughters at all, much less to name them. To look for Ælfwynn as *Æðelflædes dohtor Myrcna hlæfdiges* would be too much to ask.

But the information of the 919 *Mercian Register* does tell us that Ælfwynn succeeded her mother in Mercia after her mother's death, if only for a short time. The annal reads in full:

919. Her eac wearð Æþelredes dohtor Myrcna hlafordes ælces anwealdes on Myrcum benumen, ond on West Sexe aleded. þrim wucum ær middan wintra. seo wæs haten Ælfwyn.

[Here also the daughter of Æðelred, Lord of the Mercians, was deprived of all power in Mercia, and carried off into Wessex, three weeks before midwinter. She was called Ælfwynn.]

Wainwright and others have noted that this entry is "heavy with resentment" at Ælfwynn's forced deportation;[94] the verb *alædan* has connotations of coercion (Bosworth and Toller list "to lead, lead out, withdraw, take away" for their primary definitions of *alædan* as a transitive verb[95]). There is some dispute about exactly how long she held Mercia; the Anglo-Saxon calendar is notoriously confusing, and the New Year started variously on 24 September, Christmas Day, or midwinter (21 December, the solstice). She seems to have succeeded her mother for only six months, as the year change from 918 to 919 likely occurred before midwinter.[96] Sturdy remarks that Edward "rounded her up and took her into custody in Wessex, thus putting a firm stop to any prospect of a dynasty of powerful female governors in the midlands."[97]

Ælfwynn's assumption of her mother's role as *myrcna hlæfdige*, if only briefly, points to just such a dynasty. It also provides what I venture to suggest is the only secular maternal genealogy apparent in the textual record. Ælfwynn's brief "reign" in Mercia has provided the impetus for her inclusion in the textual record in such a way that this mother-daughter relationship does not need to be constructed from bits of other texts. It is part of the recorded history.

Its recording in patriarchal history, however, raises interesting questions about maternal genealogy, in the same way that the maternal succession in the Kentish minsters did. What is the purpose of maternal genealogy, if it only recreates and shabbily imitates the goals of paternal/patriarchal genealogy? Do Æðelflæd and Ælfwynn make up an Irigarayan mother-daughter "couple," or are they a female pretense of patrilineage? What is the maternal success of ruling a kingdom to be passed in entirety (if only briefly) to a daughter? Isn't the Æðelflæd-Ælfwynn genealogy just another reinscription of patriarchy, a celebration of inherited power and property that defies everything maternal practice works for?

I argue that the Æðelflæd-Ælfwynn maternal genealogy, despite its appearance in the patriarchal record, does provide us with a model of successful maternal practice. I make this claim because Æðelflæd included her daughter in her public actions, which were unceasingly focused on compromise, teaching, and strengthening and defending her community. Even at her most aggressive, her goals were the protection of her people and the reclamation of territory previously taken by the Vikings. She showed no objection to peaceful settlement near the Chester area, but strongly countered the invasion and attempted conquest of the city.[98] She endowed and helped to administer and protect religious houses that flowered in the tenth century, most notably Worcester and Gloucester. In addition, she made the countryside safe for endeavors like these monasteries. She worked with her brother, father, and husband, and the *witan* to keep order. She protected her kingdom, she nurtured it back to strength after years of ignominy, and she taught her people and her foster son as well as her daughter. Stansbury points out that the Mercians had more than enough advance notice of Æðelred's death for them to have chosen another leader.[99] They followed Æðelflæd because they flourished under her rule. Her country was enormously more prosperous and peaceful at the time of her death than it was at the time of her marriage.

She is a successful maternal performer also because her objectives as mother to her daughter were fulfilled. Textual evidence that refers to Ælfwynn, scanty as it is, shows that Æðelflæd had trained her daughter with many of the skills that she herself had learned from maternal performers before her, as well as from her more-recognized father Alfred the Great. Ælfwynn's deposition ultimately provided her with a modicum of safety—and I suggest that it also may have provided her with another entry into her maternal genealogy, because it is likely that she entered a nunnery after being "carried off."

The notion that Ælfwynn entered a nunnery seems logical; a number of scholars have suggested it.[100] Edward would probably not have wanted her at court, where she could be publicly seen as a symbol of what Wainwright calls "separatist tendencies in Mercia."[101] The nunnery founded by Ælfwynn's grandmother Ealhswið, Nunnaminster, would have been an ideal choice for her: it was in Winchester, where Edward could easily be kept aware of her actions, and it was closely linked in other ways to the royal family. Like Minster-in-Thanet and Wimborne and Ely, Nunnaminster depended on biological as well as spiritual relationship for its governance and maintenance. Not only had it been founded by her grandmother, but by 918 it was inhabited by Ælfwynn's cousin Eadburg, Edward's daughter who was canonized and venerated at Nunnaminster after her death.[102] Ælfwynn and Eadburg, if they did find their own form of matrilineality at Nunnaminster, were reenacting the construction of maternal genealogy at the royal nunneries of Kent two hundred years before.

We cannot be sure that Ælfwynn entered the community at Nunnaminster, but this suggestion is not pure and simple speculation. Nunnaminster (founded by Ealhswið), the Old Minster (founded by Alfred), and New Minster (founded by Edward) were the three prominent and related religious foundations in Winchester. In 1031, the abbot of New Minster, Ælfwine, made a liturgical book for his community. This *Liber Vitae* contains a list of *NOMINA FEMINARUM ILLUSTRIUM,* notable women who have been associated with the abbey in some way. It includes the name Ælfwynn, with no epithet to describe her.[103] The list seems to be in a mixed order of social class and chronology. Five royal women, from Ealhswið to Ælfgifu/Emma, begin the list. They are followed by six abbesses, and then a variety of other women described as the wives, sisters, or mothers of prominent men. The last of these described women is *Santslaue, soror CNVTI regis nostri;* a series of unepitheted names follows this entry. Ælfwynn's is the penultimate name in this series; after *Ælfwynn* comes *Aldgyð,* and then the scribal handwriting changes (the other entries are "somewhat later"[104]).

Ælfwine, the scribe of the *Liber Vitae* and the abbot of New Minster, had a sister named Ælfwynn, and this entry in the list could very well be a reference to her. He did not include his other two sisters, however, and it is unclear whether the sister of the abbot would have had enough social standing to be included in the list.[105] If it is a reference to Ælfwine's sister, it shows the continued association of the use of the name Ælfwynn within the upper classes and in the religious establishment of Winchester. However, it could also be a reference to Æðelflæd's daughter. Ælfwynn is an unusual name—unlike the other female names used in the dynasty, Ælfwynn is not repeated throughout and within the generations for the endless confusion of historians (as a contrast, there are five Æðelflæds in the *Liber Vitae* list). Inclusion of Ælfwynn's name in the New Minster *Liber Vitae* list—without an epithet, as she appears in the three charters—engenders the possibility that she and her cousin Eadburg ended their days together in the house founded by their grandmother.

Æðelflæd's maternal genealogy, then, reveals a number of similarities to the Kentish matrilinealities I discussed in chapter 2. Æðelflæd had a number of female family members that would have provided role models for her as mother and as queen and in the intersections between those roles. The Æðelflæd-Ælfwynn mother-daughter couple is not a failure because Ælfwynn did not wield public power; it is a success because the mother taught the daughter, who was (most likely) safely placed within the monastic, maternal genealogy of Wessex and Mercia. In reconstructing Æðelflæd's maternal genealogy—which flows from Osburh to Æðelswið and Ealhswið, then to Æðelflæd and finally to Ælfwynn—I want to place her in a vibrant female community that has been overlooked by scholars who continually place her as an anomalous female isolated in a patriarchal community of her father, husband, and brother. Æðelflæd's maternal genealogy does not and should not replace historians' views of her relations with the male members of her family. However, it needs to be recognized and included as a crucial part of her historical contribution to Anglo-Saxon culture.

Too often, scholars assume that the goal of any historical figure was to accrue as much power as possible and to pass that power on to descendents. In contrast, it is quite likely that Æðelflæd, after a lifetime of battles and negotiations, may have wanted a different kind of life for her daughter. We cannot know, but as I turn to the maternal performers of the poem *Beowulf,* I want to question more emphatically the assumption that royal parents, especially mothers, want succession—rather than a different sort of success—for their children.

CHAPTER 4

THE MOTHERS OF *BEOWULF*

To move from historical to literary texts in Anglo-Saxon studies is often not much of a leap, as the two categories tend to collapse into one another. Hagiography, history, and poetry reside amicably together in Bede's *History,* for example. But for a maternal genealogist to turn from real mothers with real children to mothers in literary texts necessitates a change in focus. The mothers who populate Old English poetry reveal the metaphorical propensities of texts that try to make them disappear after they reproduce, to "occlude" their maternity (to use Newton's term, as I discussed in chapter 1). The mothers of *Beowulf* tend to resist such occlusion, however, and perform maternal work in the face of the heroic code.

Because it is a culture artificially constructed within a text, the world of *Beowulf* is more stringently heroic than the historical cultures of tenth-century Wessex and seventh-century Kent. There is no organized Christian church in which a matrilineal community can flourish for mother-daughter couples, for example, and no words of praise for the types of compromise and acceptance of ransom (as opposed to murder) favored by Æðelflæd. The mothers of *Beowulf* exist in a textual world that consistently attempts to efface them.

Even more so than other female characters of Old English poetry, the women of *Beowulf* have been subject to much critical scrutiny in the past 20 years as women's studies and feminist theory gradually made an impact in Anglo-Saxon studies. While more postmodern analyses like Gillian Overing's *Language, Sign, and Gender in Beowulf*[1] now sit on the shelf by more traditional source-based or new critical studies like Helen Damico's *Beowulf's Wealhtheow and the Valkyrie Tradition,*[2] these texts and others like them leave intact the equation of women with the feminine and men with the masculine. No critic has yet used the maternal as a theoretical focal point to group together the mothers of *Beowulf* to see how an analysis of those five women specifically as mothers might affect our understanding of the poem.

The mothers of *Beowulf* engage in a number of performances, most designed to mother their children in Ruddick's sense of the word—they desire to protect, nurture, and teach their children, and in the heroic world of *Beowulf*, the protective aspect of maternal performance becomes paramount. Modþryðo, Grendel's mother, Hildeburh, Hygd, and Wealh-þeow all strive to protect their children in a poetic world governed by the principles of feud and violence. The analyses that follow will argue that only Wealhþeow succeeds in the poem as a mother—only Wealh-þeow manages not to validate and enact the violence of the masculine, heroic ethos and still keep her children alive.

Jane Chance Nitzsche first noted in 1980 that the women in *Beowulf* tend to cluster at the middle of the poem, where their stories can parallel and magnify one another.[3] Others have built upon Chance's foundation, analyzing the specific textual relationships among the female characters. At the feast celebrating Beowulf's victory over Grendel, the scop sings the tale of Hildeburh's woe in Frisia right before Wealhþeow's attempt to neutral-ize Hroðgar's possible adoption of Beowulf; immediately after that feast, Grendel's mother kills Æscher, and Beowulf's killing of her follows soon after. When Beowulf then returns to Geatland, the queen Hygd is intro-duced with her shadow, Modþryðo, and Beowulf gives his analysis of the marriage of Hroðgar and Wealhþeow's daughter Freawaru. All of these women live in a world where the balance of power is determined by vio-lence, where death is a daily possibility, where most of them see family members die and hear death celebrated in song.

Their vulnerability in a violent world initially seems their most salient characteristic; as Elaine Hansen argued 20 years ago, the women in the poem do not function as love interests but nonetheless are appealing be-cause of "their inherent vulnerability" and their presentation "chiefly as the objects of either idealization or lyric compassion."[4] Richard Schrader sim-ilarly argues that "Nearly every woman in *Beowulf* is presented as a vic-tim,"[5] while Paull Baum notes the poet's "sympathy with weak and unfortunate beings" in his patronizing summarizing of the function of the women in the poem.[6] More evenhandedly, Chance says of Grendel's mother, "Most of the other female characters figure as well in this middle section so that the female monster's adventures are framed by descriptions of other women for contrast."[7] The experiences of the women inform and build upon each other, so that the reader cannot escape the constant re-minders throughout the middle of the poem that these women live in a precarious and violent world that, for the most part, they cannot influence.

Modþryðo

The five mothers of the poem cluster even more closely towards its cen-ter. The most enigmatic of the five, Modþryðo, is the only one whose child

grows into adulthood within the text of the poem. As such, it would seem
that she is the poem's only successful mother—her adult son Eomer follows her husband Offa on the throne. But Modþryðo is not maternal—
she does not protect, nurture, or teach Eomer; instead, her performance
within the poem is masculine. In *Beowulf,* masculinity is power, specifically
the power to control the actions of others. Modþryðo, the violent queen,
illustrates Judith Butler's rubric of gender performativity, as discussed in
chapter 1; her performance shows that action, rather than biological sex, is
the determinant of gender in *Beowulf.* Modþryðo, though female and a
mother, is ultimately masculine since she wields power in the same way
that Beowulf does.

Although Overing's discussion of gender in *Language, Sign, and Gender
in Beowulf* ultimately focuses on women and the feminine, her discussion
of the "masculine economy" of *Beowulf* provides entree into my analysis of
Modþryðo as a figure who wields power to enact a masculine performance. For Overing, masculinity in *Beowulf* entails dominance and resolution; no ambiguity, of hierarchy, of gender, of decision, is permissible. She
argues: "A psychoanalytic understanding of desire as deferred death, of the
symbolic nature of desire in action, is often not necessary in *Beowulf;* death
is continually present, always in the poem's foreground: the hero says, 'I will
do this or I will die.' Resolution, choice, satisfaction of desire frequently
mean literal death."[8] Men in *Beowulf,* for Overing, live in a world of ab-
solutes: they will fight the monsters or die, they will avenge a death or die.
Overing reads Beowulf himself to trouble this absolute assertion, but acknowledges that the absolute resolution is intact even at the end of the
poem. The masculine characters define themselves against an unfavorable
Other: men are strong, noble, generous; the Other is weak, ignoble,
miserly—and might as well be dead, for within the masculine economy of
this poem, those attributes have no value. Within the terms of Overing's
analysis, Modþryðo is masculine; she forces an acknowledgement that masculinity is not "natural" but constructed, when she shows that a woman
can say, "I will do this or I will die."

After surveying critical views of Modþryðo and her role, I will examine two words, *mundgripe* and *handgewriþene,* which reveal
Modþryðo's lexical association with Beowulf and show that she cannot
merely be dismissed as an evil queen who becomes good after marrying the right man. She is neither a reformed peace pledge nor a heroic
Valkyrie. Instead, her character both confirms and denies a masculine
economy that depends on women as commodities. In the terms described in Luce Irigaray's *Women on the Market,* Modþryðo's masculine
performance manages to subvert the usual use of women as objects in
exchanges between men.

The brief episode in question tells the story of Modþryðo's actions before and after her marriage to Offa; it appears abruptly in the text after a description of the Geat queen Hygd (see complete text and translation of lines 1925 to 1962 in the notes).[9] Critics have tended to view this story of Modþryðo only within the larger context of the poem, usually reading Modþryðo as a foil to Hygd, Higelac's queen, who is described in the lines leading up to the Modþryðo episode (1925–1931) as a good queen, young, beautiful, wise, and generous. Unlike Hygd, Modþryðo was not initially good, wise, and generous, a model queen. Modþryðo orders men who dare to look on her to be killed (1933–1940). However, after her marriage to Offa, Modþryðo changes to become like Hygd, generous, loved, and fertile: a good queen who managed to overcome her wicked tendencies.[10]

A different "explanation" of the episode is patristic and reads the Modþryðo story as a Christian allegory, with Offa as Christ the bridegroom, to whom Modþryðo submits and finds happiness much like the good Christian does in submission to Christ.[11] Masculinist readings view the Modþryðo episode as a triumph, within the context of the poem, of the right, "natural" order of male over female, focusing on the "tamed shrew" aspect of the passage and revealing the critical desires of their authors to naturalize male domination of women, at least in the world of the text.[12]

One focus of formalist critics is the abrupt transition to the Modþryðo story. In order to show the passage's stylistic similarity to the rest of the poem, critics have sought other points in Beowulf at which the subject matter swings suddenly from one narrative to another without warning.[13] Similarly, Fr. Klaeber and others fit the "digression" into a moral vision of the poem wherein the story of Modþryðo is an opportunity for the poet to make a moral exemplum like others in the poem.[14]

Modþryðo's name, her very existence, and possible historical precedents for her have as well provoked considerable critical discussion. The crux "mod Þryðo wæg" (l.1931) can be read to include or not to include a name; if there is a name, it can be read as Modþryðo or as Þryðo. Historical critics, who stress the documented precedents for a number of the characters in Beowulf, search for Modþryðo among a number of candidates who include the violent and exiled Queen Drida; Cyneþryð, the notoriously cruel wife of Offa II; and Hermethruda, a Scottish queen who has a minor part in Saxo Grammaticus's story of Amleth.[15]

The political aims of feminist critics are quite different from those of the traditional (mostly male) critics noted above, but feminists, with the notable exception of Overing, also tend to shape Modþryðo and her story into a unified vision of Woman, be it in Beowulf, Old English literature, or Anglo-Saxon culture at large, to "explain her."[16] This sort of thematic, structural, moral, historical, or even feminist analysis illustrates Overing's postmodern contention about criticism of the Modþryðo passage, that "a place is found for the unmannerly queen in the larger context of the poem, one that connects, and assimilates her through opposition."[17]

Modþryðo does act as a foil to Hygd, and historical precedents for her character do exist. However, two distinctive if ambiguous words in the Modþryðo passage reveal a Modþryðo who is not so easily subsumed into patterns of the poem or of Old English literature that most critics present. These words, *mundgripe* (1938) and *handgewriþen* (1937), link Modþryðo with Beowulf in such a way that the categories of good and evil, masculine and feminine, become much harder to distinguish. Although lexically she is linked to the hero, the narrator tells us that she performed criminal acts (*firen ondrysne*, 1932). She deprives beloved men (*leofne mannan*, 1943) of life, but she is an excellent queen of the people (*fremu folces cwen*, 1932).[18] It seems that even the poet cannot quite make up his mind about her.

Modþryðo's strongest lexical links with Beowulf appear in lines 1937 and 1938, *handgewriþene* and *mundgripe*, literally translated as "twisted by hand" and "handgrip." *Handgewriþene* describes a deadly bond, *wælbende* (l.1936). Klaeber says *handgewriþene* "seems to be meant figuratively" since Modþryðo probably manipulated the events "by hand" and did not literally forge deadly bonds. However, the other two uses of forms of *wriþan* in the poem are decidedly literal: in lines 963–4, Beowulf literally twists Grendel to his deathbed (*Ic hine hrædlice heardan clammum / on wælbedde wriþan þohte*) and in line 2982 the Geats, presumably including Beowulf, bind up the wounds and the corpses on the Swedish and Geatish battlefield (*Ða wæron monige, þe his mæg wriðon*).

Here, forms of *wriþan* associate Modþryðo with Beowulf in instances where he is heroic (conquering Grendel, assisting his wounded comrades) and she is evil. Of course words have different connotations in different narratives, but the lexical association with the hero and his actions questions two usual critical assumptions: first, of Modþryðo's all-encompassing evil and, second, of a purely figurative translation of *handgewriþene*. Since Beowulf the noble hero is also associated with forms of *wriþan*, the use of the word in the Modþryðo passage clouds a reading of her as a pure termagant. The other uses in the poem are literal; why must the word be translated figuratively here? A literal translation does not necessarily mean that an Amazonian Modþryðo engaged in combat with the offending man; it could more simply mean that she bound him or executed him herself, rather than ordering someone else to do it for her. Modþryðo, the queen with the ambiguous motives and character, could indeed forge or twist deadly bonds. The lexical, literal association of Modþryðo with Beowulf through *handgewriþene* allows, even encourages, such an interpretation.

A similar problem with literal and figurative translations arises with the other word that associates Modþryðo and Beowulf: *mundgripe* (l.1938), both a clear link from Modþryðo to Beowulf and one of the most ambiguous words in the section. *Mundgripe* occurs only in *Beowulf*;[19] there are no other usages in the Old English corpus that might guide us to a wider interpretation of the word. Beowulf is the only other character in the poem with *mundgripe,* twice in the fight with Grendel and once in the fight with Grendel's mother:[20]

> 379b–81a: *he þritiges / manna mægencræft on his mundgripe / heaþorof hæbbe*
> (he [Beowulf], famed in battle, has the strength of 30 men in his handgrip)

> 751–53a: *he ne mette middangeardes, / eorþan sceata on elran men / mundgripe maran*
> (he [Grendel] has not met in middle earth, in the earth's district, than Beowulf's:any man with a stronger handgrip)

> 1533b–34b: *strenge getruwode, / mundgripe mægenes*
> (he [Beowulf] trusted strength, the might of the handgrip [rather than the sword Hrunting]).

While it is easy to translate *mundgripe* in these instances, scholars have had much more trouble with it in relation to Modþryðo. Klaeber says that it could be "an allusion to a fight between maiden (or father) and suitor" but prefers instead to translate it as "seized" or "arrested." Similarly, Constance Hieatt refers to it as "the method she uses, *presumably by proxy,* to pin down her victims" (emphasis added); Chance translates *mundgripe* as "arrest," Helen Damico as "hand-seizure."[21] If there is bodily contact, Klaeber suggests maybe the father is involved (though he gives no reason at all for this speculation); Hieatt assumes that Modþryðo would not engage in physical contact with the men who dared to look at her.

Perhaps they do not want to think of actual contact between Modþryðo and her suitors, although the word is most definitively literal in its other uses. Even though the word is literal in reference to Beowulf the hero and his good deeds, it is assumed to be figurative when referring to a woman and her bad deeds. Hieatt does remark on the link between Modþryðo and Beowulf through the word: "elsewhere, this word is associated with Beowulf alone, and its use here may be an indication of the misuse of strength and power in contrast to Beowulf's own exemplary use, recalling the contrast between Beowulf and Heremod."[22] Contrast or no, *mundgripe* associates Modþryðo with the hero just as *wriþan* does, and those associations suggest—but do not confirm—literal uses of the word in the Modþryðo story as well.

And what is the story of Modþryðo? The associations of these two words (which link Modþryðo to Beowulf) enable us to acknowledge and play with ambiguities rather than to totalize or eliminate them. Is Modþryðo really evil? Did she wrestle with men? Did her father pack her off to Offa? Does she illustrate an antitype of peace weaver? Is she an Eve figure who becomes a Mary figure? The ambiguities in the text show that Modþryðo cannot be dismissed as simply another example, albeit extreme, of a tamed shrew.

The usual assumption of Modþryðo's evil is that she has repudiated the conventional female role of passive peace weaver and taken matters of violence, best left to men, into her own hands. The traditional view of the passive peace pledge complements the traditional view of the active hero in this male/female opposition. Within this opposition, power belongs to the masculine. Except for Modþryðo, only men have the power of violence and the power of wealth in the social systems described in *Beowulf.*

Modþryðo, in the first half of her story—and in the second half, though less obviously—not only disrupts the construction of gender in the poem but manages to take control of it briefly. This control both comes from and produces the power she wields. Modþryðo has the ultimate power, that of life and death, over the men in her hall. This power is masculine in terms of the gender construction of the text; those who wield power are men, like Beowulf or Higelac, and those who are completely powerless are women, like Hildeburh or Freawaru. Although Hieatt thinks that Modþryðo's linguistic associations with Beowulf serve as a contrast involving the use and misuse of power, Modþryðo's lexical associations with Beowulf underscore the masculinity of her actions. Because she is wielding power as she arranges—or possibly carries out—the death sentences of the men who have offended her, she is constructing her gender, and that gender, within the terms of the poem, is masculine. Modþryðo is making an absolute, masculine statement, in Overing's terms, but with an interesting twist: You will not look at me or you will die.

Butler says that the construction of gender is an ongoing, circular process that builds upon itself: "'Intelligible' genders are those which in some sense institute and maintain relations of coherence and continuity among sex, gender, sexual practice, and desire."[23] In these terms, it is usual to assume that Modþryðo is evil (as Hieatt does) since she is acting against the usual assumptions about females, both within and without Anglo-Saxon texts. However, Butler also emphasizes that gender is constructed by the discourse that contains it. Simply because Anglo-Saxon scholars have most usually discussed the feminine gender in terms of passive peace pledges and a Mary/Eve opposition is no reason to continue to do so. We can view Modþryðo's gender as masculine, a gender she has the power to construct on her own. Modþryðo's gender is determined not by the author calling her a *cwen,* a queen (a noun feminine in grammatical gender as well definition),[24] but by her violent, authoritative, and powerful action.

While critics have not wanted to consider the possibility of literal contact between Modþryðo and men, a masculine construction of gender allows, even encourages that interpretation. Since Modþryðo is masculine, why should she not attach *wælbende* [deadly bonds] to those who have offended her, literally put them in chains with her own hands? This would not be a feminine action, according to the text's definition of femininity, but I read Modþryðo to construct her own gender, to assume power that is unfeminine within the context of the poem. In doing so, she "reveals a trace of something that we know cannot exist in the world of the poem: the trace of a woman signifying in her own right."[25] To achieve power, Modþryðo has had to assume the masculine gender, for her society does not permit the feminine to put offenders in chains and kill them.

The culture of the poem defines Modþryðo by her biological sex, sees her as feminine; her assumption of the masculine gender defines her deeds as *firen ondrysne,* a terrible crime in her society. The ambiguity of her gender and her sex seeps into the poet's narrative. Modþryðo is evil but also *fremu* [excellent], she performs *leodbealewa* [harms to people] but is also *aenlicu* [peerless]—the poet cannot condemn her completely with his language. She has disrupted the masculine economy, the binary definition of gender, on which the poem and its culture depend.

That economy is one that depends on women defined as commodities to be traded between and passed among men. Irigaray states, "The society we know, our own culture, is based upon the exchange of women."[26] While Anglo-Saxon England or early medieval Scandinavia may not be "the society we know," it is markedly similar in that an even more obvious exchange of women formed its basis—witness the recording of the transaction between Æðelwulf and Burgred in the *Anglo-Saxon Chronicle* that does not mention the name of the bride (Æðelswið) who seals the alliance. In *Beowulf,* Freawaru and Hildeburh are traded like commodities to their families' enemies to buy an alliance, a tenuous peace. Irigaray could be counseling Hroðgar when she says, "Wives, daughters, and sisters have value only in that they serve as the possibility of, and potential benefit in, relations among men."[27] Hroðgar's wife Wealhþeow, his daughter Freawaru, and his unnamed sister ("Healfdane's daughter") are all products in the masculine peace-pledge economy, traded for political alliance. Overing points out that women in *Beowulf* are so thoroughly objectified that most of them do not have names: of the 11 women in the poem, only 5 are named (Wealhþeow, Freawaru, Higd, Hildeburh, Modþryðo); the rest remain nameless (the old woman at Beowulf's funeral) or defined simply as a man's wife, mother, or daughter.[28]

Irigaray points out that within this masculine economy a woman is worthless unless at least two men are interested in exchanging her.[29] Modþryðo's marriage can be viewed in this light; she goes to Offa's hall *be fæder lare,* by father-counsel (l.1950). *Lare* here could be translated to mean an order of her father rather than advice (although I do not interpret it that way).[30] With such a translation, Modþryðo seems to acquiesce to the masculine economy that defines her society when she thus is exchanged between two men.

However, Modþryðo does rebel against that economy, especially in the first half of her story, when she performs within the masculine gender. Within the first 13 lines of her narrative, she refuses to become a commodity like those defined in Irigaray's essay. Overing emphasizes that Modþryðo will not allow the men in the hall—presumably potential husbands—to gaze at her. While most women are commodities, "the gold-adorned queens who circulate among the warriors as visible treasure," Modþryðo refuses to become one. "At the center of Modþryðo's rebellion is her refusal to be looked at, to become an object."[31] While Overing attributes Modþryðo's rebellion to her momentary disruption of the social and textual structures of *Beowulf,* I prefer to interpret Modþryðo more specifically as an active subject who has constructed her own gender. Her masculine gender both allows and forces her to be an active subject; thus, she cannot be an object. Modþryðo has the power to rebel, to refuse, since she has assumed the masculine gender.

Her refusal of commodification points even more strongly to literal readings of *handgewriþene* and *mundgripe;* the implications of bodily contact show the physical nature of the way the men wanted to view her and she refused to be viewed. Since Modþryðo performs within a masculine gender, we can now read the passage as a story of a queen who bound and decapitated with her own hands those men who offended her.

The literal translation of *mundgripe* allows even another interpretation of the story, and I wish to allow for a multiplicity of interpretations and acknowledge that version as well. While all critics assume that the *mundgripe* is probably figurative (even Overing translates it as "seizure"[32]) and either Modþryðo's or her father's, I would argue that the *mundgripe* could not only be literal but could be the man's. This interpretation calls for a translation of *æfter* (*æfter mundgripe,* l.1938) as "on account of" or "because of": because of an actual physical handgrip (a man touching this powerful woman), the sword was appointed. In this reading, Modþryðo has the power to refuse to be touched as well as looked at, which in Irigaray's terms rejects both the culture's definitions and commodifications of women.

The poet does not see the situation as a woman asserting her right not to be looked at and possibly touched: he refers to the men's actions as "pretended injury" (*ligetorne,* 1.1943). *Ligetorne* is unique in Old English to Modþryðo's story;[33] the narrator needs an unusual word, a compound of "lie" and "trouble" to emphasize that the actions of men concerning women's bodies are not injuries in the terms of the culture to which the men are accustomed.[34] Critics have tended to agree with the poet, that these injuries are pretended; Edward Irving says, "it is evident that these men are innocent victims of her accusations."[35] Evident? To whom? Perhaps to another man, within or without the text, who sees nothing wrong with examining the possible merchandise, as it were. Herein lies Modþryðo's ultimate disruption: she refuses to agree that the actions of the men are *ligetorne,* and wields her power to punish the offenders.

However, it is generally agreed that Modþryðo changes into a more conventional Anglo-Saxon woman upon her marriage to Offa. Since she has been given to Offa, the poet tells us, the ale drinkers tell a different story; Modþryðo lives well on the throne, good and famous, loving her husband (ll.1945–1953). Traditional critics call her change a reform: Modþryðo has become more like Hygd, the traditional gold-adorned queen. Feminist critics seem a bit saddened by the passing of the man-killer and the assumption of the traditional role; even Overing says that Modþryðo rebels against but does not conquer the masculine symbolic order.[36] However, I want to argue that Modþryðo not only disrupts the masculine symbolic order but continues to rebel against it even after her disappearance from her own story.

It is easy to see Modþryðo as a conventional woman, silent and passive at the end of her narrative. The traditional view sees Modþryðo sent to Offa *be fæder-lare* as a gold-adorned peace pledge. After three and half lines (1951b–1954) praising her as a good, traditional queen, the poet moves on to praise her husband and does not mention Modþryðo again.

However, after her marriage to Offa, Modþryðo may not be the conventional gold-adorned queen that she seems to be on the surface. Close examination of the description of her life at Offa's court shows her unconventionality in a continued "rebellion" against the binary oppositions that defined her as virago and now as passive peace weaver. First of all, although she went *be fæder lare,* she specifically *gesohte,* sought, Offa's hall. I choose to translate *lare* as "advice," without the authority-laden translation of "order,"[37] so that considering advice from her father, Modþryðo actively sought (journeyed to) Offa's hall. Once there, she is *in gumstole,* on the throne, not walking among the warriors serving them drink; the tableaux shows her in the place of power, not in the position of attendance or servitude. Modþryðo's place on the throne is especially unusual when contrasted with that of the consorts of ninth-century Wessex in Æðelflæd's maternal genealogy: Ealhswið and Osburh had no place on the throne, Asser says, and were not even called "queen."[38] On her throne, Modþryðo is described as *mære* [famous] in line 1952, an adjective normally reserved for (male) heroes.[39] These phrases all hint that Modþryðo is not the typical queen the critics have taken her to be after her marriage.

Most important is her success in that marriage. Modþryðo rebels against the system by succeeding in its terms, terms that are (as Overing and others point out) set up to ensure women's failure within the terms of patriarchal society.[40] In a society that values war, killing, violence, and glory in battle, the peace-weaver actually strives against everything the society values.

The cornerstone of Modþryðo's unconventionality is her success in the role in which the others fail. She resists and disrupts the system both before and after her marriage. Unlike the other marriages described in the poem, Modþryðo's succeeds both emotionally and politically. Offa is not embroiled in a blood feud; he is

> þone selestan   bi sæm tweonum,
> eormencynnes;   Forðam Offa wæs
> geofum ond guðum,   garcene man,
> wide geweorðod,   wisdome heold
> eðel sinne (1956–1960)

[the best between the seas of mankind. Because Offa was, with gifts and battles, a spear-bold man, widely exalted, he held with wisdom his native land].

With this great king Modþryðo *hiold heahlufan* (l.1954), held the high love; they obviously have a good marriage. Modþryðo's supposed acquiescence to the status quo actually undermines it; her success as a queen (not a peace pledge predestined to failure) defies the system that devalues yet necessitates the woman as peace weaver.

Modþryðo's gender performance in *Beowulf* thus shows that gender within the poem is not "natural" but dependent upon agency and power wielded over others. Modþryðo as masculine performer forces us to discard conventional notions of gender in the poem—the active hero, the passive peace pledge, the tamed shrew. But in her masculine success, as she sits on her throne, loves her husband, and presides over a peace that Hildeburh and Freawaru will never know, Modþryðo is not maternal. She has subverted but at the same time endorsed the ideals of the masculine economy; Overing says that "the violent form of her rebellion confronts the system on its own death centered terms."[41] Modþryðo does not try to protect, nurture, or teach, although she is quite good at wielding a sword and protecting her honor.

Indeed, she is textually separated from her son, who is defined as Offa's son rather than hers. While it is certainly possible that Eomer was Offa's son by another woman, the poem's definition of Eomer as Offa's rather than Modþryðo's son does not mean that she was not his mother (even if she were not, she was his stepmother). Anglo-Saxon texts are simply uninterested in matrilineage; for example, the genealogy of Adam, in the Junius 11 *Genesis* sequence, refers to Seth as only Adam's son, although we know he was Eve's as well.[42] Modþryðo is the only possible woman included the text who could be Eomer's mother, and I will present her as such in the argument that follows, although her role as possible maternal performer would be equally valid as biological mother or as stepmother. Ruddick's *Maternal Thinking* emphasizes that a biological relationship is not necessary for a maternal relationship, as adoptive parents and others well know.[43]

Readers do not think of Modþryðo as a mother. Critics have never argued for motherhood as one of her textual identities. The poet tells us of her son:

> þonon Eomer woc
> hæleðum to helpe,   Hemminges mæg,
> nefa Garmundes,   niða cræftig (1960b–1962).

[From him Eomer was born as a help to warriors, Hemming's kinsman, nephew of Garmund, powerful against evils.]

Modþryðo has disappeared from a story that is supposedly hers. Her body disappears as well as her name; Eomer is born not from her but *þonon* (l.1960), from him, Offa. Like the celebrated kings of the *Anglo-Saxon Chronicle,* Modþryðo's son has a purely masculine genealogy here; the poet emphasizes his father, his kinsman, and his uncle. The text severs any bodily or emotional connection between son and mother. Modþryðo succeeds in the terms of patriarchal violence, but the price is her maternity. She does not mother Eomer, in Ruddick's terms or in the terms of the text itself, and as such she cannot be viewed as a maternal performer within the poem. Her immensely successful masculine gender performance, with its violence and its disruption, precludes any textual relationship with her child.

The Seawolf

Violence is a determinant in the lives of all the mothers of *Beowulf,* but perhaps none more so than Grendel's mother, the ultimate maternal fantasy and horror, defined completely by and devoted completely to her son. Like Modþryðo, the monster-mother turns to the masculinist heroic code and its ethos and glorification of violence; unlike Modþryðo, the monster-mother must endure the death of her child and the realization of her failure to mother her son—to protect him.

Grendel's mother's critical reputation has climbed steadily throughout the twentieth century since J. R. R. Tolkien notoriously left her out of his analysis of the poem in his 1936 essay "Beowulf: The Monsters and the Critics."[44] While other critics occasionally dismiss her importance as well,[45] her integral position within the poem seems critically assured 60-some years after Tolkein's initial neglect.

Grendel's mother, like Modþryðo, has fit neatly into a number of critical paradigms. Her ancestral descent from Cain places her firmly in an exegetical reading, wherein Beowulf's descent to her mere is like Christ's descent into Hell.[46] Chance, whose reading is more broadly focused, also reads Grendel's mother as a grotesque parody of the Virgin Mary both in the mysteries of their sons' begettings and in their responses to their sons' deaths.[47] She is celebrated by admirers of *Beowulf*'s heroic code, who stress that her motive for killing Æscher—revenge for her son's death—is completely acceptable within the feud terms governing the poem.[48] Folk- and myth-oriented critics read Grendel's mother as a matriclan mother goddess or Great Mother figure who demands sacrifice;[49] in a somewhat similar vein, one scholar has gone so far as to argue that Grendel and his mother are remnants of a primitive indigenous matrilineal people left over from the Scandinavian invasions of the migration period.[50]

Most usual is a reading of Grendel's mother that stresses her similarities to the other women in the poem—the cluster of femininity at the poem's center. Chance sees Grendel's mother as "Epic Anti-Type of the Virgin and Queen" (the title of her book's chapter on *Beowulf*), who appropriates the normally masculine role of warrior-retainer-avenger.[51] Mary Kay Temple analyzes the word *ides* (noblewoman), which is used to describe Grendel's mother, Wealhþeow, and Modþryðo, to show how the three "queens" attempt to consolidate and wield power;[52] similarly, Damico sees Grendel's mother, Wealhþeow, and Hildeburh forming a "mother triptych" in which the characters act as foils to one another as they react to their various political and emotional situations.[53] While I too will examine how these mothers' performances resonate with one another, first I would like to concentrate on Grendel's mother as an individual character.

Such individual attention that had already been paid to her has a mostly psychoanalytic focus. She seems to have become a primal, female essence in the minds of critics who see her not just as Grendel's mother but as Mother in the psychoanalytic sense of the word. As John Niles views her and Grendel as an "incestuous primal couple,"[54] and Jacqueline Vaught reads her to be "primal, chaotic energy,"[55] a reading of Grendel's mother as Mother is almost inescapable. She is defined in the text only as a series of epithets and termed *grendles modor* four times (ll.1258, 1282, 1538, and 2139) and *his modor* once (l.1276). Edward Irving points out that "fanatical and vengeful mother-love is her sole human characteristic";[56] like Kiernan, who defines Grendel as "a boy only a mother could love,"[57] Irving views her as an embodiment of her relationship, both physical and emotional, with her son.

The mother-as-monster motif recurs in psychoanalysis: the monstrous mother impedes her child's development; the monstrous mother smothers her child; she does not nurture enough; she emasculates. Yet Grendel's mother's actual monstrosity has been questioned only very recently. Christine Alfano has brilliantly argued that modern editors and translators make her monstrous or animalistic in their choices of modern English words to describe her so that they "transform an avenging mother into a bloodthirsty monster,"[58] a process Alfano argues those same critics find necessary because Grendel's mother "disrupts convenient gender stereotypes."[59] Gillian Overing points out that part of the grendelkin's monstrosity is that there is no patriarch in their household.[60] These social and cultural disruptions, more than any actual physical description in the text, has led to the common critical perception of Grendel's mother as a monster, subliminally a monstrous mother to be feared.

John Hill's psychoanalytic reading of Grendel's mother, like most psychoanalyses, focuses on the child—here Beowulf, Grendel, or the reader— at the expense of the Mother, who becomes objectified as she plays her part in the child's oedipal drama. Hill reads the poem as a realization of Beowulf's superego; the fight with the Mother is an oedipal renunciation, made worthwhile by the treasure and glory given by the Father.[61] Hill's stunning analysis, despite its constant reference to Grendel's mother, remains firmly focused on Beowulf and his oedipal drama, never intimating that Grendel's mother has a drama, and a story, of her own.

James Hala has invoked this almost inadvertent focus on the son in his recent Kristevan analysis of Grendel's mother, when he argues for the "necessity of repressing the mother-as-subject" as he reads Grendel's and Beowulf's journeys to the mere as their urges to seek "the mere, the mother, and the *joissance* of primary narcissism."[62] Hala ultimately escapes the trap of focus on the child at the expense of the mother, however, and argues for mutual necessity in the relationships among the mother as a figure of abjection, the need for the phallic sword of the Father to inscribe Beowulf into patriarchal history, and the loss of the "creative power of poetry" as "the *ides* and all she is associated with are sublimated into a perfected history."[63] Hala forces an acknowledgement of the indispensability of the monster-mother to the impetus of the poem; even he, however, cannot avoid swerving into Beowulf's narrative and reinscribing the mother as minor participant rather than primary actor.

Grendel's mother's primary narrative is shrouded in the levels of narrative that present her to the poem's readers and listeners. The poet's third-person narratives of her visit to Heorot and of Beowulf's subsequent visit to her underwater hall are separated by Hroðgar's narrative telling of her history and describing her mere to Beowulf; much later in the poem, Beowulf briefly mentions her in his retelling to Hygelac of his adventures in Denmark. Occasionally, however, her point of view seeps into the poet's narrative and reveals most basically a scared, angry mother who could not protect her grown child.

Hroðgar and Beowulf, along with the poet, tend to define Grendel's mother's actions within the terms of the code they understand—the heroic code of vengeance. She is first introduced (by the poet) as a *wrecend,* an avenger, at line 1256; Hroðgar states that *wolde hyre mæg wrecan,* she wished to avenge her kin (l.1339); Beowulf tells Hygelac that *wif unhyre / hyre bearn gewræc,* the frightful woman avenged her child (ll.2120b–2121a). By focusing on her as an avenger, they can avoid focus on her as a bereaved mother who might arouse pity. By defining her within the bounds of the heroic code of feud, Beowulf can kill her with impunity. Simply killing a bereaved mother seems distinctly un-heroic behavior.

Yet during her visit to Heorot the poet—almost inadvertently—shows a more sympathetic side to Grendel's mother, one that focuses on a mother's grief that she failed to protect her child. While the poet first introduces her as an avenger, he also provides some details about her life:

>   þætte wrecend þa gyt
> lifde æfter laþum,   lange þrage,
> æfter guðceare;   Grendles modor,
> ides aglæcwif   yrmþe gemunde,
> se þe wæteregesan   wunian scolde,
> cealde streamas. . . . (ll.1256b–1261a)

[That an avenger then yet lived for a long time on account of hatred, on account of battle-care. (It was) Grendel's mother, noble lady, formidable woman, thinking on misery, she who must dwell in terror-water, in cold streams. . . .]

While much has been written about her as an *ides acglæcwif,* a noble lady, a formidable woman, at line 1258a,[64] the second half of that line has received surprisingly little critical attention. Grendel's mother is also *yrmþe gemunde,* thinking on misery, at line 1258b, and I argue that the misery is her own—she is dwelling on her loss. These lines focus wholly on her and her past, not on her subsequent actions. The *yrmþe* could conceivably refer to misery she plans to inflict on the Danes, but it is not likely in a series of lines that tell us also that she has lived for a long time worrying about the hatred between her son and the Danes and that she lives in a cold, watery place. This misery is hers. She travels to Heorot on a *sorhfulne sið,* a sorrowful voyage (l. 1278a), thinking about her loss.

These clues point towards a mother desperately trying to react to her child's death—and what is the correct reaction, in any culture? She makes her way to Heorot, not with bluster and shouting but in sorrow and misery. Once she is there, the poet informs us in one of the poem's similes that she is not as fearsome and terrifying as a man:

> Wæs se gryre læssa
> efne swa micle,   swa bið mægþa cræft,
> wiggryre wifes   be wæpnedmen,
> þonne heoru bunden,   hamere geþruen,
> sweord swate fah   swin ofer helme
> ecgum dyhttig   andweard scireð (ll. 1282b–1287)

[Was the terror less, even as great as is the skill of women, as is the battle-horror of women, beside that of the weaponed men, when the sword, metal-bound with hammer forged, blood-shining, cuts with strong edge against the boar-over-the-helmet].

This image of violence—a bloody sword cutting through a helmet—is one matched with masculinity. It is the weaponed men who can produce such an image with their swords, not the women, who seem to have their own, undescribed, sort of battle horror. This masculine violence precedes a description of the Danes waking and grabbing their swords. In this confusion, Grendel's mother feels only fear: "Heo wæs on ofste, wolde ut þanon, / feore beorgan, þa heo onfunden wæs" (she was in haste, she wished [to go] out of there to preserve her life when she was discovered ll. 1292–93).

The poet lets us see her desire. We may be intended to scorn her reaction—after all, fighters are not supposed to worry about their own lives, as the poet tells us during Beowulf's fight with Grendel's mother (ll. 1534–1537)—but we can certainly understand it. In this moment of fear and confusion, she takes Æscher: "hraðe heo æþelinga anne hæfde / fæste befangen, þa heo to fenne gang" [Quickly she had snatched one retainer fast, then she went to the fen, ll. 1294–95]. In her haste, she randomly takes

Hroðgar's trusted counselor, although when Hroðgar tells the story later, it sounds like she carefully chooses her victim to exact maximum revenge with a high-level killing.

Grendel's mother is "doing" revenge, but she does it wrong. Her femininity, her maternity, her monstrousness (psychological or otherwise)—they all impede her supposed heroism as she avenges her son's death. Full of her own misery, scared of the noise, and weaker than her opponents, her main goal by the time of her exit is to get back to her mere in one piece. Her performance here does point up the flaws in the heroic ethos, as Kiernan so ably argues, because her performance can never right her injury. An avenging mother, much as her portrait touches deep psychological chords, is ultimately a failure.

That mother's world is actually one of dramatic, alluring landscape, albeit in a way that does not fit neatly into the rest of the poem. It is described by Hroðgar:

> Hie dygel lond
> warigeað wulfhleoþu,   windige næssas,
> frecne fengelad,   ðær fyrgenstream
> under næssa genipu   niþer gewiteð,
> flod under foldan.   Nis þæt feor heonon
> milgemearces,   þæt se mere standeð;
> ofer þæm hongiað   hrinde bearwas,
> wudu wyrtum fæst   wæter oferhelmað.
> Þær mæg nihta gehwæm   niðwundor seon,
> fyr on flode. (ll.1357b–1366a)

[They guard a secret land, a wolf-slope, winding cliffs, terrible fen-paths, where mountain streams go downward under mist cliffs, a flood under the earth. That is not far from here, of mile-marks, that where the mere stands; over that hang frosted trees, wood with roots fast overhangs the water. There each night one may see an evil-wonder, fire on a flood.]

Overlooking Hroðgar's editorializing about evil wonders and terrible fen-paths, we can read Grendel and his mother to have lived together in a setting of cliffs, trails, streams, and craggy trees. While some critics have tried to set up for the poem an opposition between nature/culture and mere/Heorot in which nature and mere are both construed as evil,[65] once we read Grendel's mother more sympathetically, we can see her environment—fierce and extreme as it is—more sympathetically as well.

In Grendel's mother's final scene, Beowulf invades this space, which Chance says "symbolically projects the mystery and danger of female sexuality run rampant."[66] Grendel's mother is much more powerful and

aggressive here than she was the night before in Heorot; I read this re-
newed vigor to indicate her anger at his entrance. She is trying to defend
her home, and feels no indecision about her action in this scene.

This scene also provides Grendel's mother with a possible name. She is
now *seo brimwylf,* the Seawolf (l.1506), an epithet that has received much
critical attention in discussion of her human or monstrous qualities. No
critic has suggested that *brimwylf* functions as a name for this character
whose namelessness has contributed to critical perception of her monstrosity. Hroðgar says at line 1351 that Grendel's mother has "idese onlic-
næs" [a noblewoman's likeness], so she is recognizably human rather than
animal. But just as the humans Beowulf and Eofor have names derived
from animals, so might she have an animal epithet or name that suits her
fierceness in defending her home. Alfano argues that *brimwylf* "could function as an epithet such as those applied to warriors and figures in battle,"
rather than a reference to "Grendel's mother's literal resemblance to a female water-wolf."[67] I would like to take her argument one step further and
argue that in this section of the poem, Brimwylf functions as a name of
sorts for Grendel's otherwise nameless mother. The word is unique to *Beowulf* in the corpus, and its two occurrences describe only Grendel's
mother.[68] She is also referred to as *seo brimwylf* at line1599 when the Danes
on the banks of the mere think she has killed Beowulf; she defends her
natural landscape and the body of her dead son in the underwater hall with
the ferocity of a wolf. I will refer to her as "the Seawolf" in the remainder
of this book to name this mother who tries to avenge her child's death.

Indeed, despite the poet's previous protestations that women are less
terrible in battle than men, his second fight is much harder than Beowulf's
first. After she grabs him and drags him down into the dry part of the hall
(sea creatures poking at him all the way), he swings his sword at her only
to find that its blade is useless (ll.1519b–1528). He throws her down with
his bare hands, but she gets up and retaliates by throwing him on the floor
(ll.1537–1544). What follows has occasioned some critical comment:

> Ofsæt þa þone selegyst,   ond hyre seax geteah
> brad ond brunecg;   wolde hire bearn wrecan,
> angan eaferan (ll.1545–1547a).

[Then she set upon the hall-guest and drew her short sword, broad and
bright-edged, she wished to avenge her child, her only offspring.]

Generations of translators and readers have squirmed or laughed at the
image of Grendel's mother sitting on Beowulf—since *ofsaet* is usually translated "sat upon." But Fred Robinson's work on *ofsittan* allows the more

seemly translation of "set upon" or "beset," which does add to the fervor
of the fight without being ludicrous.[69]

More importantly for my reading of the Seawolf as a partially sympathetic portrait, however, are the lines that follow this besetting; her motives
are clear, even to the poet, and they do not concern herself. While Beowulf
talks of glory and treasure, she still thinks of her child. Even in death, Grendel is mentioned twice in these lines, his uniqueness emphasized: "hire
bearn . . . angan eaferan" [her child . . . only offspring]. As she defends her
home and herself, she thinks about her son. Her action here could be
termed specifically maternal (unlike her visit to Heorot) since she is engaging in a form of protection. She must know that Beowulf will desecrate
her son's corpse.

Masculine heroism will win out, however, as we all know, and the
mother must die. Beowulf is "aldres orwena" [despairing of life, 1.156],
when he takes the giant sword. The language of the poem breaks Grendel's
mother into pieces even before the sword itself does; she is described as
only a neck just as the "banhringes bræc" [the bone-rings broke, 1.1567].
Beowulf, somewhat monstrous himself, glories in the gore: "secg weorce
gefeh" [the man rejoiced in his work, 1.1569b]. The Seawolf is dead.

Reading Grendel's mother as a maternal performer elucidates some of
the odd inconsistencies that crop up when she is read merely as a vengeful monster. Through hints in the text during her approach to Heorot, we
can imagine her worrying about her son as he carries out his own bloodthirsty feud with the Danes; we can see her consumed by her own misery
at the death of her son; we can imagine her standing in silent Heorot,
grieving, and then bolting into confused action as she is discovered. As the
Seawolf, she defends from an invader both her territory, beautiful in its
own way, and the corpse of her only child. Her motives during the mere
fight are maternal in that they center on protection of her home and her
son's body, even in death.

Grendel's mother, almost inadvertently, uses the tools of violent masculine heroism when she kills Æscher. In doing so, she unleashes the forces
of that violence on herself. Her maternal drama lacks the resolution that
her death so neatly provides for Beowulf's oedipal drama, however. For if
the terrible mother is dead, the son can continue to reap the rewards of
the fathers. The drama of Grendel's mother tells us that if the son is dead,
there is no recourse. Violence simply leads to more violence and the
mother herself is killed. Killing Æscher does not return Grendel to his
mother; it leads only to her own death. To appropriate a phrase from Overing's analysis of Modþryðo, Grendel's mother too has "confronted the system on its own death centered terms."[70] A profitable contrast might be
drawn with Æðelflæd, who reacted to murder by taking hostages rather

than inflicting more murder on the culture.[71] Unlike Æðelflæd's nonlethal show of force, the Seawolf's violent revenge (John Hill suggests that she has eaten Æscher's body and left the head) is ultimately ineffectual, indicating that successful maternal performance will need other tools in the world of *Beowulf.*

Hildeburh

But the other prominent mother of a dead son in *Beowulf* finds herself in much the same trap, that once the child is dead there is no adequate maternal performance. Hildeburh's narrative shows us that, for mothers, mourning and vengeance are not the opposites Beowulf thinks they are. Rather than an opposite of the Seawolf, Hildeburh shows another facet of the defeated maternal. Both mothers grieve for their inescapable failure to protect their sons in a violent world.

Hildeburh's critical stature, like the Seawolf's, has been on the rise in the past few years. Martin Camargo has amply demonstrated the critical history of lines 1063 to 1159 to be one of inherent misogyny that has only recently paid attention to Hildeburh, the central figure in the drama. Often called "The Tragedy of Finn and Hengest," now usually referred to as "The Finn Episode," these lines tell the story, through the framed narrative of a bard's song in Hroðgar's hall, of the feud between the Danes and the Frisians.

While the murky place of the Jutes in the course of the fighting is still a crux,[72] the outlines of the narrative are generally clear. The Danish princess Hildeburh has married Finn, king of Frisia, as part of a political alliance. When her brother Hnæf comes to Frisia for a visit, a fight ensues in which Hildeburh's brother and son both die. Their joint funeral precedes a gloomy winter and a tenuous truce, at the end of which Hengest, now leading the Danes, begins a fight against the Frisians. In this second battle, Finn, Hildeburh's husband, is killed, and the Danes take her back to Denmark with them. Critical focus on this section has centered mostly on "Hengest's dilemma as to whether to take revenge for Hnæf and thereby break faith with Finn."[73]

In *Beowulf* criticism, Hildeburh is generally regarded as minor and pitiful. Camargo's argument for Hildeburh's critical primacy over Hengest hinges on the inherent injustice of her life; for him, her tragedy "cast(s) doubt on the revenge ethic at the very point in the narrative where such a code appears most glorious."[74] Hildeburh is the representative suffering woman in Old English poetry. Joyce Hill describes her as "a stereotype of the sorrowing woman, the victim of a situation not of her own making" so that she "gains in imaginative stature from her still dignity in mourning" even as "the only initiatory act attributed to her is the command to place her brother and her son shoulder to shoulder on the funeral pyre," which Hill terms "a powerful but ultimately futile gesture."[75] Hill notes that the poet seems to somehow approve of this female suffering, as the phrase *þæt wæs geomuru ides* (l.1075) parallels the description of Scyld Scefing, *þæt wæs god cyning* (l.11). As such, Hildeburh's function as indicator of "the tragic implications of heroic life"[76] is firmly endorsed by Hill and, she seems to think, by the poet.

Chance and Damico present similar readings of Hildeburh as an acceptably pitiful figure. Chance argues that Hildeburh shows how the mother should "passively accept and not actively avenge the loss of her son" in the world of the poem.[77] For Chance, Hildeburh is heroic in her endurance of her loss. Damico calls Hildeburh a "mother-victim."[78] Both of these analyses are part of comparisons with Grendel's mother; both critics see the mothers as opposite: one does and one does not try to avenge the death of the son.

Only two critics see Hildeburh to be successful in some way, and their readings are very different. John Hill reads Hildeburh's narrative within the context of the many different social transactions that take place within *Beowulf* to find Hildeburh somewhat vindicated at the end of the episode: "Hildeburh's grief and her bitterness about dark crime must cry for settlement, for revenge. . . . the poet does not say so but she may now feel some relief. . . . the urging of revenge is by no means an unnatural act for an aggrieved woman. . . . Very likely she still grieves but at least she is partly compensated."[79] Hill reads Hildeburh's loyalty to her tribe and its interests to take precedence over her personal loyalties to her husband, brother, or son; indeed, his reading even necessitates a bad relationship between Hildeburh and Finn, an assumption of emnity and dissatisfaction before Hnæf even arrived. Hill points out that Hildeburh is defined as her father's daughter (*Hoces dohtor,* l.1076) rather than as the queen or lady of the Frisians; she also places *her* (rather than their) son, *hire selfre sunu* (l.1115), on the funeral pyre. Hill sees these genitive uses to indicate Hildeburh's loyalty to her blood rather than to her marriage.[80] For Hill, Hildeburh's return to her homeland is a success of sorts, the best possible outcome of a bad situation.

Gillian Overing also reads Hildeburh to succeed in the course of the narrative, but not because she gets to go home with her dowry at the end of it. Overing argues even more strongly than previous critics that Hildeburh indicates the flaws in the heroic system. While Camargo or Joyce Hill may see Hildeburh to "question" the heroic code, Overing uses gender theory to show how the silenced feminine, specifically in the silent figure of Hildeburh, "serves to indict the system which ostensibly champions her as its cause, and to expose its paradoxical demands."[81] That silence becomes "actively experienced"[82] so that the reader, like the masculine actors in the poem, cannot experience closure and satisfaction of desire.

All of these critics see in Hildeburh a number of parallels to the other female figures in the poem (as I mentioned at the beginning of this chapter); most discuss her reaction to her son's death as "opposite" to that of the Seawolf. But the situations of the two mothers are too similar to be construed as opposite; Hildeburh is simply another version of the bereaved mother. Like the Seawolf, she is angry and confused; unlike the Seawolf, she gets no chance to defend her home against those who have wronged her.

The shock of Hildeburh's loss makes her plight immediate. In a short nine and a half lines, the poet forces us to see her loss and reiterates the violence of the system that caused it:

> Ne huru Hildeburh   herian þorfte
> Eotena treowe;   unsynnum wearð
> beloren leofum   æt þam lindplegan,
> bearnum ond broðrum;   hie on gebyrd hruron
> gare wunde;   þæt wæs geomuru ides!
> Nalles holinga   Hoces dohtor
> meotodsceaft bemearn,   syþðan morgen com,
> ða heo under swegle   geseon meahte
> morþorbealo maga,   þær heo ær mæste heold
> worolde wynne (1071–1080a)

[In need, Hildeburh did not think to praise the trust of the Jutes; she was :guiltless, she lost loved ones in that shield-play, son and brother; they rushed into (their) fate, wounded by swords. That was a sorrowing lady. Not without care did Hoc's daughter mourn the workings of God, when morning came, when she under clouds could see murdered kin, where she before had held the world's greatest joy.]

The poet not only tells of her loss, but refers to her happy life before the feud—the world's greatest joy was hers. The importance of her maternity is hinted at in line 1074; the word *gebyrd* is translated "fate" by Klaeber but literally means "birth." While the word may have had both meanings, intermingling in their connotations, *gebyrd* allows the poem's reader or listener to imagine Hildeburh's birthed son cut down in his fate. The narratives in *Beowulf* and its companion piece, *The Finnsburgh Fragment*,[83] do not reveal the age of Hildeburh and Finn's son. A number of possibilities present themselves—that this unnamed son was fully grown, that he was almost grown, that he was just a young child who was killed for his lineage or because he was in the wrong place at the wrong time. No matter his age, his mother must grieve because she could not protect him.

Her grief manifests itself in Hildeburh's "only initiatory act" (Joyce Hill's phrase), her order that her son and her brother be placed next to each other on the funeral pyre:

> Het ða Hildeburh   æt Hnæfes ade
> hire selfre sunu   sweoloðe befæstan,
> banfatu bærnan,   ond on bæl don
> earme on eaxle.   Ides gnornode,
> geomrode giddum (ll.1114–1118a).

[Hildeburh then ordered her own son set in flames at Hnæf's pyre to burn the bone-case, and (ordered them) to place in the fire the arm on the shoulder. The lady mourned, she lamented with songs.]

The logistics of this pyre have occasioned some critical comment; an unnecessary emendation at line 1117 has clouded Hildeburh's similarities to the Seawolf. Klaeber's and others' emendation of the manuscript reading of *earme* [arm] to *eame* [maternal uncle] appropriately emphasizes the relationship of the dead but ignores the very clear manuscript reading of *earme*.[84] Kevin Kiernan's suggested literal translation (which I have adopted) indicates that Hildeburh's son died in the same way that Grendel did. His arm was severed from his body; in her last, futile gesture of protection, Hildeburh orders the severed arm placed at her son's shoulder on the pyre.[85]

This restoration of the manuscript reading reveals that both Hildeburh and the Seawolf are bereaved mothers whose sons die by having their arms torn from their bodies. Both engage in final maternal performances, the Seawolf's to defend her home and her son's body, Hildeburh's to dignify her son's death and reassemble his corpse. Both mothers fade into the larger narrative of the poem as their final performances conclude; Hildeburh becomes a direct object in the grammar of the poem as she is taken back to Denmark, while the Seawolf is mentioned only briefly in Beowulf's recapitulation of events to Hygelac. Both, even, have names that indicate their failed maternal performances: just as the Seawolf needs to defend her aquatic home with the fierceness of a wolf, so Hildeburh becomes, in the brevity of her shocking narrative of loss, a "battle-town" or "war-fortification," for these literal translations of her name show how feud has imbedded itself in her maternal body, how inescapable violence is for her, despite her efforts to cling to "the world's greatest joy."

Hildeburh's maternal performance concludes with the funeral of her son, as the Seawolf's did with her death, both abruptly terminated by the heroic code. The only difference is that the Seawolf briefly attempted to use the code against itself, to enact revenge for the death of her child. The inadequacy of that revenge becomes more poignant when it is compared with the grief of the Seawolf's human counterpart, the war-town of Hildeburh. Both mothers have failed, their children are dead, and protection seems impossible. After examination of these two mothers, the critical assumption of the mother-as-victim seems chillingly accurate.

Hygd

Is there a possibility of positive maternal performance in *Beowulf?* Is the heroic code so suffocating of protection and nurturance that the maternal becomes futile and hopeless? Is textual separation from the child and the use of violence the best a mother can hope for, as in Modþryðo's case? An analysis of the final two mothers of *Beowulf,* the queens Hygd and Wealhþeow, shows that there is a possibility for a maternal performer that will end in love rather than grief, in the world's greatest joy rather than in songs of mourning.

Hygd's maternity in *Beowulf* is especially interesting because she has a daughter, although this unnamed daughter is called only Hygelac's in the text. Norman Eliason states that Hygelac's daughter is from an earlier marriage to another woman; he provides no evidence for this claim, however, beyond his desire for Hygd to have been married to Offa before she was married to Hygelac.[86] Like Modþryðo's relationship with Eomer, Hygd's with this unnamed daughter must be assumed rather than argued because of the poem's neglect of maternal genealogy; Hygd is the most likely candidate in the text to mother the Geatish princess. In a poem full of mothers of sons (even Beowulf's mother gets a backhanded compliment from Hroðgar at ll.942b–946), Hygd and Wealhþeow are the only mothers of daughters, although they have sons as well.

However, these queens do not interact with their daughters. Matrilineality from mother to daughter is simply not viable in *Beowulf* the way it is in seventh-century Kent, suggesting, perhaps, the necessity of a cultural institution (the double monastery) parallel to the court in which such mother-daughter couples can exist. There is no social world in *Beowulf* outside the hall and the heroic ethos, so there is no space for mothers and daughters to create a female community.[87] Wealhþeow and Freawaru never meet in the text—the audience discovers that Wealhþeow and Hroðgar have a daughter only after Beowulf returns to Geatland and tells Hygelac about Freawaru's proposed marriage to Ingeld the Hathobard.

Similarly, Hygd and her unnamed daughter never interact; the girl is defined strictly as her father's to give away as a battle prize. After Eofor the

Geat kills Ongenþeow, king of the Swedes, he receives land, treasure, and finally the princess, who is defined as her father's: "ond ða Iofore forgeaf angan dohtor, / hamweorðunge, hyldo to wedde" [and then he gave to Eofor his only daughter, a home-ornament, as a pledge of (his) favor, ll.2997–2998]. It is worth noting, however, that as the bride of a Geatish warrior, Hygd's daughter will stay in Geatland, with her mother and her people, and not find herself married into a feud as Hildeburh did and Freawaru will.

But the sons of these mothers are the focus of the poet, and as such it is to these mother-son relationships that we must return. Hygd's son Heardred dies in battle like Hildeburh's; in Hygd's case, however, we see her both before and after her son's death, and can thus comment on her maternal performance of protection. Hygd tries to protect her son in a brilliant display of diplomatic and maternal negotiation that makes clear her power; rather than enact the heroic ethos, as Modþryðo does or the Seawolf attempts, Hygd uses persuasion and arguments of nurturance as she tries to keep Heardred alive.

Hygd is first introduced as a celebrated queen who appropriately decorates her husband's hall, passes the cup to his retainers, and rewards them with treasure for their service. The poet tells us:

> Bold wæs betlic,   bregorof cyning,
> heah in healle,   Hygd swiðe geong,
> wis welþungen,   þeah ðe wintra lyt
> under burhlocan   gebiden hæbbe,
> Hæreþes dohtor;   næs hio hnah swa þeah,
> ne to gneað gifa   Geata leodum,
> maþmgestreona (ll.1925–1931a).

[The hall was splendid, the king very valiant, high in the hall, Hygd very young, wise, accomplished, although she few winters in the hall-enclosure had resided, Hareth's daughter. She was not lowly thus, however, nor too niggardly of gifts, of treasures, to the people of the Geats.]

Soon after, she is shown passing the mead cup:

> Meoduscencum hwearf
> geond þæt healreced   Hæreðes dohtor,
> lufode ða leode,   liðwæge bær
> hæleðum to handa (ll.1980b–1983a).

[Hareth's daughter bore mead-vessels around that hall-building, then she treated kindly the people, bore strong drink in hand to the warriors.]

Critics agree unanimously with the poet in their approval of Hygd; she lives up to the meaning of her name—"wise" or "thoughtful"—as this Geatish queen engages in the making of harmony in her husband's hall.[88]

Hygd is often contrasted with the masculine, sword-wielding Modþryðo, whose story abruptly interrupts the poet's initial praise of Hygd at line 1931b. Bruce Moore is typical in his opposition of the two figures when he states that their contrast "reveals the human capacity for good (Hygd) and for evil (Thryth)."[89] Norman Eliason goes so far as to argue that Thryth does not exist and Hygd was first a "wicked girl" who was tamed by her first husband, Offa, with whom she had Eomer, before marrying Hygelac and assuming her place as a wise, treasure-dispensing queen.[90]

Her wisdom has been cited in discussion of her offer of the throne to Beowulf after her husband's death, although some critics tend to ignore this brief episode, probably because it is difficult to fit into the male-dominated world of the poem.[91] In a traditional critical view—the kind that explains away unruly women like Modþryðo into patterns—kings decide on succession and queens pass cups. Hygd, like Modþryðo, defies this sort of analysis at the end of the poem when she tries to convince Beowulf to rule Geatland:

> þær him Hygd gebead   hord ond rice,
> beagas ond bregostol;   bearne ne truwode,
> þæt he wið ælfylcum   eþelstolas
> healdan cuðe,   ða wæs Hygelac dead (ll.2369–2372).

[There Hygd offered to him the treasure and the kingdom, the rings and the throne, she did not believe of her child that he against foreign people could hold the native seat when Hygelac was dead.]

Only Kemp Malone has discussed the implications of this offer, wherein Hygd has the power to *gebeodan* Beowulf to take the throne. He says, "Here the poet represents Hygd as having in her hands the bestowal of the Geatish throne. Such a state of things presupposes a woman of unchallenged authority, and such authority could hardly be hers simply as the widow of the king. Personal competence and a devoted following would seem to be necessary implications here."[92] Malone seems to envision a coterie of followers that supports Hygd in her political maneuvers beyond cup passing and treasure giving. Such power is perhaps reminiscent of Seaxburh, the abbess of Ely and Minster-in-Sheppey who served as regent for her son, or of Æðelflæd, who ruled Mercia by herself for seven years. Indeed, Hygd's power within the hall and the culture of the government is evident in the poem's other mention of her, Beowulf's gift to her of the fabulous necklace and three of the horses he received in Denmark:

> Hyrde ic þæt he ðone healsbeah   Hygde gesealde,
> wrætlicne wundurmaððum,   ðone þe him Wealhðeo geaf,
> ðeodnes dohtor,   þrio wicg somod
> swancor ond sadolbeorht;   hyre syððan wæs
> æfter beahðege   breost geweorðod (ll.2172–2176)

[I heard that he gave the neck-ring to Hygd, the wrought wonder-treasure, which to him Wealhþeow had given, the prince's daughter, together with three horses supple and saddle-bright. After ring-receiving was her breast adorned.]

In a world where treasure indicates power, Hygd controls a large portion of Beowulf's Danish reward.

Hygd's offer of the kingship to Beowulf also indicates a masculine sort of power, and here echoes of her abruptly introduced shadow, Modþryðo, resound most loudly. Modþryðo's masculine performance enacted the masculine heroic ethos, using swords and thrones to exercise power in the halls she shared with her father and with her husband. Although she does not wield a sword, Hygd's power in the hall initially seems similar—someone's swords, as Malone intimates, are ready to back up Hygd's desires. She has treasure and can offer the throne.

But the similarities stop there, for Hygd's performance is maternal, not masculine, and Beowulf foils its success. The offer itself may even be read as a remnant of some element of matriclan society, when the queen as consort or dowager had the power to award the throne. Despite her valiant attempt to protect and nurture her son, Hygd reveals another, different kind of failed maternal performance—her son dies just as the Seawolf's and Hildeburh's do.

Analysis of Hygd's offer to Beowulf as a maternal performance requires readers to discard a long-held but never-examined premise: that queens want their sons to be kings. Just as analysis of Æðelflæd and Ælfwynn as a mother-daughter couple necessitates the rejection of matrilineal dynastic goals in the patriarchal arena, understanding of maternal performance in *Beowulf* shows that queens may not want their sons to succeed to the throne of the father. While Stafford and Parsons have ably discussed the queen mother as power broker for herself and her son in early and late medieval courts,[93] the queens of *Beowulf* seem to shy away from such roles, preferring to broker power for the explicit purpose of keeping their sons safe. I argue here that a mother, a figure primarily interested in protection of her son, would want him as far away from a throne as possible in *Beowulf.* Such mothers know that feuds within and without the poem tend to center on the royal house, personified in the king. Hygd's offer to Beowulf considers the Geatish people, who would doubtless have fared better if Heardred had never ruled, but focuses on her son.

Close reading of the passage reveals that Hygd thinks primarily of her child and keeping him alive. The passage (quoted earlier) begins with a description of Beowulf's return from the battlefield where Hygelac died; Beowulf is *earm anhaga,* wretched and alone. Upon his return, Hygd offers him the kingship, with *hord and rice, / beagas ond bregostol,* treasure and kingdom, rings and throne. The kingship must seem especially tantalizing to Beowulf in contrast to his wretched loneliness after the death of his king.

Also important is the word *gebead,* which seems to connote "showing" rather than "ordering"; in its other two uses in the poem (as forms of *gebeodan*), it refers to Beowulf *showing* Grendel the strengths of the Geats (l.603) and Wiglaf's helpers *announcing* the building of Beowulf's pyre (l.3110). While Klaeber also offers "bid" or "command" as translations, they are secondary to "offer," "show," and "announce"; Hygd is *offering* Beowulf the throne, hoping he will take it. The connotations of *gebeodan* show that while she has the power to offer Beowulf the throne, she does not have the power to force him take it.

Ultimately, it is the use of the word *bearn* in line 2370 to describe Heardred that confirms Hygd's maternal performance here. With his father dead, Heardred could be referred to as king, lord, prince, leader, or warrior; such terms occur repeatedly throughout the poem to describe men who, for better or worse, are in a position to lead their people. Instead, he is described as a child.

The word *bearn,* of course, does not necessarily mean that the person so designated is a child. Beowulf, robustly adult as he is, is called *bearn ecgþeowes* 14 times in the poem.[94] Indeed, most of the usages in the poem refer to adults, and the word's function in these uses is identification of that adult—invariably male[95]—with a specific tribal or familial lineage, usually a grammatical genitive. Phrases like *æðelinges bearn* [nobleman's son] or *geata bearn* [son of the Geats] are intended to show affiliation or status, not to designate the man in question as a child.[96]

There are only three uses of the word *bearn* in *Beowulf* that are not part of a genitive phrase. They refer to Heardred, Hygd's son; Hildeburh's unnamed son; and to Ohthere and Onela, sons of Ongenþeow. Each of these sons is in need of defense against forces without the tribe; each is in need of protection. Hildeburh, as I discussed earlier, has already failed to protect her son—he is described starkly with no genitive qualifier as she orders *bearnum ond broðrum* (l.1074a) placed on the pyre. When Ohthere and

Onela are similarly with their mother at line 2956, their father Ongenþeow is strategically planning to protect them from his feuding with the
Geats:

> Gewat him ða se goda   mid his gædelingum,
> frod felageomor   fæsten secean,
> eorl Ongenþio   ufor oncirde;
> hæfde Higelaces   hilde gefrunen,
> wlonces wigcræft;   wiðres ne truwode,
> þæt he sæmannum   onsacan mihte,
> heaðoliðendum   hord forstandan,
> bearn ond bryde;   beah eft þonan
> eald under eorðweall (2949–2957a).

[The good earl Ongenþeow departed then with his companions, wise, very
much saddened, to seek a stronghold, to turn up higher. He had heard of
Hygelac's warring, of his bold war-craft. He did not trust (his own) resis-
tance so that he with his sea-men might fight against the ocean-warriors,
might defend the hoard, the children and the bride. Old, he turned back
from there, to his earth-wall.]

It seems that in the text of *Beowulf,* any *bearn* without a genitive to define
or anchor him is in trouble. Even Grendel is connected—he is *hyre bearn*
and *hire bearn*—when described after his battle with Beowulf. Onela and
Ohthere of course lose their father despite his withdrawal to his earth-
works; Hildeburh's son is already dead by the time we see him.

Heardred too is a *bearn* without a genitive to claim him. With his father
dead, he is in peril, as his mother Hygd knows too well. Indeed, the phras-
ing that describes her position is identical to that describing Ongenþeow's:
she "ne truwode" (does not trust) that he can lead the Geats. As such, she
wants her child—defined by the very diction of the poem to be cut off
from the necessary protection of family and tribe—as far from the *epelsto-
las,* the throne, as possible. She does not demonstrate, as Malone argues,
"calculating, cold-blooded decision" in her offer to Beowulf.[97] She
demonstrates a maternal performance that does not incorporate violence,
like the Seawolf's, or mourning, like Hildeburh's, but uses persuasion and
negotiation to keep her child safe. The audience of the poem might ad-
mire Beowulf's modesty and loyalty as he refuses "þæt he Heardrede
hlaford wære" (that he would be lord to Heardred, l.2375), but Hygd's maternal strategy has failed.

Heardred dies in the course of the Swedish feud, and Hygd disappears
from the poem as swiftly as Modþryðo, Hildeburh, and the Seawolf do.[98]
The proto-masculine absolutist who will kill the monster or die, Beowulf

foils the maternal as he rejects Hygd's diplomacy and offer of power. By upholding patrilineage, he resists successful maternal performance. In Geatland, son succeeded father, but at the expense of the life of the son.

Wealhþeow

The assumption that mothers want their sons to be kings must also be discarded in discussion of the final, and most important, mother of *Beowulf*. Wealhþeow is the only mother—indeed the only woman—who speaks in the poem. For my purposes, she is also the only successful mother in the poem. To read her this way necessitates an investigation of the murky relationships among the members of the Danish royal house; analysis of her speeches and actions regarding the relationship of Beowulf to that house; and a realization that she, like Hygd, wants to keep her sons off the throne in order to keep them safe.

As the most prominent woman in the poem, Wealhþeow has frequently been the object of critical discussion, most of it unanimous that she is celebrated, decorative, and generous. Her main functions seem to be serving drink and ensuring harmony ("peaceweaving") in Heorot.[99] Many feminist critics use her as a focal point in their analyses of the resonances among the women of *Beowulf;* she is a queen like Hygd and Modþryðo, a mother like Hildeburh and the Seawolf. The proximity of their narratives forces an acknowledgement of their parallels; Wealhþeow's prominence makes her the central woman in these "triptychs" (Damico's word) or "foils" (Chance's) and similarly makes her the prominent mother of the poem.

Indeed, her maternity is the focus of much of the critical speculation about Wealhþeow, and her role in the hall and in the protection of her sons has led to a critical dialogue that seems to argue for or against her relative strength in the hall. Wealhþeow has an army of sympathetic detractors who see her as "a conscious but helpless victim," to use Edward Irving's phrase;[100] other critics argue for her strength and power in the social transactions in the hall—Carmen Cramer has noted Wealhþeow's forceful and continuous use of the present tense and the imperative voice[101] while Leslie Stratyner sees her final words as a thinly veiled threat to Beowulf.[102] Helen Damico, whose study of Wealhþeow is a book-length analysis of the Danish queen's strength in the hall, argues that Wealhþeow is a valkyrie figure with all the power and glamour which that semi-divine role entails.[103] Critics have thus manipulated Wealhþeow in much the same manner that Modþryðo was "explained"; using the opposition of weak-strong or doomed-powerful to examine this intriguing and maternal queen, critics have reinscribed yet another polarized methodology of the sort against which Overing has warned the poem's readers.

Overing's analysis of Wealhþeow, like her reading of Modþryðo, both exposes and manipulates this critical penchant for opposition. She states: "There has been a perhaps equally overwhelming binarism coming from without the poem. The push for definition and resolution, often resulting in a reductive either/or classification, has in the past been reflected with most alarming clarity and rigidity in critical assessments of women, not only in *Beowulf*, but in Old English poetry in general."[104] Overing indeed rejects both the views of Wealhþeow as passive victim (and its binary complementarity to aggressive hero) and as valkyrie figure (for the "valkyrie essentially *participates* in the death-centered, male definition of power").[105] Overing reads Wealhþeow as a hysteric who points up the inability of language to describe the world of the speaker; she asks, "At what point does she believe the world will match her words, or even that language itself will control the violence which continually threatens her world?"[106] Overing's analysis forces readers to acknowledge that we cannot know if Wealhþeow engages in "pleading or commanding" when she tells Beowulf that he should be good to her sons because the warriors in Heorot do what she tells them.[107]

The speeches in question are not spoken at Wealhþeow's first appearance in the poem. The poet's initial introduction of Wealhþeow leaves her strangely silent as she passes the cup in the hall. We "hear" her words only in indirect statement: "bæd hine bliðne æt þære beorþege" [she bade him be glad at that beer-fest, l.617]; at the same feast, we listen as Beowulf in direct statement makes his hyper-masculine boast that he will kill Grendel or die (ll.632–638). It seems as though she has no need to speak in her first appearance; events are progressing in her favor—a hero has come to rid the Danes of a monster.

Her speeches—and, I argue, her maternal performance—follow Beowulf's fight with Grendel and are spoken at his victory feast. She enters just three and a half lines after the *scop*'s tale ends with Hildeburh's return to Denmark, juxtapositioning the two Danish queens. Her two speeches superficially present very different content, but work together to achieve her purpose of keeping her sons off the throne and relatively safe.

Her first speech is addressed to her husband and can be divided into two parts. First (ll.1169–1180a), the *ides scyldinga* urges her husband to leave his kingdom to his kin, rather than to Beowulf, whom, she has heard, Hroðgar wishes to adopt:

> Onfoh þissum fulle,   freodrihten min,
> sinces brytta!   þu on sælum wes,
> goldwine gumena,   ond to Geatum spræc
> mildum wordum,   swa sceal man don!

Beo wið Geatas glæd,   geofena gemyndig,
nean ond feorran   þu nu hafast.
Me man sægde,   þæt þu ðe for sunu wolde
hererinc habban.   Heorot is gefælsod,
beahsele beorhta;   bruc þenden þu mote
manigra medo,   ond þinum magum læf
folc ond rice,   þonne ðu forð scyle,
metodsceaft seon (ll.1169–1180a)

[Accept this cup, my noble lord, treasure-king. May you be in health, gold-
friend of warriors, and speak to the Geats with mild words, as a man must
do. Be glad with the Geats, remembering the gifts you now have from near
and far. To me men say that you this warrior wish to have for a son. Heorot
is cleansed, the bright beer-hall; rejoice while you may in these many gifts
and leave to your kin the folk and the kingdom, when you must look forth
on death.]

In this section of her first speech, Wealhþeow does not seem to do anything extraordinary. She passes the cup to her lord and reminds him of his
duty to his kin; she does not want Beowulf to inherit the Danish throne.[108]
    In the second half of this speech, she refers to her nephew Hroðulf and
his part in the Danish political drama, and it is these words that have occasioned so much critical comment on Wealhþeow as a mother trying to
save her sons (and their succession) from their supposedly evil, usurping,
older cousin. She says:

                    Ic minne can
glædne Hroþulf,   þæt he þa geogoðe wile
arum healdan,   gyf þu ær þonne he,
wine Scildinga,   worold oflætest;
wene ic þæt he mid gode   gyldan wille
uncran eaferan,   gif he þæt eal gemon,
hwæt wit to willan   ond to worðmyndum
umborwesendum ær   arna gefremedon (ll.1180b–1187)

[I know my good Hroðulf, that then he will hold the youths in honor, if you,
friend of the Scyldings, before him then leave the world; I expect that he will
repay with goodness our sons, if he remembers all that help which we two
for his desire and for his honor provided before when he was a child.]

The conventional reading here entails a reference to the destruction of
Heorot (alluded to at ll.83–84) and an assumption that Hroðulf murdered
his cousins Hreðric and Hroðmund to gain the throne.

Within such a critical rubric, Wealhþeow becomes a desperate, pleading mother, trying to enlist Beowulf and the entire Danish comitatus to support the claims of her sons to the throne even as the audience knows her attempts will fail. Margaret Goldsmith comments that Wealhþeow knows "the dangerous position of a child heir to the throne,"[109] while Joyce Hill refers to Wealhþeow's "support of her own sons against the possibly older Hroðulf."[110] Hildeburh's textual proximity underscores the danger to Wealhþeow's sons; Chance says, "As if reminded of her own role as mother by hearing of Hildeburh's plight, Wealhþeow demonstrates maternal concern in an address to Hroðgar immediately after the scop sings this lay."[111]

Most recently, this reading of the speech has been championed by Rolf Bremmer, who states that "evidence from outside the poem reveals that after Hroðgar's death Hroðulf indeed seized the throne" and "Queen Wealhþeow fears for the future and tries to secure Beowulf's support for her son Hreðric."[112] Bremmer has investigated uncle-nephew relationships throughout Old English poetry, and has discovered that the father's brother–brother's son relationship is often fraught with tension while the mother's brother–sister's son relationship provides mutual satisfaction and harmony.[113] As such, Bremmer has critical capital invested in a Hroðgar-Hroðulf feud and is inclined to accept extratextual evidence that accords with his theory of familial relationship. Such critical acceptance of this "evidence" has led to statements like Richard Schrader's observation that the guest list at the feast provides "a listing of potential enemies."[114]

That evidence is by no means secure, however; Chickering calls it "tricky, to say the least."[115] Extratextual evidence relies on Saxo Grammaticus's thirteenth-century story of how Roluo (Hroðulf?) killed Røricus (Hreðric?); Chambers admits that "Saxo is here translating an older authority, the *Bjarkamál* (now lost) and he did not know who Røricus was."[116] Further extratextual evidence (cited by Chambers and others) relies on a modern correction to a twelfth- century Danish royal genealogy, the text of which actually states that Hrærek (Hreðric) *followed* Rolf (Hroðulf) on the throne; modern historians, using the intratextual "evidence" of *Beowulf,* switch these names and then argue that Rolf killed Hrærek to gain the throne.[117]

But that intratextual evidence is by no means assured; critical assumption of Hroðulf's treachery depends on two ambiguous adverbs. The poet tells us that:

> fægere geþægon
> medoful manig   magas þara
> swiðhicgende   on sele þam hean,
> Hroðgar ond Hroðulf.   Heorot innan wæs

> freondum afylled;   nalles facenstafas
> Þeod-scyldingas   þendon fremedon (ll.1014b–1019).

[Courteously they partook of many mead-cups there, the strong-minded kin in the high hall, Hroðgar and Hroðulf. Within, Heorot was filled with friends; no treacheries did the Scylding-princes then perform.]

The word *þendon* becomes a crux. Does it imply (as it is conventionally read) that Hroðulf did not *then* perform treachery but would in the future? Or does it simply refer to the past? Kenneth Sisam translates *þendon* to mean "in the age of heroes" or "in the great days of Heorot," implying a sense of past-ness but not a reversal of fortune—he states that the word *þendon* has "the simple connotation that those glorious times were past."[118] A similar adverbial crux occurs at Wealhþeow's second entrance, immediately before her speeches. The poet tells us:

> Þa cwom Wealhþeo forð
> gan under gyldnum beage   þær þa godan twegen
> sæton suhtergefæderan;   þa gyt wæs hiera sib ætgædere,
> æghwylc oðrum trywe (ll.1162b–1165a).

[Then Wealhþeow came forth, shining under golden rings, where the two good ones sat, uncle-nephew; then yet was their peace together, each to the other true.]

Just as in the case of *þendon* at line1019, *þa gyt* can be read to imply future treachery—there was *yet* peace between the uncle and nephew, but that peace would soon end. Sisam again argues that the adverb is temporal, implying past greatness; he points out that "There was a natural limit to their alliance, which must end when one or the other died."[119]

Acceptance of Sisam's temporal implications of these adverbs means that Hroðulf did not murder Hreðric or Hroðmund even though he succeeded Hroðgar. Such a reading accords with John Niles's argument that "Hroðulf's supposed treachery against members of the Danish court is another motif whose importance has been exaggerated . . . if it is not an outright invention of modern readers."[120] Gerald Morgan has pointed out that "strict primogeniture" was not the general rule in medieval Scandinavia or in Anglo-Saxon England; only critical assumption of such primogeniture has impeded our view of Hroðgar as a king like Alfred the Great, who inherited the throne of Wessex after his brothers had ruled in their turn rather than receiving it directly from his father. Morgan argues for "hereditary succession" in the royal Danish line, whereby a male with royal blood, although not necessarily the king's son, would inherit, so that Hroðulf's assumption of the throne after Hroðgar's death is not at all controversial, especially in light of the relative youth of Hroðgar's and Wealhþeow's sons.[121]

As a member of the family, then, Hroðulf seems to be approved by the queen and probably by the court as Hroðgar's heir apparent.[122] Rather than protecting the rights of her sons against Hroðulf in her first speech, then, we need to see Wealhþeow to protect Hroðulf's rights against Beowulf in the first part of the speech. She tells Hroðgar to *þinum magum læf folc ond rice,* leave to your kin the folk and the kingdom. The word "kin" is certainly wide enough to include Hroðulf; had she meant their sons specifically, she could have designated them as she does later in her first speech: *uncran eafaran,* the sons of us two, using the dual pronoun to emphasize the bond that she and Hroðgar share.

Morgan's description of the second part of the speech is accurate, then—Wealhþeow is speaking "to protect the rights of her sons as members of the Scylding royal *family,* not as sole heirs to Hroðgar's throne."[120] She envisions Hreðric and Hroðmund to be primary members of Hroðulf's warband when he is king and they are fully grown. This vision is primarily a maternal one, as I stated earlier. She wants Hroðulf to be king because her children will be safest in that social structure. They will have honor as sons of the former king but not act as lightning rods for feud— and the audience of the poem, like Wealhþeow and the Danish comitatus, knows that the feud with the Hathobards is far from settled.

Wealhþeow's view of Beowulf, then, is as a threat to her maternal vision because he could threaten Hroðulf's kingship and her sons' subsequent lesser political and military importance. With Hroðulf dead, her sons would be the (probably doomed) leaders of a vengeful retaliation against the Geats. These speeches show that the queen is not concerned that her sons' claim to the throne is jeopardized by their dangerously older cousin—because she does not want them even to have a claim to that throne.

Michael Drout and John Hill have already noted this intra-familial loyalty of Wealhþeow towards Hroðulf. Hill reads Wealhþeow's gift of the necklace to Beowulf to have sexual overtones. He says the gift "may be a subliminal offer of herself if Beowulf will simply fade away, refuse the conqueror's role, and reject Hroðgar's effort to adopt him."[124] Drout argues that Wealhþeow engages in *realpolitik* and decides to support Hroðulf's claim to throne although she "would support Hreðric and Hroðmund for the throne if there were any chance of them succeeding to it and surviving."[125] Drout sees inheritance systems in *Beowulf* guided by the dual principles of "blood and deeds," and argues that Wealhþeow and other women in the poem have a vested interest in inheritance by blood, since "it is the only system in which a female character may exercise her will to power."[126] Hill and Drout agree that for Wealhþeow, Hroðulf is a better successor to Hroðgar than Beowulf.

Wealhþeow's actions after her first speech and before her second speech underscore this antipathy she feels for Beowulf. While my analysis of this speech and these actions does not negate Drout's and Hill's readings, it adds a maternally motivated dimension. Wealhþeow is willing to use all the ritual and verbal tools of power accessible to her to protect what she views as the safest course for her children—the ascension of Hroðulf. As such, she curses, prays to, and threatens Beowulf to ensure that he leaves Denmark with no designs on the throne.

Wealhþeow begins her second speech with the presentation of the "healsbeaga mæst" (the most high necklace), at line 1216, when she says, "bruc ðisses beages" (rejoice in this ring). It is a perfectly acceptable and conventional phrase of gift-giving, but it does not sound like it to the poem's audience, for the poet has just given the past and future history of the necklace. The poem's diction blends the Danish necklace with the famous Brosing necklace, and relates the doom associated with both. After stating that Hama died after receiving the Brosing necklace, the poet relates the events future to the banquet in Heorot, when the Geatish king Hygelac wore the neck-ring to his death on a Frisian battlefield (ll.1197–1214; see note for text and translation).[127]

The Brosing necklace and its Danish counterpart bring death and sorrow, right down to the odd echo of line 1214b—"heal swege onfeng"—with other funerals in Beowulf: at the funeral of Hildeburh's son and brother "lig ealle forswealg" (l.1122b) and at Beowulf's own funeral "heofon rece swealg" (l.3155b). Wealhþeow gives Beowulf a ring that might be "an offer of herself," especially considering the sexual connotations of the Old Norse Brising necklace, which was made for the fertility goddess Freyja; it seems more likely, in the context of the poem, to be a necklace of doom. Her injunction to "rejoice in the ring" seems more like a curse than a sexual invitation; in giving him one of her richest treasures, she also gives him the death and feud that accompany it.

As if to insure that her purpose is accomplished, however, she adds both a prayer and a threat to this curse in her second speech. Her prayer is that he will act as protector to her sons: she asks him "þyssum cnyhtum wes / lara liðe" (to these boys be kind in counsel, ll.1219b–1220a) and says, "Beo þu suna minum / dædum gedefe" (be you seemly in deeds to my sons, ll.1226b–1227a). Interspersed with these prayers are reminders of her gifts to him; in addition to the (cursed) necklace, she has given him a corslet (l.1217b) and other treasures.

She concludes her speech with a threat that the Danes will do as she asks them: "þegnas syndon geþwære, þeod ealgearo, / druncne dryhtguman doð swa ic bidde" [the thanes are united, the nation prepared; having drunk, the warriors do as I bid, ll.1230–1231]. This threat is perhaps hollow, as Beowulf has shown that he exceeds all the Danes in military prowess, but adds to the many layers of purpose in Wealhþeow's second speech, addressed to Beowulf rather than to her husband, although both speeches are of course delivered publicly and heard by all the assembled company.

Overing argues that Wealhþeow's speeches force us to examine the relationship between her words and her world; I agree with her, but see Wealhþeow as a maternal performer rather than a hysteric. She works actively to protect her children and uses a three-fold approach of curse, prayer, and threat to ensure her children's safety—not their claim to the throne. Unlike the way he behaves towards Hygd, Beowulf supports Wealhþeow's maternal performance in the poem, constantly affirming his loyalty to Hygelac (and thus his lack of interest in Hroðgar's throne) and amicably inviting Hreðric to visit Geatland. Beowulf thus does not threaten Hroðulf's succession or Wealhþeow's maternal desires. Wealhþeow's seemingly opaque performance in her two speeches becomes understandable in light of her maternal goals. When critics realize that her main purpose is to protect her sons, not their supposed claims to their father's throne, her manipulations of social relationships in the hall make sense. She affirms the primacy of Hroðulf because she wants him to succeed, not because she sees him as a threat of future treachery. Beowulf is her only obstacle, and with a curse, a prayer, and a threat, she effectively assures he will leave what Drout calls "inheritance by blood" an intact institution in Denmark.

As such, we can see Wealhþeow as the only successful mother in the poem. She has manipulated social interaction in the hall with words and generosity. She has not enacted a masculine performance, like Modþryðo; she has not engaged in a revenge feud as does the Seawolf, however inadvertently; she need not mourn her child's death, like Hildeburh; she does not fail to keep her young children off the throne, like Hygd. Wealhþeow protects her sons from the violence of the heroic, patriarchal world. She engages in maternal action and still sees her children grow up.

Wealhþeow's performance also reveals the connections among the three aspects of maternal performance, according to Ruddick's ahistorical rubric; she is the only mother in the poem to protect successfully, and she actively nurtures and teaches as well. In her performance in the hall, she illustrates that another system of value and action exists, one other to the dominant system guided by principles of honor and treasure that defines the masculine world of the poem. While I would not go so far as to argue that this set of maternal values overcomes, even momentarily, the masculinist violence that threatens her children, Wealhþeow's performance indicates that another set of principles is possible even as it is not primary. In her performances, she teaches that there is a different way of viewing the world.

Similarly, Wealhþeow manages to nurture. She reminds the company of her kindnesses to Hroðulf when he was a child. She uses the word *arna,* help, showing Hroðulf's past need, which she and Hroðgar fulfilled. The hapax legomenon *umborwesendum* is an ungainly gerund that literally translates child-being-ness. Bosworth and Toller translate *umbor* as "child," Clark-Hall suggests "infant"; the subsequent connotations of vulnerability are thus transferred to Hroðulf when he was a child. Hroðgar and Wealh-þeow have nurtured this previously vulnerable child and helped him when he needed it so that he is now ready to assume the kingship. There is no textual separation between Wealhþeow and her sons or Wealhþeow and her nephew; we hear in her own voice how she has met their needs, nurtured and taught them when they were young, protected them from the violence of their world. Wealhþeow's performance seems to show that a mother figure can nurture and teach if she can protect, that once the inevitable challenge of keeping a child alive has been overcome, the other facets of maternal performance will follow.

Beowulf's Mother/Maternal Conclusions

At the beginning of this chapter, I indicated that an examination of mothers in *Beowulf* within the rubric of maternal performance might shift critical understanding of the poem as a whole. I hope I have added to critical views of each of the individual mothers in the poem: that Modþryðo's performance is masculine and literal; that the Seawolf has a name as she incorrectly practices patriarchal revenge; that Hildeburh has no alternative but to mourn as she reassembles her son's corpse, marked by its lack of a genitive tribal marker; that Hygd attempts to protect her son, similarly lacking a genitive in his description as a *bearn;* and that Hygd and Wealh-þeow explicitly *do not* want their sons to be kings as they work against their ascensions to the throne.

Hroðgar's comment about Beowulf's mother, to which I alluded earlier, accurately sums up the place of maternity and maternal performance in the heroic world of the poem:

> Hwæt, þæt secgan mæg
> efne swa hwylc mægþa   swa ðone magan cende
> æfter gumcynnum,   gyf heo gyt lyfað,
> þæt hyre Ealdmetod   este wære
> bearngebyrdo (ll. 942b–946a).

[Lo, that one who brought forth this man among man-kin, even as each of women (does), might tell, if she yet lives, that the God of Old was kind to her in child-bearing.]

Literal translation of the ungainly half-line at line 943a reveals patriarchal expectations about reproduction; *as each woman does,* Beowulf's mother brought forth a specifically male child to dwell among specifically male kin. Hroðgar reveals the reliance of patriarchy on maternity in this vision of a masculine king who imagines that Beowulf's mother would be proud of his masculine heroism. Beowulf's mother, defined entirely by her biological function in producing Beowulf, is the ideal mother for Hroðgar and the masculinist heroic ethos he represents.

The fleeting appearance of Beowulf's mother can be contrasted to the more developed maternal performances in the poem to lead to an understanding of the place of the maternal in the social world of *Beowulf,* and of the way that protection, nurturance, and teaching are not simply undervalued but actively discouraged in the poem. Only one mother succeeds in the course of a poem that catalogues both the horrors and the glories of war. Wealhþeow's performance is a disruptive reminder of the price of heroic glory and the necessity of maternity to the heroic code—for mothers are needed to produce heroes but remain as uncomfortable reminders of nurturance and love in a world of killing and glory.

AFTERWORD

THE POLITICS OF MOTHERHOOD

The abbess-mothers of Kent, the queen-mothers of Wessex and Mercia, and the fictional mothers of *Beowulf* clarify the goals of maternal practice both in Anglo-Saxon England and in the late-twentieth-century United States. Desires of mothers for their children—for medical care, safety, education, self-determination—speak across the gulf of a thousand years and illuminate our own society, where schoolyard shootings, lack of health insurance, inequitable school systems, and drug-related violence challenge maternal performers. Judith Butler, Sara Ruddick, and Luce Irigaray provided the theoretical basis for much of the vocabulary in the introduction of this study; that vocabulary will illuminate the actions not just of Wealhþeow and Mildrið, I hope, but also of all maternal performers, men and women, biological mothers and not, who endeavor to protect, nurture, and teach children in any culture. Irigaray's search for mother-daughter couples is not simply an exercise appropriate to mythology, history, and literature but a reminder of the continuing patrilineal focus of our own culture, in which children are automatically given the last names of their fathers at birth.

The previous chapters have served to remove, at least partially, the occlusion of motherhood from the included Anglo-Saxon texts. These specific examinations of mothers in Old English poetry and Anglo-Saxon history have interrogated what mothers do and how they do it—how they make their value systems and nurturing structures work in a patriarchal culture that occludes motherhood even as it celebrates fathers, patrilineal genealogy, violence, and heroic death. The maternal performances of all these mothers, both literary and historical, might serve as guides for late-twentieth-century culture.

In *Beowulf*, Modþryðo gives notice that biological motherhood does not guarantee maternal performance as her masculine, sword-wielding performance precludes any maternal relationship with her child. Hildeburh enacts a maternal performance as she officiates at the funeral of her son whom she could not protect. Hygd's (failed) diplomatic negotiations to keep her son off the throne and the Seawolf's (failed) revenge and defense of her home both indicate the ways in which a mother can try to achieve agency in textual and cultural worlds governed mainly by masculine prerogative. Finally, Wealhþeow demonstrates a successful challenge to the heroic code as she negotiates to keep her sons safe with a value system based on relationships rather than conquests.

Similarly, Æðelflæd's tenth-century defense of her kingdom and training of her daughter can be read as a maternal performance. Æðelflæd's performance of compromise and avoidance of unnecessary violence demonstrates a mediation of patriarchal goals even as she performs within a patriarchal system. Analysis of Æðelflæd's maternal genealogy reveals that she had a maternal community composed of her grandmother, aunt, mother, and daughter as well as the more-recognized paternal community of her father, husband, and brother. Her daughter may have entered a maternal community with her cousin Eadburg at Nunnaminster, a religious house founded by Ealhswið, Æðelflæd's mother.

The abbess-mothers of seventh- and eighth-century Kent also provide evidence of a viable cultural system based on maternal performance of protection, nurturance, and teaching rather than acquisition of power and wealth. These women demonstrate a pattern in their lives in which a widow founds a double monastery on land she controls, through either her dowry or her widow's inheritance. This monastery, with a link to the similar houses of Frankish Gaul, then becomes a house for the female members of the royal family, with the abbacy passed from the founder to her biological sister, daughter, or niece, who was either a widow or a virgin. The incomplete textual histories of these monasteries hint at specifically female and maternal communities within the patriarchies of church and state. Folio 210 of Lambeth Palace MS 427 shows a maternal ritual of greeting and consecrating a daughter, indicating structures within the minster that were different from, but not exclusive of, more conventional Christian institutions.

One issue hovering over any analysis of mothers, motherhood, mothering, or maternal performance is the possibility of men as maternal actors. Does a celebration of maternal performance exclude men? Ruddick says that it does not—and indeed men are slowly coming to accept traditional maternal roles in the late-twentieth-century United States. One question I hope this study will raise is the possibility of male maternal performers in Anglo-Saxon England.

In addition, I hope this study raises some awareness about maternal work in our own culture, which, while different from Anglo-Saxon England, has its own occlusions of motherhood. Daycare and education are still considered "women's issues," and hence not as important as other top-

ics on the national agenda. To acknowledge and seek out maternal performers (male and female), to celebrate them and their work, would in-
vigorate our culture and revalue some beliefs that are now not much more
than platitudes. A reexamination of the maternal as a viable, empowering
subject position for women and men can then move from academic the-
orizing to actual political practice.

Such acknowledgement of maternal performance might also allow
(since men can be maternal performers as well) the possibilities and acceptance of other sorts of performances. The maternal provides an initial
point from which to depart the hierarchical and limiting opposition of
masculine/feminine. To read maternal performances within Anglo-Saxon
poetic and historical texts as well as in contemporary culture reveals not
only their own disruptive possibilities but the possibility of reading other
genders, as yet undescribed and untheorized. Our general rather than our
academic society limits itself to two genders, masculine and feminine, as-
signed respectively to the male and female sex. But such stringent patrol of
gender roles has resulted in the loss of infinite opportunity in our country,
most obviously in the loss of involved parenting by men, which is still considered more a topic for the comics page and slapstick movies than for real
life. To say that a man can be a maternal performer is a radical statement
in the late-twentieth-century United States.

Suggestions for such fluid possibilities of gender performance raise a variety of questions: If the maternal can be construed as a performance separate from the feminine, can the paternal be separate from the masculine
as well? How would "the paternal" be different from "the patriarchal"? Is
there a performance of androgyny or asexuality? Are different types of ho-
mosexual performance actually different gender performances? For that
matter, is there not a range of viable performances within that seemingly
monolithic construct, heterosexual masculinity?

Analysis of maternal performance engenders a vision of a society where
the maternal is enacted by both women and men, where it is respected but
not worshipped (and thus neutralized). In that society, the term "working
mother" has become obsolete because all its members recognize that all
mothers work, usually 12- to 14-hour unpaid days. In that society, the politics of maternity, complicated as they are by race and class, are not just
"women's issues" but issues acknowledged to affect all facets of society. The
maternal, embraced and accepted along with other gender performances
that reach beyond traditional paradigms of masculinity and femininity, can
become an example of nonhierarchical, nurturing, and empowering performance for women and men.

APPENDIX: FAMILY TREES

The Family Tree of Æðelberht and Bertha of Kent

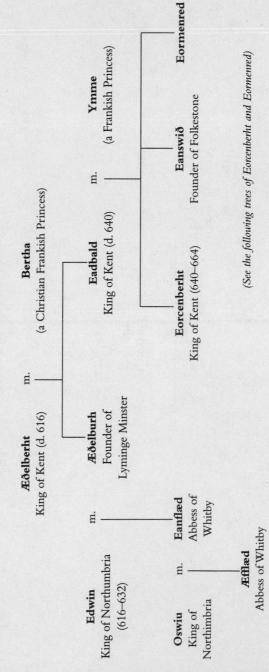

Æðelberht
King of Kent (d. 616)

m.

Bertha
(a Christian Frankish Princess)

Æðelburh
Founder of
Lyminge Minster

Eadbald
King of Kent (d. 640)

m.

Ymme
(a Frankish Princess)

Edwin
King of Northumbria
(616–632)

m.

Eanflæd
Abbess of Whitby

Eorcenberht
King of Kent (640–664)

Eanswið
Founder of Folkestone

Eormenred

Oswiu
King of
Northimbria

m.

Æfflæd
Abbess of Whitby

(See the following trees of Eorcenberht and Eormenred)

The Family Trees of the Brothers Eorcenberht and Eormenred
(Their sister, Eanswið, founded Folkestone Minster and left no decendents.)

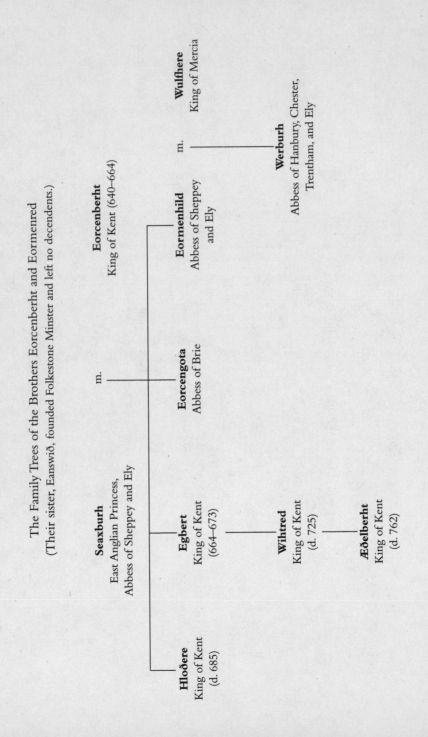

Hloðere
King of Kent
(d. 685)

Seaxburh
East Anglian Princess,
Abbess of Sheppey and Ely

m.

Eorcenberht
King of Kent (640–664)

Egbert
King of Kent
(664–673)

Eorcengota
Abbess of Brie

Eormenhild
Abbess of Sheppey
and Ely

m.

Wulfhere
King of Mercia

Wihtred
King of Kent
(d. 725)

Werburh
Abbess of Hanbury, Chester,
Trentham, and Ely

Æðelberht
King of Kent
(d. 762)

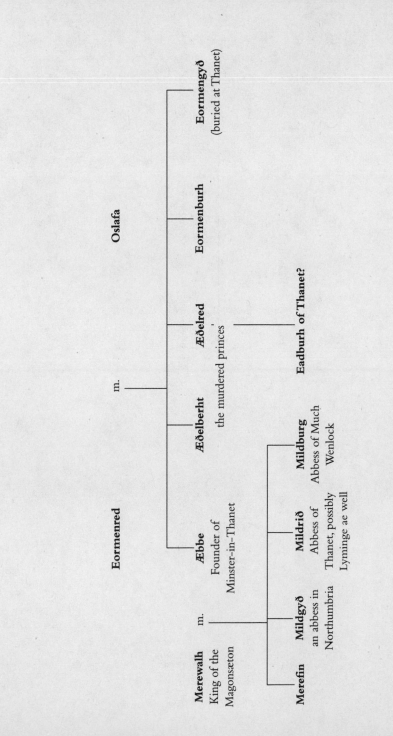

The Family Tree of the East Anglian King Anna, with His Holy Daughters

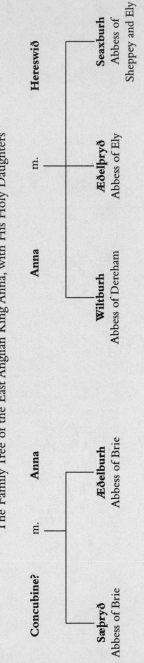

NOTES

Preface

1. For a discussion of the impossibility of objectivity in scholarship, specifically in relation to Anglo-Saxon studies, see Allen J. Frantzen's *Desire for Origins* (New Brunswick, NJ: Rutgers University Press, 1990), especially chapter 2.
2. Stephanie Hollis's *Anglo-Saxon Women and the Church* (Woodbridge, UK: Boydell, 1992) is the most thorough of these studies.
3. Gillian Overing and Clare Lees, "Birthing Bishops and Fathering Poets: Bede, Hild, and the Relations of Cultural Production," *Exemplaria* 6 (1994): 35–66.
4. The Æðelþryð sections are in Book IV, chapters 19 and 20 of the *History*. Throughout this book, I refer to the Latin/English edition of Bertram Colgrave and R.A.B. Mynors, eds., *Bede's Ecclesiastical History of the English People* (Oxford: Clarendon Press, 1969).
5. Since Bede does not provide this information, scholars must seek it in the little-known text referred to as *Þa Halgan,* a history of early royal Kentish saints that includes their resting places. It has been edited by Franz Liebermann, *Die Heiligen Englands* (Hanover: Hahn, 1889) and is also included in Walter de Grey Birch, ed., *Liber Vitae: Registry and Martyrology of New Minster and Hyde Abbey* (London: Simpkin, 1892), 83–87.

Chapter 1

1. Adrienne Rich mentions specifically Simone de Beauvoir and Shulamith Firestone, who completely reject biological motherhood as they "perceive women's maternal function as, quite simply and precisely, the root of our oppression" in *Of Woman Born: Motherhood as Experience and Institution,* 2nd ed. (New York: Norton, 1986), 72.
2. Allen J. Frantzen, "When Women Aren't Enough," *Speculum* 68 (1993): 446.
3. Judith Bennett, "Medievalism and Feminism," in the same *Speculum* volume as n.2; the essays in this volume were subsequently released as *Studying Medieval Women: Sex, Gender, Feminism,* ed. Nancy Partner (Cambridge, MA.: Medieval Academy of America, 1993).

4. A typical example is *Sanctity and Motherhood: Essays on Holy Mothers in the Middle Ages,* ed. Anneke B. Mulder-Bakker (New York: Garland, 1995). An exception is the collection *Medieval Mothering,* eds. John Carmi Parsons and Bonnie Wheeler (New York: Garland, 1996), which includes historical analyses of mothers with growing children as well as investigations of pregnancy, spiritual motherhood, and maternal tropes in religious discourse.

5. Clarissa Atkinson, *The Oldest Vocation: Christian Motherhood in the Middle Ages* (Ithaca: Cornell University Press, 1991), 94 and 115.

6. Ibid., 162 and 195; see all of chapters 5 and 6.

7. Caroline Walker Bynum, *Jesus as Mother: Studies in the Spirituality of the High Middle Ages* (Berkeley: University of California Press, 1982).

8. Christine Fell, *Women in Anglo-Saxon England* (Oxford: Basil Blackwell, 1984).

9. Jane Chance, *Woman as Hero in Old English Literature* (Syracuse: Syracuse University Press, 1986).

10. Helen Damico and Alexandra Hennessy Olsen, eds., *New Readings on Women in Old English Literature* (Bloomington: Indiana University Press, 1990).

11. A sampling of gender-theoretical readings of Anglo-Saxon poetry in the past decade would surely include Gillian Overing, *Language, Sign, and Gender in Beowulf* (Carbondale: University of Illinois Press, 1990); Clare Lees, "Men and *Beowulf*" in *Medieval Masculinities,* ed. Clare Lees (Minneapolis: University of Minnesota Press, 1994), 129–138; James Hala, "The Parturition of Poetry and the Birthing of Culture: The *Ides Aglæcwif* and *Beowulf,*" *Exemplaria* 10 (1998): 29–50; Karma Lochrie, "Gender, Sexual Violence, and the Politics of War in the Old English *Judith,*" in *Class and Gender in Early English Literature: Intersections,* eds. Britton J. Harwood and Gillian R. Overing (Bloomington: Indiana University Press, 1994), 1–20. The other essays in these collections, as well as those in *Speaking Two Languages: Traditional Disciplines and Contemporary Theory in Medieval Studies,* ed. Allen J. Frantzen (Albany: SUNY Press, 1991), address concerns of postmodern theory as well.

12. Clare A. Lees and Gillian R. Overing, "Birthing Bishops and Fathering Poets: Bede, Hild, and the Relations of Cultural Production," *Exemplaria* 6 (1994): 35–66.

13. See M. L. Cameron, *Anglo-Saxon Medicine* (Cambridge: Cambridge University Press, 1993).

14. Judith Butler, *Gender Trouble: Feminism and the Subversion of Identity* (New York: Routledge, 1990), 25.

15. The indented quote and quotations in the paragraph following from Butler, *Bodies That Matter: On the Discursive Limits of "Sex"* (New York: Routledge, 1993), x and 9.

16. Quotations in this paragraph from Butler, *Bodies,* 2, 14, 12.

17. Quotations in this sentence from Butler, *Bodies,* 4 and 15; Butler, *Trouble,* viii.

18. Quotations in the sentence and the previous from Butler, *Bodies,* 2 and 4; *Trouble,* viii and 33.

19. Sara Ruddick, *Maternal Thinking: Toward a Politics of Peace* (Boston: Beacon Press, 1989, repr.1995), 41.

20. Ibid., 17.

21. Ruddick expands her vision of birthgiving as distinct from mothering in "Thinking Mothers/Conceiving Birth," in *Representations of Motherhood,* eds. Donna Basin et al. (New Haven: Yale University Press, 1994), 29–45.

22. This quotation from *Maternal Thinking,* xi; the quotation from the sentence previous from *Maternal Thinking,* 22.

23. Ibid., 22.

24. Ibid., 19.

25. Ibid., 21.

26. Ibid.

27. Ibid., xvi.

28. Luce Irigaray, *Sexes and Genealogies,* trans. Gillian C. Gill (New York: Columbia University Press, 1993), 188.

29. Ibid., 12.

30. Ibid., 189.

31. Ibid., 131.

32. Allyson Newton, "The Occlusion of Maternity in Chaucer's *Clerk's Tale,*" in *Medieval Mothering* op.cit. (see n.4), 63–76.

Chapter 2

1. Roberta Gilchrist, *Gender and Material Culture* (New York: Routledge, 1994), 66.

2. Monika Otter, "The Temptation of St. Æthelthryth," *Exemplaria* 9 (1998): 152.

3. For example, see Mary Bateson, "Origin and Early History of Double Monasteries," *Transactions of the Royal Historical Society,* n.s. 13 (1899): 137–98; Joan Nicholson, "Feminae Gloriosae: Women in the Age of Bede," in *Medieval Women,* ed. Derek Baker (Oxford: Blackwell, 1970), 15–29; Jane Tibbetts Schulenberg, "Female Sanctity: Public and Private Roles, ca.500–1100," in *Women and Power in the Middle Ages,* eds. Mary Erler and Maryanne Kowalski (Athens: University of Georgia Press, 1988), 102–125. For a more cautious (perhaps too cautious) analysis of the achievements of women in the double monasteries, see Carol Neuman de Vegvar, "Saints and Companions to Saints: Anglo-Saxon Royal Women Monastics in Context," in *Holy Men and Holy Women: Old English Prose Saints' Lives and their Contexts,* ed. Paul E. Szarmach (Albany: SUNY Press, 1996), 51–94.

4. Textual citations to and translations of Bede throughout this chapter will be by book and chapter in the edition of Bertram Colgrave and R. A. B. Mynors, eds., *Bede's Ecclesiastical History of the English People* (Oxford: Clarendon Press, 1969).

5. Patricia Coulstock, *The Collegiate Church of Wimborne Minster* (Woodbridge: Boydell, 1993), 68.

6. Nicholson, "Feminae Gloriosae," 18.
7. Schulenberg, "Female Sanctity," 107. This argument is similar to that of Barbara Yorke in "'Sisters Under the Skin'? Anglo-Saxon Nuns and Nunneries in Southern England," *Annual Proceedings of the Graduate Centre for Medieval Studies in the University of Reading* 15 (1989) 95–117, wherein Yorke argues that the double monasteries were "regarded as possessions of the royal house throughout their existence."
8. Nicholson, "Feminae Gloriosae," 28.
9. Stephanie Hollis, *Anglo-Saxon Women and the Church* (London: Boydell, 1992), 67 and 125.
10. Clare Lees and Gillian Overing, "Birthing Bishops and Fathering Poets: Bede, Hild, and the Relations of Cultural Production," *Exemplaria* 6 (1994): 47.
11. Ibid., 56.
12. Bede, 1.25–26 and 2.5.
13. K. P. Witney suggests that Æðelburg's foundation of and burial at Lyminge is legendary rather than historical in "The Kentish Royal Saints: An Enquiry into the Facts behind the Legends," *Archaeologia Cantiana* 101 (1984): 2–5.
14. For a highly colored description of Eanswith's abbey, see Dame Eanswythe Edwards, *Eanswythe of Folkestone: Her Life, Her Relics, and Her Monastery* (Folkestone, Kent: Folkestone Parish Church, 1980). The appendix includes details of exhumation of a skeleton identified with Eanswythe.
15. For discussions of Ely's refoundation and the gender implications of a female saint as patron of a monks' house, see chapter 6 of Susan Ridyard's *The Royal Saints of Anglo-Saxon England: A Study of West Saxon and East Anglian Cults* (Cambridge: Cambridge University Press, 1988) as well as Monika Otter, "The Temptation of Saint Æthelthryth," (see n.2).
16. References to Bede are to 4.19–20.
17. Lina Eckenstein, *Woman Under Monasticism* (Cambridge: Cambridge University Press, 1896): 98; Barbara Mitchell, "Anglo-Saxon Double Monasteries," *History Today* 25 (1995): 35.
18. David Rollason, *Saints and Relics in Anglo-Saxon England* (Oxford: Blackwell, 1989), 41.
19. James Bentham, *The History and Antiquities of the Conventual Church of Ely* (Norwich: Stevenson, Matchett, and Stevenson, 1812), 45. This edition is actually a revision of the original 1762 history by James Bentham Sr., and is something of a tribute by James Bentham Jr.
20. While some of the *Legend* texts list Seaxburh as regent for her son Hloðere (Lotharius) rather than for Egbert, the dates of kingships in the seventh century make it more likely that she was Egbert's regent in the mid to late 660s before founding Sheppey and moving to Ely (Eorcenberht died in 664, Egbert in 673). She was at Ely by 679, the date of Æðelþryð's death; Hloðere died in 685.
21. Witney, in "Kentish Royal Saints," argues that Wihtburh of Dereham was a Kentish rather than an East Anglian princess, daughter of Eormengyth/

Eangyth (there is some confusion about her name) and Centwine of Wessex rather than of Anna of East Anglia. He relies on some tenuous connections through Eddius's *Life of Wilfrid*, however; *Þa Halgan* states quite clearly that Wihtburh was Anna's daughter.

22. Text from M. J. Swanton, "A Fragmentary Life of St. Mildred and Other Kentish Royal Saints," *Archaeologia Cantiana* 91 (1975): 15–27; translation is my own but checked against his and that of O. S. Cockayne in *Leechdoms, Wortcunning, and Starcraft of Early England,* vol. 3 (London: Longman, 1864), 422–433. Cockayne provides the Old English text as well.

23. K. P. Witney, *The Kingdom of Kent* (London: Phillimore, 1982), 142.

24. Swanton, "Fragmentary Life," 23; Cockayne, *Leechdoms,* 431. For discussion of *wales* as "slaves," see Margaret Lindsay Faull, "The Semantic Development of Old English *wealh*," *Leeds Studies in English* n.s.8 (1975): 20–44; David Pelteret, *Slavery in Early Medieval England* (London: Boydell, 1995), 321.

25. Text and translation from Bede 3.8.

26. All *Chronicle* text in this chapter, unless otherwise noted, is from the E Text, the Peterborough Chronicle (Oxford, Bodleian Library, Laud MS 636) edited by B. Thorpe, *The Anglo-Saxon Chronicle,* Rolls Series vols. 23a and 23b (London: Longman, 1861). Translation is my own, but I have checked it against Thorpe's and against that of Dorothy Whitelock in *The Anglo-Saxon Chronicle* (New Brunswick: Rutgers University Press, 1961).

27. This sister's daughter–mother's sister relationship echoes the important mother's brother–sister's son relationship discussed by Rolf Bremmer in "The Importance of Kinship: Uncle and Nephew in Beowulf," *Amsterdamer Beitrage zur Alteren Germanistik* 15 (1980): 21–38.

28. See Lees and Overing, "Birthing Bishops," 43; Hollis, *Anglo-Saxon Women and the Church,* 249, as well as discussion on 125–135; Christine Fell, "Hild, Abbess of Streonaeshalch," in *Hagiography and Medieval Literature,* eds. Hans Bekker-Nielsen et al. (Odense: Odense University Press, 1981), 79.

29. Fell, "Hild," 87.

30. Bede, 4.23–24. All references to and quotations from Bede in this discussion of Whitby are from these chapters of the *Ecclesiastical History.*

31. Hollis, *Anglo-Saxon Women and the Church,* 126.

32. Eckenstein, *Woman Under Monasticisim,* 82.

33. Hollis, *Anglo-Saxon Women and the Church,* 183.

34. Charles Peers and C. A. Ralegh Radford, "The Saxon Monastery at Whitby," *Archaeologia* 89 (1943): 41–42.

35. Frank Stenton, *Anglo-Saxon England,* 2nd ed. (Oxford: Clarendon Press, 1947, repr. 1955), 161.

36. Bede, *Ecclesiastical History,* 4.18.

37. Stenton, *Anglo-Saxon England,* 184.

38. Stephanie Hollis, "The Minster-in-Thanet Foundation Story," *Anglo-Saxon England* 27 (1998): 61 and throughout.

39. All references to *Þa Halgan* in this chapter are to Franz Liebermann, ed., *Die Heiligen Englands: Angelsaechsisch und Lateinisch* (Hanover: Hahn, 1889),

1–7. This is the only scholarly edition of the work, but it is also printed in Walter de Grey Birch, ed., *Liber Vitae: Registry and Martyrology of New Minster and Hyde Abbey, Winchester* (London: Simpkin, 1892), 83–87. This manuscript (BL Stowe 944) is now available in facsimile: Simon Keynes, ed., *The Liber Vitae of the New Minster and Hyde Abbey Winchester (British Library Stowe 944)*, Early English Manuscripts in Facsimile 26 (Copenhagen: Rosenkilde and Bagger, 1996).

40. David Rollason, *The Mildrith Legend: A Study in Early Medieval Hagiography in England* (Leicester: Leicester University Press, 1982), 28.

41. Hollis, "Minster-in-Thanet Foundation," 45 and throughout.

42. These conflicts are discussed in specific relation to Kent in chapter 8 of Witney's *Kingdom of Kent*.

43. I will reference charters by their numbers in Walter de Grey Birch, ed., *Cartularium Saxonicum*, vol. 1 (London: Whiting and co., 1885). All of the charters I will be referencing in the following discussion have been judged authentic according to the annotations in P. H. Sawyer, ed., *Anglo-Saxon Charters: An Annotated List and Bibliography* (London: Royal Historical Society, 1968); each is also discussed in detail in Susan Kelly's new edition, *Charters of St. Augustine's Abbey and Minster-in-Thanet,* Anglo-Saxon Charters 4 (Oxford: Oxford University Press, 1995). Unfortunately, Birch, Sawyer, and Kelly all use different reference numbers for each charter, so that Kelly 40 is Sawyer 10 and Birch 42.

44. Kelly, *Charters,* 143 and 144

45. Barbara Yorke, *Kings and Kingdoms of Early Anglo-Saxon England* (London: Seaby, 1990), 32–35.

46. Kelly, *Charters,* 141.

47. Ibid., 141. The possible identity of Oswine as a son of one of the murdered princes is discussed by both Witney, *The Kingdom of Kent,* 155–157; and Gordon Ward, "King Oswin—A Forgotten Ruler of Kent," *Archaeologia Cantiana* 50 (1933): 60–65.

48. Kelly, *Charters,* 155–157.

49. Three charters with dates previous to that of #86 have one female witness each—all of these have been termed spurious or forged, however; they are Birch #8, #13, and #22, corresponding to Sawyer #5, #6, and #68.

50. Witney, *Kingdom of Kent,* 180.

51. Rollason, *The Mildrith Legend,* 47–49.

52. Another charter of Wihtred—Birch #99—exempts the monasteries of the kingdom from public taxation; it invokes the names of four abbesses—Hirminhilda, Irminburga, Aeaba, and Nerienda. While Gordon Ward is at pains to prove the charter's originality ("King Wihtred's Charter of AD 699," *Archaeologia Cantiana* 60 [1947]: 1–14), Sawyer's annotations indicate that this charter is spurious or dubious (Birch #99 is Sawyer #20).

53. The *Chronicle* version of the Bapchild Synod is in the notes of the AD 694 F Text entry in Thorpe, *The Anglo-Saxon Chronicle,* op.cit. For Latin versions, see in Birch, *Cartularium Saxonicum,* #91–#95. The best discussion is

in Arthur West Haddan and William Stubbs, eds., *Councils and Ecclesiastical Documents Relating to Great Britain and Ireland,* vol. 3 (Oxford: Clarendon Press, 1871, repr. 1964), 238–242, in their notes to the text.

54. Witney, *Kingdom of Kent,* 171–173, discusses the specifically Kentish political and ecclesiastical repercussions of the Bapchild Synod.

55. Rollason, *The Mildrith Legend,* 24–25.

56. Witney, *Kingdom of Kent,* 156.

57. For a full discussion of the implications of these documents in mercantile history, see S. E. Kelly, "Trading Privileges from Eighth-Century England," *Early Medieval Europe* 1 (1992): 3–28.

58. Kelly, *Charters,* 174. For full discussion, 168–175.

59. Ibid., 175.

60. Hollis, "Minster-in-Thanet Foundation," 60.

61. There is nothing in the text of the Boniface correspondence that absolutely identifies Boniface's Eadburh with Thanet's Eadburh. The editors of the Bonifatian letters simply refer to her as "Eadburh of Thanet." See Ephraim Emerton, ed. and trans., *The Letters of St. Boniface* (New York: Octagon Books, 1973), as well as Reanhol Rau, ed., *Briefe des Bonifatius* (Darmstadt: Wissenschaftlice Buchgesellschaft, 1968). Helmut Gneuss as well accepts the identification of Thanet's Eadburh with Boniface's Eadburh in "Anglo-Saxon Libraries from the Conversion to the Benedictine Reform," *Books and Libraries in Early England* (Aldershot, Hampshire: Ashgate Publishing, 1996), essay II, pages 643–688 (this essay collection retains the pagination of the original journal printings; the original publication date of this essay is 1984).

62. Witney, "The Kentish Royal Saints," 16.

63. Coulstock, *Collegiate Church,* 55; Hollis, *Anglo-Saxon Women and the Church,* 271–300.

64. Rollason, *The Mildrith Legend,* 35–36.

65. Emerton, *The Letters,* 60–61. Boniface calls Eadburh "abbess" in the text of this letter, indicating that Mildrith was dead by this time. This letter then helps us to date Mildrith's death more accurately—she must have died between 732, the date of her last charter appearance, and 736, the latest possible date of this letter.

66. Ibid., 64–65.

67. Ibid., 121–122.

68. Latin text from Rau, *Briefe,* 30.

69. For text, translation, and discussion of what he calls "St. Mildburg's Testament," see H. P. R. Finberg, *The Early Charters of the West Midlands* (Leicester: Leicester University Press, 1961), 195–216.

70. David Hugh Farmer, ed., *The Oxford Dictionary of Saints,* 2nd ed. (Oxford: Oxford University Press, 1987), 302.

71. For example, see Hollis, *Anglo-Saxon Women and the Church,* 258; and Eckenstein, *Woman Under Monasticism,* 112; as well as the introductory remarks to the *De Virginitate* in Michael Lapidge and James Rosier, eds. and trans.,

Aldhelm: The Poetic Works (Cambridge: Brewer, 1985), and Michael Lapidge and Michael Herren, eds. and trans, *Aldhelm: The Prose Works* (Cambridge: Brewer, 1979).

72. Farmer, *The Oxford Dictionary of Saints,* 147.

73. Dorothy Whitelock, *Some Anglo-Saxon Bishops of London* (London: HK Lewis, 1974), 5.

74. Rau, *Briefe,* 104

75. Coulstock, *Collegiate Church,* 41 and 74.

76. Witney, *Kingdom of Kent,* 245–247. Witney shakily relies on the letter of the mother-daughter pair Eangyð and Heaburg to Boniface (in which they plead with him to help them pilgrimage to Rome as they describe the sorrow in their lives) as a letter from Eormengyð/Eangyð and Eadburh. There is no reason why Eadburh of Thanet, a wealthy, influential, and secure abbess or abbess-in-training, would have felt the need to complain to Boniface about her situation. Most editors of the Bonifatian correspondence do not even entertain an identification of Heaburg with Eadburh; indeed, as far as I know, only Witney does so.

77. Swanton, "Fragmentary Life," 23, n.34.

78. Rollason, *The Mildrith Legend,* 21–24.

79. Gordon Ward, "King Oswin—A Forgotten Ruler of Kent," *Archaeologia Cantiana* 50 (1938): 62–63. Ward's argument that Eormengyð was the wife of the murdered Æðelberht and mother to the enigmatic Osuuini ignores *Þa halgan*'s explicit statement that Eormengyð was Æbbe's sister. Ward's argument is echoed somewhat by Barbara Yorke, who remarks that "The two princes are presented as young children, but in fact are more likely to have been adults," in *Kings and Kingdoms of Early Anglo-Saxon England,* 35.

80. Rollason, *The Mildrith Legend,* 79.

81. Jane Tibbetts Schulenberg, in "Women's Monastic Communities, 500–1100: Patterns of Expansion and Decline," *Signs* 14 (1989): 261–292, chronicles the gruesome deaths of nuns at the hands of the Vikings.

82. Goscelin, *Vita Mildrithae,* in Rollason, *The Mildrith Legend,* 142.

83. Helmut Gneuss, "Liturgical Books in Anglo-Saxon England," in *Learning and Literature in Anglo-Saxon England,* eds. Michael Lapidge and Helmut Gneuss (Cambridge: Cambridge University Press, 1985), 114–116.

84. This hymn has been edited by E.V. K. Dobbie as "A Prayer" in *The Anglo-Saxon Minor Poems,* ASPR vol. 6 (New York: Columbia University Press, 1942), 94–95. Dobbie uses the longer text from London, British Library, MS Cotton Julius A.ii; the first 15 of its 79 lines correspond almost exactly to the 15-line Lambeth text.

85. N. R. Ker, ed., *Catalogue of Manuscripts Containing Anglo-Saxon* (Oxford: Clarendon Press, 1957) 342–43. Folios 1–209 are Ker's entry #280, while folios 210–211 are #281.

86. This deduction first noted by Montague Rhodes James, the editor of *A Descriptive Catalogue of the Manuscripts of the Library of Lambeth Palace* (Cambridge: Cambridge University Press, 1932), 589.

87. Stephanie Hollis, "The Old English 'Ritual of the Admission of Mildrith' (London, Lambeth Palace 427, fol.210)," *Journal of English and Germanic Philology* 97 (1998): 313.

88. Ker, *Catalogue,* 343.

89. Cockayne, *Leechdoms,* 428–433.

90. Swanton, "Fragmentary Life," 15–17.

91. Hollis, "Minster-in-Thanet Foundation," 43.

92. Swanton, "Fragmentary Life," 15–17.

93. Rollason, *The Mildrith Legend,* 29 and 14.

94. Hollis, "Minster-in-Thanet Foundation," and "Old English Ritual."

95. Rollason, *The Mildrith Legend,* 29.

96. Ibid., 30–31.

97. Hollis, "Old English Ritual," 319–321.

98. Text from Swanton, "Fragmentary Life," 26; translation is my own although I have checked it against Swanton's, "Fragmentary Life," 22, and Cockayne's, *Leechdoms,* 429.

99. Cockayne, *Leechdoms,* 404.

100. Quotations in this paragraph from Cockayne, *Leechdoms,* 405.

101. Ibid., 429.

102. Swanton, "Fragmentary Life," 22, n.29.

103. Hollis, "Old English Ritual," 314, n.8.

104. David Knowles, *The Monastic Order in England* (Cambridge: Cambridge University Press, 1950), 21.

105. Justin McCann, ed. and trans., *The Rule of Saint Benedict in Latin and English* (London: Burns Oates, 1952), 118–119.

106. Hollis, "Old English Ritual," 314.

107. Ibid., 319.

108. Quotations and comments about Thedore in this paragraph from Stenton, *Anglo-Saxon England,* 131.

109. Ibid., 140, n.1.

110. On the authenticity of *Theodore's Penitential,* see Haddan and Stubbs, *Councils and Ecclesiastical Documents,* 173–174; Allen Frantzen, *The Literature of Penance in Anglo-Saxon England* (New Brunswick: Rutgers University Press, 1983), 69; and John T. McNeill and Helena M. Gamer, *Medieval Handbooks of Penance* (New York: Columbia University Press, 1938), 179.

111. Thomas Charles Edwards, "The Penitential of Theodore and the Iudicia Theodori," in *Archbishop Theodore,* ed. Michael Lapidge (Cambridge: Cambridge University Press, 1995), 141–174.

112. All of the quotations in this discussion of *Theodore's Penitential* from Haddan and Stubbs, *Councils and Ecclesiastical Documents,* 196; all translation from McNeill and Gamer, *Medieval Handbooks,* 205.

113. The most thorough discussion of medieval uses of the word *oblatio* is in J. F. Niermeyer, ed., *Mediae Latinitatis Lexicon Minus* (Leiden: Brill, 1976).

114. I am indebted to Dr. Julie Ann Smith of Massey University in New Zealand for guiding me to these mosaics, which are reproduced in H. W.

Janson, *The History of Art,* 3rd ed. (New York: Harry Abrams, 1986), 219 and colorplate 29.

115. McCann, *The Rule of Saint Benedict,* 134.
116. Hollis, "Old English Ritual," 315.
117. Quotations in this paragraph from Lees and Overing, "Birthing Bishops," 57–60.
118. Lees and Overing clearly disagree with such celebrations of feminine power; they argue that "It has become conventional among feminist historians to point to the kinship ties of royal women who, as abbesses, nuns, and saints, achieve a considerable degree of prominence in the period" ("Birthing Bishops," 57). Unfortunately, they do not footnote this sentence.

Chapter 3

1. Charles Plummer, ed., *Two of the Saxon Chronicles Parallel,* revised ed. based on that of John Earle (Oxford: Clarendon Press, 1889), 18. Text of the *Anglo-Saxon Chronicle* throughout this chapter will be cited by year; text is from the Parker Manuscript unless otherwise designated. Translations are my own, although I have checked them against Dorothy Whitelock's in *The Anglo-Saxon Chronicle: A Revised Translation,* eds. and trans. Whitelock et al. (New Brunswisk: Rutgers University Press, 1961).
2. Latin quotations cited by chapter are from *Asser's Life of Alfred,* ed. William Henry Stevenson (Oxford: Clarendon Press, 1904; repr. 1959); translations are my own, although I have checked them against Albert S. Cook in *Asser's Life of Alfred* (Boston: Ginn and Co., 1906) and against Simon Keynes and Michael Lapidge in *Alfred the Great* (Hammondsworth: Penguin, 1983).
3. Cook, *Asser's Life of Alfred,* v.
4. Dorothy Whitelock, "The Genuine Asser," *The Stenton Lecture 1967* (Reading: University of Reading, 1967).
5. Alfred Smyth, *King Alfred the Great* (Oxford: Oxford University Press, 1995).
6. See Simon Keynes' review article, "On the Authenticity of Asser's Life of Alfred," *Journal of Ecclesiastical History* 47 (1996): 529–51, as well as Bernard Bachrach's review in *The Journal of Military History* 61 (1997): 363–64.
7. Allen Frantzen, "Alfred's Alfred: The Cultural Meaning of Alfred P. Smyth's *King Alfred the Great,*" MLA Paper given on 26 December 1997 at the Annual Meeting of the Modern Language Association, Toronto. Quoted by permission of the author.
8. Smyth, *Alfred the Great,* 182–83.
9. The argument and quotations from this and the following paragraph are from pp. 181–185 of Smyth, *Alfred the Great.*
10. Ibid., 184.
11. P. G. W. Glare, ed., *The Oxford Latin Dictionary* (Oxford: Clarendon Press, 1982, repr. 1983), 731.

12. Smyth, *Alfred the Great,* 11.

13. Stevenson, *Asser's Life of Alfred,* 4 (chapter 2).

14. Pauline Stafford, "The King's Wife in Wessex, 800–1066," in *New Readings on Women in Old English Literature,* eds. Helen Damico and Alexandra Hennessey Olsen (Bloomington: Indiana University Press, 1990), 60–61.

15. For example, see Smyth, *King Alfred the Great,* 11.

16. Whitelock, *The Anglo-Saxon Chronicle,* 53, n.1.

17. Information about the Brescia *Liber Vitae* from *The Liber Vitae of the New Minster and Hyde Abbey (British Library Stowe 944),* EEMF 26, ed. Simon Keynes (Copenhagen: Rosenkilde and Bagger, 1996), 51.

18. As in chapter 2, I will here refer to charters by their reference numbers in Birch, although I will be relying on Sawyer for scholarly judgment about their authenticity: Walter de Gray Birch, ed., *Cartularium Saxonicum: A Collection of Charters Relating to Anglo-Saxon History,* vols. 1–3 (London: Whiting and Co., 1885); P. H. Sawyer, *Anglo-Saxon Charters: An Annotated List and Bibliography* (London: Royal Historical Society, 1968). The six authentic charters of Burgred in which Æðelswið appears as a witness are numbers 487, 488, 492, 503, 513, and 535; 488 is doubled in 489, which I did not include in my count. Number 514, also a charter of Burgred witnessed by Æðelswið, is "spurious." The two jointly issued and witnessed charters are #509 and #524; the sole charter issued by Æðelswith is #522. In 872, Burgred and Æðelswið appear as witnesses as well in a "doubtful" and "interpolated" charter (#537) of Æðelred, "dux merciorum," probably the same Mercian leader who became Æðelflæd's husband in the 880s. The only charter of Burgred not witnessed by Æðelswið is #521. Sawyer's numbering system is different from Birch's, although there is a correspondence chart in Sawyer's introduction.

19. Birch, *Cartularium Saxonicum,* #589.

20. The ring is described most thoroughly in David M. Wilson, *Anglo-Saxon Ornamental Metalwork 700–1100 in the British Museum* (London: Trustees of the British Museum, 1964), 117–119. Wilson provides line drawings of the shoulder animals and of the inscription as well as photographic reproduction of the main face of the ring (no. 1, plate xi).

21. Quotations in this and the previous sentence from Wilson, *Anglo-Saxon Ornamental Metalwork,* 56.

22. R. I. Page, "Appendix A: The Inscriptions," in Wilson, *Anglo-Saxon Ornamental Metalwork,* 80.

23. Ibid., 83.

24. Leslie Webster, catalogue entry for "244: Finger-ring," in *The Making of England: Anglo-Saxon Art and Culture A.D. 600–900,* eds. Leslie Webster and Janet Backhouse (Toronto: University of Toronto Press, 1991), 269. Please note that Webster and Backhouse switched the caption and catalogue numbers of the two rings in their texts; Æðelswið's ring, captioned as #243, is catalogued as #244.

25. Ibid.

26. Don Stansbury, *The Lady Who Fought the Vikings* (Devon, England: Imogen Books,1993), 21. Stansbury's book has not been reviewed at all, as far as I can tell; its uneven quality mars its interesting points.

27. Asser, chap. 29, states that Ealhswið's mother "Eadburh nominabatur, de regali genere Merciorum regis" (was called Eadburh, of the royal line of Mercian kings). Smyth disputes the Mercian ancestry of Alfred's wife, referring to "Alfred's supposed Mercian in-laws" as he argues that Ealhswið was more likely West Saxon as part of his larger argument that Asser's *Life of Alfred* is a tenth-century forgery by Bryhtferth of Ramsey, (in Smyth, *King Alfred the Great,* 24–28).

28. David Sturdy, *Alfred the Great* (London: Constable, 1995), 169.

29. Sawyer, *Anglo-Saxon Charters,* #349; in Birch, #571.

30. Pauline Stafford, "The King's Wife in Wessex, 800–1066," 57–59.

31. Birch #589, Sawyer #363.

32. For a discussion of this facet of the will, see Smyth, *King Alfred the Great,* 401–420.

33. References to Alfred's *Will* throughout this chapter are to the text in Birch, *Cartularium Saxonicum,* #553; translation is my own although I have checked it against that of Dorothy Whitelock in *English Historical Documents,* 2nd ed. (London: Routledge, 1996), 534–536.

34. Reference to Ealhswið's founding of Nunnaminster can be found in *Liber Vitae: Register and Martyrology of New Minster and Hyde Abbey, Winchester,* ed. Walter de Gray Birch (London: Simpkin, 1892), 5–6, in which she is called *aedificatrix monasterii.*

35. Walter de Gray Birch, ed., *An Ancient Manuscript of the Eighth or Ninth Century Formerly Belonging to St. Mary's Abbey, or Nunnaminster, Winchester* (London: Simpkin and Marshall, 1889), text on p.96, translation on p.32.

36. Ibid., 17.

37. Helmut Gneuss includes BL Harley 2965 in his list of only five private prayer-books surviving from Anglo-Saxon England in "Liturgical Books in Anglo-Saxon England and Their Old English Terminology," in *Learning and Literature in Anglo-Saxon England,* eds. Michael Lapidge and Helmut Gneuss (Cambridge: Cambridge University Press, 1985), 138.

38. For a recent discussion of these and other "charms" as a unique blend of liturgical and folkloric medicine, see Karen Louise Jolly, *Popular Religion in Late Saxon England: Elf Charms in Context* (Chapel Hill: University of North Carolina Press, 1996).

39. Smyth, *Alfred the Great,* 513.

40. Birch, *Ancient Manuscript,* 17.

41. Asser, *Life of King Alfred,* chapter 75.

42. Smyth, *King Alfred the Great,* 419–420 discusses Æðelweard's inheritance and its complementarity with his brother's.

43. Asser, *Life of King Alfred,* chapter 75.

44. Glare, *Oxford Latin Dictionary,* 550–551.

45. The forged charter of Ælfþryð is Birch #661. Information about her life from Philip Grierson, "The Relations Between England and Flanders Before the Norman Conquest," *Transactions of the Royal Historical Society,* 4th series, 23 (1941): 83–87.

46. The charter is Birch #531 (OE) and #532 (Latin); comments in Sawyer, *Anglo-Saxon Charters,* #357. *Erie* in the Old English text is probably a mistransliteration of *erfe,* property (which I have translated "grant").

47. Smyth, *King Alfred the Great,* 266.

48. For a discussion, see J. Charles Wall, *Alfred the Great: His Abbeys of Hyde, Athelney, and Shaftesbury* (London: E. Stock, 1900), 115–118. Wall uses Birch charter #531 as authentic, although he garbles the translation of the lines referring to Æðelgifu to elide any reference to infirmity.

49. F. T. Wainwright, "The Chronology of the Mercian Register," *English Historical Review* 60 (1945): 385–392.

50. The B manuscript is British Library Cotton Tiberius A.vi; the C text is British Library Cotton Tiberius B.i, which Plummer associated with Abingdon. Plummer's comment about the "annals of Æthelflæd" in *Two of the Saxon Chronicles Parallel,* op.cit., ix.

51. Paul E. Szarmach, "Æðelflæd in the Chronicle," *Old English Newsletter* 29.1 (1995), 43. For a development of this argument for a lost Latin source for the *Mercian Register,* see Szarmach, "Æðelflæd of Mercia: *Mise en page,*" in *Words and Works: Studies in Medieval English Language and Literature in Honour of Fred C. Robinson,* eds. Peter S. Baker and Nicholas Howe (Toronto: University of Toronto Press, 1998), 105–126.

52. Joan Newlon Radner, ed. and trans, *Fragmentary Annals of Ireland* (Dublin: Dublin Institute for Advanced Study, 1978). Radner's edition replaces that used by Wainwright: John O'Donovan, ed. and trans., *Annals of Ireland: Three Fragments* (Dublin: Irish Archaeological and Celtic Society, 1860). The *Fragmentary Annals* text is a 1643 manuscript, which is a copy of an unknown annalistic manuscript now lost.

53. Wainwright, "Æthelflæd, Lady of the Mercians," in *The Anglo-Saxons: Studies in Some Aspects of their History and Culture Presented to Bruce Dickins,* ed. Peter Clemoes (London: Bowes and Bowes, 1959); reprinted in *New Readings on Women in Old English Literature,* eds. Helen Damico and Alexandra Hennessey Olsen (Bloomington: Indiana University Press, 1990), 44–55. Quotation is from Damico and Olsen edition, 46. All further citations of Wainwright's essay are to this edition.

54. The charter is Birch #547, Sawyer #217. Stevenson's remarks are from *Asser's Life of King Alfred,* 300.

55. The three charters of Æðelred witnessed by Æðelflæd are Birch #547, #557, and #561. The *witan* document is Birch #574. The jointly issued charters are Birch #579 and #587. The charters that involve Edward, Æðelred, and Æðelflæd are Birch #603, #606, and #607. The land grant from Werfrith to Æðelred and Æðelflæd is Birch #608.

56. Wainwright, "Æthelflæd, Lady of the Mercians," 46.

57. Ibid., 54.
58. Catherine Karkov, "Æðelflæd's Exceptional Coinage?" *Old English Newsletter* 29.1 (1995): 41.
59. Alistair Campbell, ed. and trans., *The Chronicle of Æthelweard* (London: Thomas Nelson, 1962), xviii.
60. Joan Ferrante, *To the Glory of Her Sex* (Bloomington: Indiana University Press, 1997), 83.
61. Æðelweard provides a table of contents for his second, third, and fourth books; the tables of books three and four show that these books are organized chronologically by kings' reigns.
62. H. P. R. Finberg, *The Formation of England* (London: Hart-Davis, MacGibbon, 1974), 145–146.
63. Sturdy, *Alfred the Great,* 219.
64. Stephanie Hollis, *Anglo-Saxon Women and the Church* (Woodbridge: Boydell, 1992), 236.
65. Stansbury, *The Lady Who Fought the Vikings,* 149.
66. Ibid., 179–180.
67. Hollis, *Anglo-Saxon Women and the Church,* 88.
68. J. A. Robinson, *The Times of St. Dunstan* (Oxford: Clarendon Press, 1923, repr. 1969), 48.
69. Jane Chance, *Woman as Hero in Old English Literature* (Syracuse: Syracuse University Press, 1986), 61.
70. Translation from J. A. Giles, ed., *William of Malmesbury's Chronicle of the Kings of England* (London: G. Bell, 1911), 123. For the Latin text, see William Stubbs, ed., *Willelmi Malmesbiriensis Monachi: De Gestis Regum Anglorum,* Rolls Series #90 (London, 1887), 136. William calls Æðelflæd a *virago.*
71. Hollis, *Anglo-Saxon Women and the Church,* 219.
72. Ibid., 92.
73. Old English text from Birch #574; translation is my own, although I have checked it against that of Florence Harmer in *Select English Historical Documents of the Ninth and Tenth Centuries* (Cambridge: Cambridge University Press, 1914), 56–57.
74. Harmer, *Select English Historical Documents,* 108.
75. Old English text from Birch #579; translation is my own although I have checked it against that of Dorothy Whitelock in *English Historical Documents c.500–1042,* 2nd ed. (London: Routledge, 1979), 540–541. Whitelock's translation gives the charter an ecclesiastical tone that I feel the Old English text does not communicate (for instance, she translates *stowe* as "foundation" while I maintain the more neutral term "place").
76. Stansbury, *The Lady Who Fought the Vikings,* 218–220.
77. Ibid., 156.
78. Radner, *Fragmentary Annals,* xix and xxii.
79. F. T. Wainwright, "North-West Mercia," in *Scandinavian England: Collected Papers by F. T. Wainwright,* ed. H. P. R. Finberg (Sussex: Phillimore, 1975), 78 and 84–85.

80. Full text and translation in Radner, *Fragmentary Annals,* 166–173.

81. F.T.Wainwright, "Inigmund's Invasion," in *Scandinavian England: Collected Papers by F.T.Wainwright,* ed. H. P. R. Finberg (Sussex: Phillimore, 1975), 144.

82. Full text and translation in Radner, *Fragmentary Annals,* 180–183.

83. Text and translation from Radner, *Fragmentary Annals,* 180–181.

84. Information and quotation in this and the previous sentence from Wainwright, "Æthelflæd, Lady of the Mercians," 49.

85. Stansbury suggests that the remark of the death of her four retainers shows that she "was thinking and feeling as a woman would feel," whatever that means (*The Lady Who Fought the Vikings,* 208).

86. Lois Huneycutt, "Public Lives, Private Ties: Royal Mothers in England and Scotland, 1070–1204," in *Medieval Mothering,* eds. John Carmi Parsons and Bonnie Wheeler (New York: Garland, 1996), 296 and 298. Huneycutt is specifically discussing historian Ralph Turner when she argues against parental ineffectiveness by public women.

87. F.T.Wainwright, "Æthelflæd, Lady of the Mercians," 53.

88. Stafford, "The King's Wife in Wessex," 59–60.

89. This information from Birch, *Cartularium Saxonicum,* 259, n.3.

90. Sturdy, *Alfred the Great,* 169.

91. Sawyer, *Anglo-Saxon Charters,* #367, provides bibliography for arguments that the charter may even be original.

92. Stansbury, *The Lady Who Fought the Vikings,* 134–135.

93. See Robinson, *The Times of St. Dunstan,* 47, n.3, and Sturdy, *Alfred the Great,* 220. Quotation from Sturdy 220.

94. Wainwright, "Æthelflæd, Lady of the Mercians," 53.

95. Joseph Bosworth and T. Northcote Toller, eds., *An Anglo-Saxon Dictionary* (London: Oxford University Press, 1898), 33.

96. See Wainwright, "The Chronology of the Mercian Register," 388–89, for a discussion of the dating of the Ælfwynn annal.

97. Sturdy, *Alfred the Great,* 220.

98. See Wainwright, "Inigmund's Invasion," op.cit., for a detailed analysis of the peaceful settlement of Scandinavians in the Wirral area.

99. Stansbury, *The Lady Who Fought the Vikings,* 177.

100. These include Stansbury, *The Lady Who Fought the Vikings,* 215, and H. P. R. Finberg, *The Formation of England,* 147.

101. Wainwright, "Æthelflæd, Lady of the Mercians," 53.

102. For the only edition of Osbert of Clare's *Life* of Edburga, see appendix 1 of Susan Ridyard's *The Royal Saints of Anglo-Saxon England* (Cambridge: Cambridge University Press, 1988).

103. Birch, ed., *Liber Vitae,* 59. For the facsimile, see Keynes, ed., *Liber Vitae,* 26r and 26v.

104. Birch, *Liber Vitae,* n.1; Birch actually states that Ælfwynn's is the last name in the original list, but Keynes argues that the last name is Aldgyð; examination of the facsimile reveals the nature of the puzzle (the two handwritings are very similar), but I must agree with Keynes.

105. We know of this sister's existence from "Ælfwine's Prayerbook," London, British Library, Cotton Titus D.xxvii and Titus D.xxvi, a personal devotional which marks her death (Keynes, *Liber Vitae*, 122).

Chapter 4

1. Gillian Overing, *Language, Sign, and Gender in Beowulf* (Carbondale: Illinois University Press, 1991).

2. Helen Damico, *Beowulf's Wealhtheow and the Valkyrie Tradition* (Madison: Wisconsin University Press, 1984).

3. Jane Chance Nitzsche, "The Structural Unity of Beowulf: The Problem of Grendel's Mother," *Texas Studies in Literature and Language* 22 (1980): 287–303; reprinted by Jane Chance in *New Readings on Women in Old English Literature,* eds. Helen Damico and Alexandra Hennessey Olsen (Bloomington: Indiana University Press, 1990), 248–261. Throughout this book I refer to this author as "Chance" since most of her work is published under that name.

4. Elaine Tuttle Hansen, "Women in Old English Poetry Reconsidered," *The Michigan Academician* 9 (1976/77): 117.

5. Richard Schrader, *God's Handiwork: Images of Women in Early Germanic Literature* (Westport, CT: Greenwood Press, 1983), 36.

6. Paull F. Baum, "The Beowulf Poet," *Philological Quarterly* 39 (1960): 393.

7. *Woman as Hero in Old English Literature* (Syracuse: Syracuse University Press, 1986), 99.

8. Overing, *Language, Sign, and Gender,* 70.

9. All text from Fr. Klaeber, *Beowulf and the Fight at Finnsburgh,* 3rd ed. (Lexington, MA: D. C. Heath and Co., 1950). Translations are my own, and tend to be literal rather than poetic. The complete text of the episode is as follows:

Bold wæs betlic,   bregorof cyning, 1925
heah on healle,   Hygd swiðe geong,
wis welþungen,   þeah ðe wintra lyt
under burhlocan   gebiden hæbbe,
Hæreþes dohtor;   næs hio hnah swa þeah,
ne to gneað gifa   Geata leodum,   1930
maþmgestreona.   Modþryðo wæg,
fremu folces cwen,   firen' ondrysne.
Nænig þæt dorste   deor geneþan
swæsra gesiða,   nefne sinfrea,
þæt hire an dæges   eagum starede;   1935
ac him wælbende   weotode tealde
handgewriþene;   hraþe seoþðan wæs
æfter mundgripe   mece geþinged,
þæt hit sceadenmæl   scyran moste,

cwealmbealu cyðan.   Ne bið swylc cwenlic þeaw   1940
idese to efnanne,   þeah ðe hio ænlicu sy,
þætte freoðuwebbe   feores onsæce
æfter ligetorne   leofne mannan.
Huru þæt onhohsnode   Hemminges mæg;
ealodrincende   oðer sædan,   1945
þæt hio leodbealewa   læs gefremede,
inwitniða,   syððan ærest wearð
gyfen goldhroden   geongum cempan,
æðelum diore,   syððan hio Offan flet
ofer fealone flod   be fæder lare   1950
siðe gesohte;   ðær hio syððan well
in gumstole,   gode mære,
lifgesceafta   lifigende breac,
hiold heahlufan   wið hæleþa brego,
ealles moncynnes   mine gefræge   1955
þone selestan   bi sæm tweonum,
eormencynnes;   Forðam Offa wæs
geofum ond guðum,   garcene man,
wide geweorðod,   wisdome heold
eðel sinne;—   þonon Eomer woc   1960
hæleðum to helpe,   Hemminges mæg,
nefa Garmundes,   niða cræftig.

(The hall was splendid, the king very valiant, high in the hall,
Higd very young, wise, accomplished, though she had resided few
winters under the hall enclosure, Hareth's daughter; she was not
lowly thus, however, nor too niggardly of gifts, of treasures, to the
people of the Geats.
    [1931b] Modthryth carried on, excellent queen of the folk, a
crime terrible. None fierce of more dear companions dared to
venture that, except a great lord, so that one of a day gazed at her
with eyes, but for him a deadly bond was ordained, was
considered, twisted by her hand; quickly thereupon a sword was
appointed on account of a hand grip, so that the ornamented
sword must settle it, [must] show the death-evil.
    [1940b] It is not such queenly custom for a noblewoman to
perform, however she may be peerless, that a peace-weaver
deprive a beloved man of life after pretended injury. Indeed the
kinsman of Hemming stopped that; the ale-drinkers another
[story] tell, that she less of harms to a people, of hostile acts
performed, since first she was given gold-adorned to the young
champion, beloved for nobilities, since by father-counsel she
sought the hall of Offa over the pale flood by a journey.

[1951b] Since she has there enjoyed well living of lives on the throne, good, famous, she has held the high love with the chief of warriors, of all the race of man as I have heard the best between the seas, of mankind. Because in gifts and in battles Offa, a spear-bold man, was widely exalted, he held with wisdom his native land; from him Eomer was born as a help to warriors, Hemming's kinsman, nephew of Garmund, powerful against evils.)

10. Such comparisons between Modþryðo and Hygd can be found in Adrien Bonjour, *The Digressions in Beowulf* (Oxford: Basil Blackwell, 1950, repr. 1965); Constance Hieatt, "Modthrytho and Heremod: Intertwined Threads in the Beowulf Poet's Web of Words," *Journal of English and Germanic Philology* 83 (1984): 173–182; Howell D. Chickering, *Beowulf: A Dual Language Edition* (New York, Anchor Books, 1977), 349–352; Norman Eliason, "The Thryth-Offa Digression in *Beowulf*" in *Franciplegius: Medieval and Linguistic Studies in Honor of Francis Peabody Magoun, Jr.,* eds. Jess Bessinger and Robert Creed (New York: New York University Press, 1965), 124–138.

11. See, for example, David Allen, "The Coercive Ideal in *Beowulf*" in *Literary and Historical Perspectives of the Middle Ages,* eds. Patricia Cummins et al. (Morgantown: West Virginia University Press, 1982), 120–32.

12. See, for example, Edward Irving, *Rereading* Beowulf (Philadelphia: University of Pennsylvania Press, 1989), 73, and Randall Bohrer, "Beowulf and the Bog People" in *Literary and Historical Perspectives of the Middle Ages,* eds. Patricia Cummins et al. (Morgantown: West Virginia University Press, 1982), 142.

13. Chickering, *Beowulf: A Dual-Language Edition,* 349–352, discusses these stylistics in depth.

14. For moral analyses of the passage, see Klaeber, *Beowulf,* 198–200; Norma Kroll, "Beowulf: The Hero as Keeper of Human Polity," *Modern Philology* 84 (1986): 117–129; and Bruce Moore, "The Thryth-Offa Digression in Beowulf," *Neophilologus* 64 (1980): 127–33.

15. See Chickering, *Beowulf,* 349–352, for summaries of the onomastic and historical arguments about Modþryðo.

16. For instance, Mary Kay Temple analyzes Modþryðo as one of a group of *ides* or noblewomen in Old English poetry in "Beowulf 1258–1266: Grendel's Lady-Mother," *English Language Notes* 23 (1986): 10–15; Jane Chance argues in *Woman as Hero in Old English Literature* (Syracuse: Syracuse University Press, 1986) that Modþryðo "begins as a type of female monster, but upon marriage to Offa changes her nature and becomes a much-loved queen" (105); Helen Damico reads her as a valkyrie-type who can be both terrible and welcoming in *Beowulf's Wealtheow and the Valkyrie Tradition* (Madison: University of Wisconsin Press, 1984).

17. Overing, *Language, Sign, and Gender,* 102.

18. Kemp Malone argues in "Hygd," *Modern Language Notes* 56 (1941): 356–58, that *fremu folces cwen* refers to Hygd, not to Modþryðo, but he is alone in this reading; the phrase is in apposition to *mod þryðo wæg.*

19. Richard Venezky and Antonette diPaolo Healey, eds., *A Microfiche Concordance to Old English* (Newark: University of Delaware Microforms), 1980, fiche M023, 164.

20. The other use of *mundgripe* listed in the concordance is actually an emendation of the manuscript reading *handgripe* at ll.965–66: "he for handgripe minum scolde licgean lifbysig" (In Beowulf's handgrip, Grendel struggles against death). All editions I have examined accept this emendation, but I have not included it in my text since the manuscript reading makes sense as it stands.

21. Klaeber, *Beowulf,* 199; Hieatt, "Beowulf 1258," 177 (italics added); Chance, *Woman as Hero,* 105; Damico, *Beowulf's Wealhtheow,* 46.

22. Hieatt, "Beowulf 1258," 177

23. Judith Butler, *Gender Trouble: Feminism and the Subversion of Identity* (New York: Routledge, 1990), 17.

24. Interestingly enough, in light of feminist arguments about women's being defined only in terms of their relations to men, Klaeber's primary definition for *cwen* is not *queen* but "wife (of a king)" (314).

25. Overing, *Language, Sign, and Gender,* 106.

26. Luce Irigaray, "Women on the Market," in *This Sex Which is not One,* trans. Catherine Porter with Carolyn Burke (New York: Columbia University Press, 1993), 170.

27. Ibid., 172.

28. Overing, *Language, Sign, and Gender,* 73.

29. Irigaray, "Women on the Market," 181.

30. Klaeber, *Beowulf,* 366, suggests "bidding," with its connotations of compulsion, as a possible translation.

31. Overing, *Language, Sign, and Gender,* 103 and 104.

32. Ibid., 104.

33. Venezky and Healy, *Concordance,* fiche L011, 201.

34. In a way, this "case" is not so different from discussion in the 1990s about sexual harassment. To many men, sexual harassment is a "pretended injury" while to many women it is a wholly legitimate grievance. It seems that Modþryðo has something in common with Anita Hill.

35. Irving, *Rereading Beowulf,* 73.

36. Overing, *Language, Sign, and Gender,* 105.

37. Klaeber, *Beowulf,* 366, suggests not only "bidding" (mentioned in note 30), but "instruction," "precept," and "counsel."

38. See W. H. Stevenson, ed., *Asser's Life of Alfred* (Oxford: Clarendon Press, 1959), 10–12 (chapter 13); for further discussion of queens in Wessex, see chapter 3.

39. Forms of *mære* occur 31 times in *Beowulf;* of these, 15 references are to a *þeoden,* a (male) prince (Klaeber 371).

40. It should be noted that Overing reads the women of *Beowulf* as hysterics who trouble rather than sanction that society, and as such questions the validity of their "failures."

41. Overing, *Language, Sign, and Gender*, 105.

42. For the Old English text of the genealogy of Adam, see A. N. Doane, ed., *Genesis A: A New Edition* (Madison: University of Wisconsin Press, 1978), ll.965–1127.

43. Sara Ruddick, *Maternal Thinking*, 2nd ed. (Boston: Beacon Press, 1995), 40–42.

44. J. R. R. Tolkien, "Beowulf: The Monsters and the Critics," *Proceedings of the British Academy* 22 (1936): 245–96; reprinted in numerous places, including *The Monsters and the Critics and Other Essays*, ed. Christopher Tolkien (London: Allen and Unwin, 1983), 5–48.

45. See, for example, Paul Beekman Taylor, "Beowulf's Second Grendel Fight," *Neuphilologische Mitteilungen* 86 (1985): 62–69, which argues that Beowulf's primary motivation in the second fight is not to kill the mother but to reclaim the trophy of Grendel's arm.

46. Margaret Goldsmith, *The Mode and Meaning of Beowulf* (London: Athlone, 1970), 118.

47. Chance, *Woman as Hero*, 101–102.

48. Nora Chadwick, in "The Monsters and Beowulf," in *The Anglo-Saxons*, ed. Peter Clemoes (London: Bowes and Bowes, 1959), 171–203, argues that the monster-mother is a valkyrie figure; Keith Taylor, in "Beowulf 1259a: The Inherent Nobility of Grendel's Mother," *English Language Notes* 31, no. 3 (1993/94); 13–25, argues that she has "inherently noble status"; and Kevin Kiernan, in "Grendel's Heroic Mother," *In Geardagum* 6 (1984); 13–33, notes that the notion of the monster-mother's heroism undermines the notion of that heroism itself; however, he confines his analysis to her monstrosity without inquiring into her gender.

49. See Randall Bohrer, "Beowulf and the Bog People," 133–147, and Gwendolyn Morgan, "Mothers, Monsters, Maturation: Female Evil in Beowulf," *Journal of the Fantastic in the Arts* 4 (1991): 54–68.

50. Signe Carlson, "The Monsters of Beowulf: Creations of Literary Scholars," *Journal of American Folklore* 80 (1967): 357–364.

51. Chance, *Woman as Hero*, 95–98.

52. Temple, "Beowulf 1258," 10–15.

53. Damico, *Beowulf's Wealhtheow*, 122.

54. John Niles, *Beowulf: The Poem and Its Tradition* (Cambridge: Harvard University Press, 1983), 231.

55. Jacqueline Vaught, "Beowulf: The Fight at the Center," *Allegorica* 5 (1980): 133.

56. Irving, *Rereading Beowulf*, 71.

57. Kiernan, "Grendel's Heroic Mother," 13.

58. Christine Alfano, "The Issue of Feminine Monstrosity: A Reevaluation of Grendel's Mother," *Comitatus* 23 (1992): 2.

59. Ibid., 3.

60. Overing, *Language, Sign, and Gender,* 73.

61. John Hill, *The Cultural World in Beowulf* (Toronto: University of Toronto Press, 1995), 128.

62. James Hala, "The Parturition of Poetry and the Birthing of Culture: The *Ides Aglæcwif* and *Beowulf,*" *Exemplaria* 10 (1998): 39, 44.

63. Hala, "The Parturition of Poetry," 50.

64. See Temple, "Beowulf 1258"; Alfano, "The Issue of Feminine Monstrosity"; and Chance, *Woman as Hero,* all op.cit.

65. For example, see John Halverson, "The World of Beowulf," *Journal of English Literary History* 36 (1969): 593–608; Michael Swanton, *Crisis and Development in Germanic Society, 700–800: Beowulf and the Burden of Kingship* (Goppingen: Kummerle Verlag, 1982); and Raymond Tripp, "The Exemplary Role of Hrothgar and Heorot," *Philological Quarterly* 56 (1977): 123–29.

66. Chance, *Woman as Hero,* 104.

67. Alfano, "The Issue of Feminine Monstrosity," 8.

68. Venezky and Healy, *Concordance,* fiche B017.

69. Fred Robinson, "Did Grendel's Mother Sit on Beowulf?" in *From Anglo-Saxon to Early Middle English: Studies Presented to E. G. Stanley,* eds. Malcolm Godden et al. (Oxford: Clarendon Press, 1994), 1–7.

70. Overing, *Language, Sign, and Gender,* 105.

71. See discussion in chapter 3; the annal is the *Mercian Register* entry for AD 916.

72. Donald Fry, ed., *Finnsburgh: Fragment and Episode* (London: Methuen, 1974), provides a thorough discussion.

73. Martin Camargo, "The Finn Episode and the Tragedy of Revenge in Beowulf," *Studies in Philology (Texts and Studies Supplement)* 78 (1981): 126.

74. Camargo, "The Finn Episode," 132. His argument is similar to but not as exegetically stressed as that of Goldsmith, *The Mode and Meaning of Beowulf,* 251; both argue that the lack of Christian compassion in the heroic code is its inherent flaw.

75. Joyce Hill, "Þæt wæs geomuru ides!: A Female Stereotype Examined," in *New Readings on Women in Old English Literature,* eds. Helen Damico and Alexandra Hennesey Olsen (Bloomington: Indiana University Press, 1990), 241.

76. Ibid.

77. Chance, *Woman as Hero,* 251.

78. Damico, *Beowulf's Wealhtheow,* 121.

79. John Hill, *Cultural World,* 26.

80. John Hill, personal communication. This argument is included in his book-in-progress.

81. Overing, *Language, Sign, and Gender,* 81.

82. Ibid., 87.

83. Also in Fry, *Finnsburgh: Fragment and Episode,* op.cit., as well as in Klaeber, 245–249.

84. Julius Zupitza, ed., *Beowulf,* EETS o.s.245 (Oxford: Oxford University Press, 1959, repr.1967), 52.

85. Kiernan, "Grendel's Heroic Mother," 29.

86. Eliason, "Thryth-Offa," 127.

87. For an analysis of female-female community in the Old English *Judith* (probably the only such community in Old English poetry), see my "Female Community in the Old English *Judith,*" *Studia Neophilogica* 70, no. 2 (1998): 165–172.

88. Kemp Malone, "Hygd," *Modern Language Notes* 56 (1941): 356–58, and Judith Weise, "The Meaning of the Name Hygd," *Names* 34 (1986): 1–10; both comment on Hygd's name.

89. Bruce Moore, "The Thryth-Offa Digression," 131.

90. Eliason, "Thryth-Offa," enters into long historical discussion to enable Offa and Hygelac, historical figures who lived more than a hundred years apart, to be married to the same woman.

91. Klaeber and Wrenn make no mention of it; Chickering focuses on the nobility of Beowulf's refusal.

92. Malone, "Hygd," 358.

93. Pauline Stafford, "The Queen's Wife in Wessex," in *New Readings on Women in Old English Literature,* eds. Helen Damico and Alexandra Hennessey Olsen (Bloomington: Indiana University Press, 1990), 56–78; John Carmi Parsons, "Family, Sex, and Power: The Rhythms of Medieval Queenship," in *Medieval Queenship,* ed. John Carmi Parsons (New York: St. Martin's, 1993).

94. Klaeber, *Beowulf,* 303.

95. At l.59, Healfdene's *feower bearn* include his unnamed daughter as well as his three sons. Generalized uses of the word, such as *yldo bearn,* children of men, can be understood generally to include women as well as men.

96. Uses of *bearn* with a genitive include *æðelinges bearn, þeodnes bearn, his/hyre/hire bearn, broðor bearn, hæleþa bearn, geato bearn, eotena bearn, yldo bearn, gumena bearn,* and *niþða bearn.*

97. Malone, "Hygd," 358.

98. Critical speculation about and desire for Hygd as the old woman at Beowulf's funeral pyre has been thoroughly debunked by Helen Bennett in "The Female Mourner at Beowulf's Funeral: Filling in the Blanks / Hearing the Spaces," *Exemplaria* 4 (1992): 35–49.

99. For such a "typical" reading of Wealhþeow and her actions within the poem as a form of peace-weaving, see L. John Sklute, "Freoðuwebbe in Old English Poetry," in *New Readings on Women in Old English Literature,* eds. Helen Damico and Alexandra Hennessey Olsen (Bloomington: Indiana University Press, 1990), 204–210, wherein he argues that "Wealhþeow's main function in the meadhall is to walk among the retainers, to pass out drink, and to give rings" (207).

100. Irving, *Rereading Beowulf,* 74. For a similar reading of Wealhþeow as powerless to control her own fate and that of her sons, see Alain Renoir, "A

Reading Context for the Wife's Lament," in *Anglo-Saxon Poetry: Essays in Appreciation,* eds. Nicholson and Frese (South Bend: Notre Dame University Press, 1975), 223–241, wherein he argues that she shows "an obsession with the protection of her doomed children" (228).

101. Carmen Cramer, "The Voice of Beowulf," *Germanic Notes* 8 (1977): 43–44.

102. Leslie Stratyner, "Wealhtheow's Threat: *Beowulf* 1228–1231," *In Geardagum* 14 (1993): 39–44.

103. Damico, *Beowulf's Wealhþeow and the Valkyrie Tradition,* op.cit.

104. Overing, *Language, Sign, and Gender,* 76.

105. Ibid., 80; italics hers.

106. Ibid., 97.

107. Ibid.

108. For a discussion of Hrothgar's attempted adoption of Beowulf, see my "Beowulf's Tears of Fatherhood," *Exemplaria* 10 (1998): 1–28.

109. Goldsmith, *The Mode and Meaning of Beowulf,* 250.

110. Joyce Hill, "Þæt wæs geomuru ides!" 238.

111. Chance, "The Structural Unity of Beowulf: The Problem of Grendel's Mother," 251.

112. Rolf Bremmer Jr., "The Germanic Context of Cynewulf and Cyneheard Revisited," *Neophilologus* 81 (1997): 449.

113. Rolf Bremmer Jr., "The Importance of Kinship: Uncle and Nephew in Beowulf," *Amsterdamer Beitrage zur Alteren Germanistik* 15 (1980): 21–38.

114. Schrader, *God's Handiwork,* 38.

115. Chickering, *Beowulf: A Dual Language Edition,* 320–322 summarizes the critical conflict and the reconstruction of later Scandinavian genealogies to "prove" that Hrothulf killed his cousins.

116. R. W. Chambers, *Beowulf: An Introduction to the Study of the Poem with a Discussion of the Stories of Offa and Finn* (Cambridge: Cambridge University Press, 1959), 26.

117. See Chambers, *Beowulf,* 26, n.3. Kemp Malone, in "Hrethric," *PMLA* 27 (1942): 268–312, uses the same evidence to argue this sequence of events: Hrothulf killed Hrothgar; Hrethric, with the help of Beowulf and the Geats, took back the throne; later, Hrothulf returned to kill Hrethric and re-ascend the Danish throne.

118. Kenneth Sisam, *The Structure of Beowulf* (Oxford: Clarendon Press, 1965), 82.

119. Ibid., 80–81.

120. John Niles, *Beowulf: The Poem and its Tradition,* 174–175.

121. Gerald Morgan, "The Treachery of Hrothulf," *English Studies* 53 (1972): 23–39. His discussion of primogeniture is on pp.30–34.

122. Helen Damico actually argues that Hrothulf is Wealhþeow's (but not Hrothgar's) son, and thus her campaign to make Hrothulf king in lines 1180 to 1187 makes sense because she wishes her son to be king (see *Beowulf's Wealhtheow and the Valkyrie Tradition,* 127–130).

123. Morgan, "Treachery," 37; italics his.

124. Hill, *Cultural World*, 75.
125. Michael D. C. Drout, "Imitating Fathers: Tradition, Inheritance, and the Reproduction of Culture in Anglo-Saxon England," Ph.D. diss., Loyola University Chicago, May 1997, 238.
126. Ibid., 239.
127. The text of the necklace description follows with translation:

Nænigne ic under swegle   selran hyrde
hordmaðum hæleþa,   syþðan Hama ætwæg
to þære byrhtan byrig   Brosinga mene,
sigle ond sincfæt,—   searoniðas fleah   1200
Eormenrices,   geceas ecne ræd.—
þone hring hæfde   Higelac Geata,
nefa Swertinges   nyhstan siðe,
siðþan he under segne   sinc ealgode,
wælreaf werede;   hyne wyrd fornam,   1205
syþðan he for wlenco   wean ahsode,
fæhðe to Frysum.   He þa frætwe wæg,
eorclanstanas   ofer yða ful,
rice þeoden;   he under rande gecranc.
Gehwearf þa in Francna fæþm   feorh cyninges,   1210
breostgewædu,   ond se beah somod;
wyrsan wigfrecan   wæl reafedon
æfter guðsceare,   Geata leode
hreawic heoldon.—   Heal swege onfeng. (ll.1197–1214)

(I have heard of none better of hoard-gifts to heroes under the sky, since Hama took the Brosing necklace, gemmed and worked, to the bright city. He earned the hatred of Eormenric, he chose eternal counsel [he died]. Then Hygelac the Geat had the ring, Swerting's nephew, on his last voyage, when he under the banner defended treasure, the spoils of killing; fate took him when he sought woe for treasure, a feud in Frisia. Then he waged feud, [wore] precious stones over the waves, the prince of the kingdom. He fell under the shield. The body of the king, the breast-treasure and the ring together, came into the Frankish kingdom. Worse warriors rifled the corpses after the battle-scarring, held the battlefield with the Geats dead. The hall took the noise.)

BIBLIOGRAPHY

Alfano, Christine. "The Issue of Feminine Monstrosity: A Reevaluation of Grendel's Mother." *Comitatus* 23 (1992): 1–16.

Allen, David. "The Coercive Ideal in *Beowulf.*" In *Literary and Historical Perspectives of the Middle Ages,* eds. Patricia Cummins et al., 120–32. Morgantown: West Virginia University Press, 1982.

Atkinson, Clarissa. *The Oldest Vocation: Christian Motherhood in the Middle Ages.* Ithaca: Cornell University Press, 1991.

Bachrach, Bernard. Review of *King Alfred the Great,* by Alfred Smyth. *The Journal of Military History* 61 (1997): 363–64.

Bateson, Mary. "Origin and Early History of Double Monasteries." *Transactions of the Royal Historical Society* n.s. 13 (1899): 137–98.

Baum. Paull F. "The Beowulf Poet." *Philological Quarterly* 39 (1960): 389–399.

Bennett, Helen. "The Female Mourner at Beowulf's Funeral: Filling in the Blanks / Hearing the Spaces." *Exemplaria* 4 (1992): 35–49.

Bennett, Judith. "Medievalism and Feminism." *Speculum* 68 (1993): 309–332.

Bentham, James. *The History and Antiquities of the Conventual Church of Ely.* Norwich: Stevenson, Matchett, and Stevenson, 1812.

Birch, Walter de Gray, ed. *Liber Vitae: Registry and Martyrology of New Minster and Hyde Abbey.* London: Simpkin, 1892.

_____, ed. *An Ancient Manuscript of the Eighth or Ninth Century Formerly belonging to St. Mary's Abbey, or Nunnaminster, Winchester.* London: Simpkin and Marshall, 1889.

_____, ed. *Cartularium Saxonicum.* 3 vols. London: Whiting and co., 1885.

Bohrer, Randall. "Beowulf and the Bog People." In *Literary and Historical Perspectives of the Middle Ages,* eds. Patricia Cummins et al., 133–147. Morgantown: West Virginia University Press, 1982.

Bonjour, Adrien. *The Digressions in Beowulf.* Oxford: Basil Blackwell, 1950, repr 1965.

Bosworth, Joseph, and T. Northcote Toller, eds. *An Anglo-Saxon Dictionary.* London: Oxford University Press, 1898.

Bremmer, Rolf Jr. "The Germanic Context of Cynewulf and Cyneheard Revisited." *Neophilologus* 81 (1997): 445–465.

_____. "The Importance of Kinship: Uncle and Nephew in *Beowulf.*" *Amsterdamer Beitrage zur Alteren Germanistik* 15 (1980): 21–38.

Butler, Judith. *Gender Trouble: Feminism and the Subversion of Identity.* New York: Routledge, 1990.

____. *Bodies That Matter: On the Discursive Limits of "Sex."* New York: Routledge, 1993.

Bynum, Caroline Walker. *Jesus as Mother: Studies in the Spirituality of the High Middle Ages.* Berkeley: University of California Press, 1982.

Camargo, Martin. "The Finn Episode and the Tragedy of Revenge in *Beowulf.*" *Studies in Philology (Texts and Studies Supplement)* 78 (1981): 120–134.

Cameron, M. L. *Anglo-Saxon Medicine.* Cambridge: Cambridge University Press, 1993.

Campbell, Alistair, ed. and trans. *The Chronicle of Æthelweard.* London: Thomas Nelson, 1962.

Carlson, Signe. "The Monsters of *Beowulf:* Creations of Literary Scholars." *Journal of American Folklore* 80 (1967): 357–364.

Chadwick, Nora. "The Monsters and *Beowulf.*" In *The Anglo-Saxons,* ed. Peter Clemoes, 171–203. London: Bowes and Bowes, 1959.

Chambers, R. W. *Beowulf: An Introduction to the Study of the Poem With a Discussion of the Stories of Offa and Finn.* Cambridge: Cambridge University Press, 1959.

Chance, Jane. *Woman as Hero in Old English Literature.* Syracuse: Syracuse University Press, 1986.

Chickering, Howell D. *Beowulf: A Dual Language Edition.* New York, Anchor Books, 1977.

Cockayne, O. S. *Leechdoms, Wortcunning, and Starcraft of Early England,* 3 vols. London: Longman, 1864.

Colgrave, Bertram, and R. A. B. Mynors, eds. *Bede's Ecclesiastical History of the English People.* Oxford: Clarendon Press, 1969.

Cook, Albert S., trans. *Asser's Life of Alfred.* Boston: Ginn and Co., 1906.

Coulstock, Patricia. *The Collegiate Church of Wimborne Minster.* Woodbridge: Boydell, 1993.

Cramer, Carmen. "The Voice of Beowulf." *Germanic Notes* 8 (1977): 40–44.

Damico, Helen. *Beowulf's Wealtheow and the Valkyrie Tradition.* Madison: University of Wisconsin Press, 1984.

Doane, A. N., ed. *Genesis A: A New Edition.* Madison: University of Wisconsin Press, 1978.

Dockray-Miller, Mary. "Beowulf's Tears of Fatherhood." *Exemplaria* 10 (1998): 1–28.

____. "Female Community in the Old English *Judith.*" *Studia Neophilogica* 70 (1998): 165–172.

Dobbie, E. V. K., ed. "A Prayer." In *The Anglo-Saxon Minor Poems,* ASPR vol.6, 94–95. New York: Columbia University Press, 1942.

Drout, Michael D. C. "Imitating Fathers: Tradition, Inheritance, and the Reproduction of Culture in Anglo-Saxon England." Ph.D. diss., Loyola University Chicago, 1997.

Edwards, Dame Eanswythe. *Eanswythe of Folkestone: Her Life, Her Relics, and Her Monastery.* Folkestone, Kent: Folkestone Parish Church, 1980.

Eckenstein, Lina. *Woman Under Monasticism.* Cambridge: Cambridge University Press, 1896.

Edwards, Thomas Charles. "The Penitential of Theodore and the Iudicia Theodori." In *Archbishop Theodore,* ed. Michael Lapidge, 141–174. Cambridge: Cambridge University Press, 1995.

Eliason, Norman. "The Thryth-Offa Digression in *Beowulf.*" In *Franciplegius: Medieval and Linguistic Studies in Honor of Francis Peabody Magoun, Jr.,* eds. Jess Bessinger and Robert Creed, 124–138. New York: New York University Press, 1965.

Emerton, Ephraim, ed. and trans. *The Letters of St. Boniface.* New York: Octagon Books, 1973.

Farmer, David Hugh, ed. *The Oxford Dictionary of Saints,* 2nd ed. Oxford: Oxford University Press, 1987.

Faull, Margaret Lindsay. "The Semantic Development of Old English *wealh.*" *Leeds Studies in English* n.s.8 (1975): 20–44.

Fell, Christine. *Women in Anglo-Saxon England.* Oxford: Basil Blackwell, 1984.

———. "Hild, Abbess of Streonaeshalch." In *Hagiography and Medieval Literature,* ed. Hans Bekker-Nielsen et al., 76–99. Odense: Odense University Press, 1981.

Ferrante, Joan. *To the Glory of Her Sex.* Bloomington: Indiana University Press, 1997.

Finberg, H. P. R. *The Early Charters of the West Midlands.* Leicester: Leicester University Press, 1961.

———. *The Formation of England.* London: Hart-Davis, MacGibbon, 1974.

Frantzen, Allen J. "Alfred's Alfred: The Cultural Meaning of Alfred P. Smyth's *King Alfred the Great.*" Paper presented at the annual meeting of the Modern Language Association, Toronto, December 1997.

———. *Desire for Origins: New Language, Old English, and Teaching the Tradition.* New Brunswick: Rutgers University Press, 1990.

———. *The Literature of Penance in Anglo-Saxon England.* New Brunswick: Rutgers University Press, 1983.

———. "When Women Aren't Enough." *Speculum* 68 (1993): 445–472.

Fry, Donald, ed. *Finnsburgh: Fragment and Episode.* London: Methuen, 1974.

Gilchrist, Roberta. *Gender and Material Culture.* New York: Routledge, 1994.

Giles, J. A., ed. and trans. *William of Malmesbury's Chronicle of the Kings of England.* London: G. Bell, 1911.

Glare, P. G. W., ed. *The Oxford Latin Dictionary.* Oxford: Clarendon Press, 1982, repr.1983.

Gneuss, Helmut. "Anglo-Saxon Libraries from the Conversion to the Benedictine Reform." In *Books and Libraries in Early England,* essay II, 643–688. Aldershot, Hampshire: Ashgate Publishing, 1996. This essay collection retains the pagination of the original journal printings; the original publication date of this essay is 1984.

———. "Liturgical Books in Anglo-Saxon England and their Old English Terminology." In *Learning and Literature in Anglo-Saxon England,* eds. Michael Lapidge and Helmut Gneuss, 114–116. Cambridge: Cambridge University Press, 1985.

Goldsmith, Margaret. *The Mode and Meaning of Beowulf.* London: Athlone, 1970.

Grierson, Philip. "The Relations Between England and Flanders Before the Norman Conquest." *Transactions of the Royal Historical Society,* 4th series, 23 (1941): 83–87.

Haddan, Arthur West, and William Stubbs, eds. *Councils and Ecclesiastical Documents Relating to Great Britain and Ireland,* vol.3. Oxford: Clarendon Press, 1871, repr. 1964.

Hala, James. "The Parturition of Poetry and the Birthing of Culture: The *Ides Aglæcwif* and *Beowulf.*" *Exemplaria* 10 (1998): 29–50.

Halverson, John. "The World of Beowulf." *Journal of English Literary History* 36 (1969): 593–608.

Hansen, Elaine Tuttle. "Women in Old English Poetry Reconsidered." *The Michigan Academician* 9 (1976/77): 109–117.

Harmer, Florence, ed. *Select English Historical Documents of the Ninth and Tenth Centuries.* Cambridge: Cambridge University Press, 1914.

Hieatt, Constance. "Modthrytho and Heremod: Intertwined Threads in the Beowulf Poet's Web of Words." *Journal of English and Germanic Philology* 83 (1984): 173–182.

Hill, John. *The Cultural World in Beowulf.* Toronto: University of Toronto Press, 1995.

Hill, Joyce. "Þæt wæs geomuru ides!: A Female Stereotype Examined." In *New Readings on Women in Old English Literature,* eds. Helen Damico and Alexandra Hennesey Olsen, 235–247. Bloomington: Indiana University Press, 1990.

Hollis, Stephanie. *Anglo-Saxon Women and the Church.* Woodbridge: Boydell, 1992.

_____. "The Minster-in-Thanet Foundation Story." *Anglo-Saxon England* 27 (1998): 41–64.

_____. "The Old English 'Ritual of the Admission of Mildrith' (London, Lambeth Palace 427, fol.210)." *Journal of English and Germanic Philology* 97 (1998): 311–321.

Huneycutt, Lois. "Public Lives, Private Ties: Royal Mothers in England and Scotland, 1070–1204." In *Medieval Mothering,* eds. John Carmi Parsons and Bonnie Wheeler, 295–312. New York: Garland, 1996.

Irigaray, Luce. *Sexes and Genealogies.* Trans. Gillian C. Gill. New York: Columbia University Press, 1993.

_____. "Women on the Market." In *This Sex Which is not One.* Trans. Catherine Porter with Carolyn Burke. New York: Columbia University Press, 1993.

Irving, Edward. *Rereading Beowulf.* Philadelphia: University of Pennsylvania Press, 1989.

James, Montague Rhodes. *A Descriptive Catalogue of the Manuscripts of the Library of Lambeth Palace.* Cambridge: Cambridge University Press, 1932.

Janson, H. W., ed. *The History of Art,* 3rd ed. New York: Harry Abrams, 1986.

Jolly, Karen Louise. *Popular Religion in Late Saxon England: Elf Charms in Context.* Chapel Hill: University of North Carolina Press, 1996.

Karkov, Catherine. "Æðelflæd's Exceptional Coinage?" *Old English Newsletter* 29, no. 1 (1995): 41.

Kelly, Susan, ed. *Charters of St. Augustine's Abbey and Minster-in-Thanet.* Anglo-Saxon Charters, vol. 4. Oxford: Oxford University Press, 1995.

_____. "Trading Privileges from Eighth-Century England." *Early Medieval Europe* 1 (1992): 3–28.

Ker, N. R. *Catalogue of Manuscripts Containing Anglo-Saxon.* Oxford: Clarendon Press, 1957.

Keynes, Simon. "On the Authenticity of Asser's *Life of Alfred.*" *Journal of Ecclesiastical History* 47 (1996): 529–51.

_____, ed. *The Liber Vitae of the New Minster and Hyde Abbey Winchester (British Library Stowe 944).* Early English Manuscripts in Facsimile, vol.26. Copenhagen: Rosenkilde and Bagger, 1996.

Keynes, Simon, and Michael Lapidge. *Alfred the Great.* Hammondsworth: Penguin, 1983.

Kiernan, Kevin. "Grendel's Heroic Mother." *In Geardagum* 6 (1984) 13–33.

Klaeber, Fr., ed. *Beowulf and the Fight at Finnsburgh,* 3rd ed. Lexington, MA: D. C. Heath and Co., 1950.

Knowles, David. *The Monastic Order in England.* Cambridge: Cambridge University Press, 1950.

Kroll, Norma. "Beowulf: The Hero as Keeper of Human Polity." *Modern Philology* 84 (1986): 117–129.

Lapidge, Michael, and James Rosier, eds. and trans. *Aldhelm: The Poetic Works.* Cambridge: Brewer, 1985.

Lapidge, Michael, and Michael Herren, eds. and trans. *Aldhelm: The Prose Works.* Cambridge: Brewer, 1979.

Lees, Clare. "Men and *Beowulf.*" In *Medieval Masculinities,* ed. Clare Lees, 129–138. Minneapolis: University of Minnesota Press, 1994.

_____, and Gillian R. Overing. "Birthing Bishops and Fathering Poets: Bede, Hild, and the Relations of Cultural Production." *Exemplaria* 6 (1994): 35–66.

Liebermann, Franz, ed. *Die Heiligen Englands: Angelsaechsisch und Lateinisch.* Hanover: Hahn, 1889.

Lochrie, Karma. "Gender, Sexual Violence, and the Politics of War in the Old English *Judith.*" In *Class and Gender in Early English Literature: Intersections,* eds. Britton J. Harwood and Gillian R. Overing, 1–20. Bloomington: Indiana University Press, 1994.

Malone, Kemp. "Hrethric." *PMLA* 27 (1942): 268–312.

_____. "Hygd." *Modern Language Notes* 56 (1941): 356–58.

McCann, Justin, ed. and trans. *The Rule of Saint Benedict in Latin and English.* London: Burns Oates, 1952.

McNeill, John T., and Helena M. Gamer. *Medieval Handbooks of Penance.* New York: Columbia University Press, 1938.

Mitchell, Barbara. "Anglo-Saxon Double Monasteries." *History Today* 25 (1995): 33–39.

Moore, Bruce. "The Thryth-Offa Digression in *Beowulf.*" *Neophilologus* 64 (1980): 127–33.

Morgan, Gerald. "The Treachery of Hrothulf." *English Studies* 53 (1972): 23–39.

Morgan, Gwendolyn. "Mothers, Monsters, Maturation: Female Evil in *Beowulf.*" *Journal of the Fantastic in the Arts* 4 (1991): 54–68.

Mulder-Bakker, Anneke B., ed. *Sanctity and Motherhood: Essays on Holy Mothers in the Middle Ages.* New York: Garland, 1995.

Newton, Allyson. "The Occlusion of Maternity in Chaucer's *Clerk's Tale*." In *Medieval Mothering,* eds. John Carmi Parsons and Bonnie Wheeler, 63–76. New York: Garland, 1996.

Nicholson, Joan. "Feminae Gloriosae: Women in the Age of Bede." In *Medieval Women,* ed. Derek Baker, 15–29. Oxford: Blackwell, 1970.

Niermeyer, J. F., ed. *Mediae Latinitatis Lexicon Minus.* Leiden: Brill, 1976.

Niles, John. *Beowulf: The Poem and Its Tradition.* Cambridge: Harvard University Press, 1983.

Nitzsche, Jane Chance. "The Structural Unity of *Beowulf:* The Problem of Grendel's Mother." *Texas Studies in Literature and Language* 22 (1980): 287–303.

O'Donovan, John, ed. and trans. *Annals of Ireland: Three Fragments.* Dublin: Irish Archaeological and Celtic Society, 1860.

Otter, Monika. "The Temptation of St. Æthelthryth." *Exemplaria* 9 (1998): 139–163.

Overing, Gillian R. *Language, Sign, and Gender in Beowulf.* Carbondale: University of Illinois Press, 1990.

Page, R. I. "Appendix A: The Inscriptions," In *Anglo-Saxon Ornamental Metalwork 700–1100 In the British Museum,* ed. David Wilson, 67–90. London: Trustees of the British Museum, 1964.

Parsons, John Carmi. "Family, Sex, and Power: The Rhythms of Medieval Queenship." In *Medieval Queenship,* ed. John Carmi Parsons, 1–13. New York: St. Martin's, 1993.

_____ and Bonnie Wheeler, eds. *Medieval Mothering.* The New Middle Ages. New York: Garland, 1996.

Peers, Charles, and C. A. Ralegh Radford. "The Saxon Monastery at Whitby." *Archaeologia* 89 (1943): 27–88.

Pelteret, David. *Slavery in Early Medieval England.* London: Boydell, 1995.

Plummer, Charles, ed. *Two of the Saxon Chronicles Parallel.* Revised ed. based on that of John Earle. Oxford: Clarendon Press, 1889.

Radner, Joan Newlon, ed. and trans. *Fragmentary Annals of Ireland.* Dublin: Dublin Institute for Advanced Study, 1978.

Rau, Reanhol, ed. *Briefe des Bonifatius.* Darmstadt: Wissenschaftlice Buchgesellschaft, 1968.

Renoir, Alain. "A Reading Context for the Wife's Lament." In *Anglo-Saxon Poetry: Essays in Appreciation,* eds. Lewis E. Nicholson and Dolores Warwick Frese, 224–241. South Bend: Notre Dame University Press, 1975.

Rich, Adrienne. *Of Woman Born: Motherhood as Experience and Institution,* 2nd ed. New York: Norton, 1986.

Ridyard, Susan. *The Royal Saints of Anglo-Saxon England: A Study of West Saxon and East Anglian Cults.* Cambridge: Cambridge University Press, 1988.

Robinson, Fred. "Did Grendel's Mother Sit on Beowulf?" In *From Anglo-Saxon to Early Middle English: Studies Presented to E. G. Stanley,* eds. Malcolm Godden et al., 1–7. Oxford: Clarendon Press, 1994.

Robinson, J. A. *The Times of St. Dunstan.* Oxford: Clarendon Press, 1923, repr. 1969.

Rollason, David. *The Mildrith Legend: A Study in Early Medieval Hagiography in England.* Leicester: Leicester University Press, 1982.

_____. *Saints and Relics in Anglo-Saxon England.* Oxford: Blackwell, 1989.

Ruddick, Sara. *Maternal Thinking: Toward a Politics of Peace.* Boston: Beacon Press, 1989, repr. 1995.

_____. "Thinking Mothers/Conceiving Birth." In *Representations of Motherhood,* ed. Donna Basin et al., 29–45. New Haven: Yale University Press, 1994.

Sawyer, P. H., ed. *Anglo-Saxon Charters: An Annotated List and Bibliography.* London: Royal Historical Society, 1968.

Schrader, Richard. *God's Handiwork: Images of Women in Early Germanic Literature.* Westport, CT: Greenwood Press, 1983.

Schulenberg, Jane Tibbetts. "Female Sanctity: Public and Private Roles, ca.500–1100." In *Women and Power in the Middle Ages,* eds. Mary Erler and Maryanne Kowalski, 102–125. Athens: University of Georgia Press, 1988.

_____. "Women's Monastic Communities, 500–1100: Patterns of Expansion and Decline." *Signs* 14 (1989): 261–292.

Sisam, Kenneth. *The Structure of Beowulf.* Oxford: Clarendon Press, 1965.

Sklute, L. John. "Freoðuwebbe in Old English Poetry." In *New Readings on Women in Old English Literature,* eds. Helen Damico and Alexandra Hennessey Olsen, 204–210. Bloomington: Indiana University Press, 1990.

Smyth, Alfred. *King Alfred the Great.* Oxford: Oxford University Press, 1995.

Stafford, Pauline. "The King's Wife in Wessex, 800–1066." In *New Readings on Women in Old English Literature,* eds. Helen Damico and Alexandra Hennessey Olsen, 56–78. Bloomington: Indiana University Press, 1990.

Stansbury, Don. *The Lady Who Fought the Vikings.* Devon, England: Imogen Books, 1993.

Stenton, Frank. *Anglo-Saxon England,* 2nd ed. Oxford: Clarendon Press, 1947, repr.1955.

Stevenson, William Henry, ed. *Asser's Life of Alfred.* Oxford: Clarendon Press, 1904, repr. 1959.

Stratyner, Leslie. "Wealhtheow's Threat: *Beowulf,* 1228–1231." In *Geardagum* 14 (1993): 39–44.

Stubbs, William, ed. *Willelmi Malmesbiriensis Monachi: De Gestis Regum Anglorum.* Rolls Series, vol. 90. London: Eyre and Spottiswoode, 1887.

Swanton, Michael J. "A Fragmentary Life of St. Mildred and Other Kentish Royal Saints." *Archaeologia Cantiana* 91 (1975): 15–27.

_____. *Crisis and Development in Germanic Society, 700–800: Beowulf and the Burden of Kingship.* Goppingen: Kummerle Verlag, 1982.

Szarmach, Paul E. "Æðelflæd in the Chronicle." *Old English Newsletter* 29, no. 1 (1995): 42–43.

_____. "Æðelflæd of Mercia: *Mise en page.*" In *Words and Works: Studies in Medieval English Language and Literature in Honour of Fred C. Robinson,* eds. Peter S. Baker and Nicholas Howe, 105–126. Toronto: University of Toronto Press, 1998.

Taylor, Keith. "*Beowulf* 1259a:The Inherent Nobility of Grendel's Mother." *English Language Notes* 31, no. 3 (1993/94): 13–25.

Taylor, Paul Beekman. "Beowulf's Second Grendel Fight." *Neuphilologische Mitteilungen* 86 (1985): 62–69.

Temple, Mary Kay. "*Beowulf* 1258–1266: Grendel's Lady-Mother." *English Language Notes* 23 (1986): 10–15.

Thorpe, Benjamin, ed. *The Anglo-Saxon Chronicle.* Rolls series, vols. 23a and 23b. London: Longman, 1861.

Tolkien, J. R. R. "Beowulf:The Monsters and the Critics." *Proceedings of the British Academy* 22 (1936): 245–96; reprinted in numerous places, including *The Monsters and the Critics and Other Essays,* ed. Christopher Tolkien (London: Allen and Unwin, 1983), 5–48.

Tripp, Raymond. "The Exemplary Role of Hrothgar and Heorot." *Philological Quarterly* 56 (1977): 123–29.

Vaught, Jacqueline. "*Beowulf:* The Fight at the Center." *Allegorica* 5 (1980): 125–137.

de Vegvar, Carol Neuman. "Saints and Companions to Saints: Anglo-Saxon Royal Women Monastics in Context." In *Holy Men and Holy Women: Old English Prose Saints' Lives and Their Contexts,* ed. Paul E. Szarmach, 51–94. Albany: SUNY Press, 1996.

Venezky, Richard, and Antonette diPaolo Healey, eds. *A Microfiche Concordance to Old English.* Newark: University of Delaware Microforms, 1980.

Wainwright, F. T. "Æthelflæd, Lady of the Mercians." In *The Anglo-Saxons: Studies in Some Aspects of Their History and Culture Presented to Bruce Dickins,* ed. Peter Clemoes, 53–69. London: Bowes and Bowes, 1959; reprinted in *New Readings on Women in Old English Literature,* eds. Helen Damico and Alexandra Hennessey Olsen (Bloomington: Indiana University Press, 1990), 44–55.

_____. "The Chronology of the Mercian Register." *English Historical Review* 60 (1945): 385–392.

_____. "Inigmund's Invasion." In *Scandinavian England: Collected Papers by F. T. Wainwright,* ed. H. P. R. Finberg, 131–162. Sussex: Phillimore, 1975.

_____. "North-West Mercia." In *Scandinavian England: Collected Papers by F. T. Wainwright,* ed. H. P. R. Finberg, 63–130. Sussex: Phillimore, 1975.

Wall, J. Charles. *Alfred the Great: His Abbeys of Hyde, Athelney, and Shaftesbury.* London: E. Stock, 1900.

Ward, Gordon. "King Wihtred's Charter of A.D. 699." *Archaeologia Cantiana* 60 (1947): 1–14.

_____. "King Oswin—A Forgotten Ruler of Kent." *Archaeologia Cantiana* 50 (1933): 60–65.

Webster, Leslie, and Janet Backhouse, eds. *The Making of England: Anglo-Saxon Art and Culture A.D. 600–900.* Toronto: University of Toronto Press, 1991.

Weise, Judith. "The Meaning of the Name Hygd." *Names* 34 (1986): 1–10.

Whitelock, Dorothy, et al., eds. *The Anglo-Saxon Chronicle: A Revised Translation.* New Brunswisk: Rutgers University Press, 1961.

Whitelock, Dorothy, ed. *English Historical Documents, c. 500–1042,* 2nd ed. London: Routledge, 1996.

_____. "The Genuine Asser." *The Stenton Lecture 1967*. Reading: University of Reading, 1967.

_____. *Some Anglo-Saxon Bishops of London*. London: HK Lewis, 1974.

Wilson, David M. *Anglo-Saxon Ornamental Metalwork 700–1100 in the British Museum*. London: Trustees of the British Museum, 1964.

Witney, K. P. "The Kentish Royal Saints: An Enquiry into the Facts behind the Legends." *Archaeologia Cantiana* 101 (1984): 1–22.

_____. *The Kingdom of Kent*. London: Phillimore, 1982.

Wren, C. L., and W. F. Bolton, eds. *Beowulf*, 4th ed. Exeter: University of Exeter, 1988.

Yorke, Barbara. *Kings and Kingdoms of Early Anglo-Saxon England*. London: Seaby, 1990.

_____. "'Sisters Under the Skin'? Anglo-Saxon Nuns and Nunneries in Southern England." *Annual Proceedings of the Graduate Centre for Medieval Studies in the University of Reading* 15 (1989) 95–117.

Zupitza, Julius, ed. *Beowulf*. Early English Text Society o.s.245. Oxford: Oxford University Press, 1959, repr. 1967.

INDEX

160   MOTHERHOOD AND MOTHERING